MW01256400

The Lo
and the N.
First Great Scandal

The Louisville Grays and the Myth of Baseball's First Great Scandal

WENDELL LLOYD JONES

McFarland & Company, Inc., Publishers
Jefferson, North Carolina

Library of Congress Cataloging-in-Publication Data

Names: Jones, Wendell Lloyd, 1963– author.
Title: The Louisville Grays and the myth of baseball's first great scandal / Wendell Lloyd Jones.
Description: Jefferson, North Carolina : McFarland & Company, Inc., Publishers, 2024. | Includes bibliographical references and index.
Identifiers: LCCN 2024006361 | ISBN 9781476694382 (paperback : acid free paper) ∞ ISBN 9781476651842 (ebook)
Subjects: LCSH: Louisville Grays (Baseball team)—History—19th century. | Sports betting—History—19th century. | Baseball—Corrupt practices—History—19th century. | Major League Baseball (Organization)—History—19th century. | BISAC: SPORTS & RECREATION / Baseball / History
Classification: LCC GV875.L62 J66 2024 | DDC 796.357/64/0976944—dc23/eng/20240216
LC record available at https://lccn.loc.gov/2024006361

British Library cataloguing data are available

ISBN (print) 978-1-4766-9438-2
ISBN (ebook) 978-1-4766-5184-2

Front cover: (clockwise from top) Etching of John Haldeman (Filson Historical Society), George Hall, Al Nichols, Bill Craver and Jim Devlin

Printed in the United States of America

McFarland & Company, Inc., Publishers
  Box 611, Jefferson, North Carolina 28640
   www.mcfarlandpub.com

Dedicated to the memory of my mother,
Betty Jane Anthony Jones, and my father,
Adrian Wilson Jones. They did not introduce me
to baseball or history, but they certainly encouraged
my love of both throughout my life. I only wish
they had lived long enough to see this.

Acknowledgments

I suppose it is possible to write a book like this completely on one's own, but why would you want to? Among the most gratifying and humbling experiences one can have in life is the assistance and encouragement of others. To that end I owe a debt of gratitude to many. First and foremost is my friend Christopher E. Hutchison who gave his time and effort into providing invaluable editorial support to this book. Hutch pointed out gaps in the story I could not have seen as well as a few writing quirks I never realized I had. His wife, and my friend, Kimberly Rodman Hutchison (a/k/a "Redman") probably involuntarily gave up some time as well while my project pulled her spouse away from other duties and chores he might otherwise have been compelled to perform.

Then there are those who showed kindness and support in the simple act of doing their jobs. I am thinking of the staff in the Kentucky History Room at the Louisville Free Public Library and, in particular, Kelly Dunnagan and Claudia Fitch. John W. Horne, Jr., the Coordinator of Rights & Reproductions at the National Baseball Hall of Fame, bent over backwards to be of assistance.

The same can be said of the curators and librarians at the Filson Historical Society here in Louisville, Kentucky, who dutifully and cheerfully fetched the countless files I felt compelled to review. Of them, none stood out more than Caitlin Hogue, the Collections Assistant who also went the extra mile to get me what I needed. I had a similar experience with the staff at the Abakanowicz Research Center at the Chicago History Museum, though I failed to get any of their names.

Finally, I would like to mention the kind words and assistance of T. Scott Brandon of the SABR Pictorial History Committee.

There are others, of course. Co-workers and friends who encouraged and cheered me on throughout. They are too countless to name.

Table of Contents

Preface

If you read this story and come away with the idea that I am critical or judgmental of the historians who came before me, that would be understandable. It is not my intent. I may have approached this story from a mindset different from those who preceded me. My personal history is in the study of history. My academic background is that of a political scientist with what could be called a history minor, only my institution did not award minors. From there I proceeded to law school and have spent the years since 1994 as a litigator. To add to the mix, I had a professor in law school who warned me to "never forget, your client is lying to you."

My professional experience since then has taught me he was right. Clients do not lie maliciously; they lie defensively. They also misremember—again, not intentionally. They leave out the parts that, in their minds, make them look bad. Sometimes, those facts are the very ones you need to properly prepare your case. That impacts my study of history, however, in that an unwritten rule of studying and researching history is that you prioritize your sources based on their immediacy to the events. Primary sources are preferred to secondary sources and secondary are preferred to tertiary sources. Normally that holds well. In this instance, it does not. That being the case, instinctively trusting the eyewitness leads to errors in telling the story.

When I first engaged in this research, I, like my predecessors, relied on the article by Charles Chase (see Prologue below). It was, after all, a primary source. Chase was there. He would know what happened. But I was unsatisfied with the explanation because it seemed to have gaps. I needed to fortify it somehow. Previous historians have stated that the truth remains elusive, and we will likely never know the full extent of the conspiracy. I wanted to close that hole or at least reduce its size and scope. So, I endeavored to compare the narrative with the secondary sources— the newspaper accounts of the games—to see if I could bolster the narrative. It is something my litigation training has taught me to do: find the holes in your argument, and then find a way to plug them with the contemporaneous evidence. What I found instead was an incongruous mess.

I will not pretend to understand how prior historians could have missed what was to me quite obvious. The simple explanation seems to be they did not look. They assumed that since Chase laid out the entire story, and he is a qualified primary source, no further exploration into the details is required. They did not approach the topic with the cynical mindset that their client is lying.

The question now becomes Why did Charles Chase lie? To be frank, I do not think he intentionally did so, but I asked the same question. Fortunately, I was able to recall some studies I had read thirty years ago about human memory and the inherent flaws we all share. Specifically, I was curious about whether we construct memories of the early stages of some life story around what we know to be the ultimate outcome. In other words, our memory of what happened on day one is impacted by what happened on day final. I will give you an example.

Do you recall the 1986 World Series between the New York Mets and the Boston Red Sox? If you do, you likely recall the famous play in which Mookie Wilson of the Mets hit a slow roller to Bill Buckner, who was playing first base for the Red Sox. Buckner inexplicably allowed the ball to roll through his legs allowing the winning run to score. I cannot tell you how many times I have had a Boston fan insist that if Buckner makes that play, the Series is over, and the Red Sox are world champs. The problem is, that is simply not true.

Boston fans remember that play and that the Mets won the World Series. But for some Boston fans, in their memory—honestly stated—but for that play Boston wins. The details of what immediately preceded that play are lost. The details are thus: It was Game Six and Boston was up three games to two. The game went into extra innings and in the top of the tenth, Dave Henderson of Boston hit a solo home run to give Boston the lead. That was followed two outs later by a Marty Barrett single to drive home Wade Boggs to make the score 5–3 Boston. If Boston could prevent the Mets from scoring in the bottom of the inning, Boston would win the title. The first two Mets batters, Wally Backman and Keith Hernandez, went down without a whimper, so Boston was now just one out away from its first title since 1918. That brought up Gary Carter, who singled to left, followed by Kevin Mitchell, pinch-hitting in the pitcher's spot, who singled to center. There were now runners on first and second with two outs and Ray Knight at the plate. Knight singled to center scoring Carter and moving Mitchell to third base. The score was now 5–4. Boston replaced Calvin Schiraldi with Bob Stanley to face Mookie Wilson. This is the part Red Sox fans forget: with the count 2–2, Stanley uncorked a wild pitch that Wilson jumped over, allowing the ball to go to the backstop and Kevin Mitchell to score. The game was now tied 5–5 in the bottom of the tenth. It was the next pitch that Wilson rolled to Buckner that ultimately allowed Knight to score the winning run and send the series to Game Seven. In other words, if Buckner makes the play, Boston does not secure the title, we all just go to the eleventh inning and play continues.

Boston fans who tell you Buckner's play cost them the Series are not lying. What they are doing is reconstructing the memory of the details around the result that so pained them. That is what Charles Chase did. He wrote from memory, and he reconstructed his memory of the details leading up to the final result. It is a mechanism for making sense of the story and we all do it. I decided to research a bit further and found a study from 1995 in which academics termed this process as "fuzzy trace theory." What they show is that we generally recall the "gist" of what happened rather than a verbatim recollection of events as they unfolded. Chase got the gist of what happened just fine, it is on the details where he completely whiffed. That is what modern Red Sox fans are doing: the gist is apparent—Buckner made an error, and the Red Sox lost the World Series (albeit due to a rain out, two days later). The details of how one thing led to another is more problematic.

I relied on the work of earlier authors to get me through much of this story. That I reached different conclusions from them may be attributable to my litigator's cynicism, which led me to question, repeatedly, whether the testimony (Chase's article) matches the documented story (newspaper accounts). This book is about how the two are woefully mismatched.

Prologue: Dilemma

John Haldeman had a dilemma. The 1877 Louisville Grays were considered the best team in the National League of Professional Base Ball Clubs.[1]* Recently, they had played a stretch of 16 games in which they won 14. The winning streak catapulted them into first place in the League and a four-game lead over the fading St. Louis Brown Stockings. Now, suddenly, they could not seem to beat anyone. Haldeman knew something was amiss.

For Haldeman, unlike perhaps the common fan, this was no minor problem. For starters, covering the team daily was his job. He was the baseball editor for the *Louisville Courier-Journal*. But he also played for the team. In exhibition games, and one major league game, he filled in occasionally when the team needed another player. To add more pressure, his father was the president of the club. His father, Walter N. Haldeman, was not only president of Louisville's National League baseball club, he was also the owner, publisher and president of the *Courier-Journal* and vice-president of the Associated Press.[2] If something was wrong within the team, and John Haldeman could figure it out, it was his responsibility to both his employer and the public to expose it. But, on the other hand, there was a risk that whatever the problem was, exposing it could potentially be embarrassing for his family.

More than anything else, however, was the risk of being wrong, and there were many ways this could go wrong. If, after all, Haldeman's suspicions were well-founded, and he said nothing, it would appear to be a cover-up. But if he alleges games are being sold, and he cannot prove it, it just looks like sour grapes. The bottom line was that Haldeman had no facts, he merely had his suspicions. How else can one explain the best team in baseball being suddenly unable to win? His suspicions were not completely out of the blue. There was a history behind professional baseball that could not be ignored. Indeed, the very problem of players selling

---

*See Notes section at the back of the book, divided by chapters.

games to gamblers ("hippodroming," it was called) was a large part of what drove the formation of the National League in the first place.[3]

A decade after the fact, the Louisville Club's vice-president in 1876 and 1877, Charles E. Chase, wrote an article for a magazine detailing the events of 1877. It was an extended narrative of the scandal. It was later republished in a collection of works about the history of sport in the United States, England and Australia.[4] In the article Chase describes a powerful, almost invincible team that had been assembled by Louisville. Chase recounted the receipt of a telegram as the moment when he first became aware that something might be wrong with his club. Chase informs the readers that the telegram cautioned there may be something amiss with the club. Later that day, he learned that the club lost to the Hartford Club and, upon closer inspection, he learned that it was due to the errors of three players in particular. The next day, the same scenario unfolded. He detailed in the narrative what steps he took, such as ordering the manager to bench one of the culprits, and he gives credit to Haldeman for ultimately uncovering the truth. Chase's narrative of the scandal became the basis upon which every history of the Louisville Grays has been written since then. No one has examined its accuracy against the objective record created by the newspapers contemporaneously with the actual events. A modest examination reveals of the Chase narrative that it is almost entirely incorrect. Consequently, every history of the 1877 Louisville Grays written based on Chase's narrative is likewise wrong.

* * *

To understand Haldeman's suspicions in August of 1877, it is helpful to remember how the game of baseball even got to that point. While there remains some disagreement over the origins of the game of baseball itself, what is generally agreed upon by baseball historians is that when it took hold, it did so as a club sport. In the 1840s social clubs would form with baseball being at the center of activities, but not the only activity. Clubs would host various social activities such as parties, dances, dinners or even literary discussions. The clubs were typically young men (and women) who were either from the same socio-economic group or, in some cases, the same profession or even workplace. The game itself was a reason to have a party. Club members would gather, both playing members and non-playing members, a game would be played for entertainment, and then all would have some type of feast. Winning was a matter of indifference.[5]

In the 1850s, clubs began to challenge one another more frequently. However, society was strictly partitioned by class, race, and ethnicity, so these match contests were really just a reason to have a party with those outside your particular baseball club, but well within your social tribe. Most people in the 21st century are familiar with the racial partition of 19th-century America. Many are less aware of the ethnic and socio-economic partitions that existed. By way of example, perhaps the most violent day in Louisville's history was Monday, August 6, 1855, when gangs of mostly Anglo-Saxon Protestants launched an attack on German and Irish Catholics. The situation turned into an all-out battle in multiple parts of the city and resulted in the deaths of at least 22 people.[6]

Because of these social divisions, a club composed of young professional men would not include tradesmen among their number. Likewise, a club comprised of members of Anglo-Saxon heritage would never consider admitting an Irishman or a German. The divisions went both ways: no club of self-respecting Germans would entertain even the mildest thought of inviting—let alone accepting—an Anglo-Saxon or any other ethnic group to join their fun. These divisions in class and ethnicity were not merely quaint. They came with a host of mutual suspicions and distrust. When the partitions were removed years later as professional baseball developed, the mutual suspicions remained and likely played a role in the Grays' scandal of 1877.

A pervasive trend in America throughout the 19th century was the organization of social clubs for one purpose or another. It was not just baseball or even sports. Clubs were formed over a wide variety of interests, such as literature, gardening, shooting, philosophy, music or even *ad hoc* charitable causes. In fact, it was so common even immigrants quickly began to take up the practice. But it was not enough to simply form a club, the club had to be organized with a president and other officers with bylaws and a constitution.[7]

This tendency of 19th-century Americans to be hyper-organized naturally spilled over into sport and led several New York clubs to conclude that if clubs were going to challenge one another, there had to be a structure in which to do it and there had to be rules—standards—for how it was conducted. Thus, in 1857 the New York clubs formed the National Association of Base Ball Players ("NABBP"), and the rules of participation and engagement were created. Among the earliest rules was that no player was to be compensated for his play.[8]

It was around the same time clubs started taking a greater and greater interest in the outcome of games so the rules of the NABBP included a rule for how to determine the championship. With championships and pride on the line, the rules surrounding paying players had little chance. By the beginning of the Civil War, a few players, Al Reach, Joe Start, Dickey Pearce and Jim Creighton, were believed to have been paid by their respective clubs.[9]

After the war, the Washington Nationals formed. The club consisted of ball players from around the country with little or no commonality other than their ability to play baseball. One of them, George Wright, was considered the best of his era. Miraculously, most of the Nationals' players found jobs working for the club's primary financial sponsor, the United States Department of Treasury. In the summer of 1867, they found themselves touring the country—the first team to do so—suggesting their positions at the Treasury Department were not entirely legitimate. With the emphasis now decisively swinging toward winning, and fans even willing to pay an admission price to watch the games, gamblers took notice.[10]

In December 1868, the NABBP finally relented, and the rules were changed to allow players to be compensated.[11] Several clubs immediately took advantage of the new rules with none more famous for it that the Cincinnati Red Stockings. The Cincinnati Club was managed by George Wright's older brother, Harry. The club originally consisted of prominent lawyers and other businessmen and a few up-and-comers. Wright, a native of England, was hired to manage the club's sporting affairs. Initially, his role was similar to that of a golf club professional. He managed the baseball affairs of the club—scheduling games, acquiring equipment, seeing to the grounds—and provided instruction to the members on playing the game. In time, he would emerge as an early genius for the game and developed many of its tactical components still in use today. The Reds were not alone. They were just one of several professional clubs. In 1869 there were a dozen professional clubs and by 1870 there were fully 20. For two seasons professional and amateur clubs alike tried to co-exist in the NABBP, but the reality was that the short-term needs and long-term goals of the two groups required far different considerations when it came to the rules. In March 1871, several of the professional clubs met in New York and formed the National Association of Professional Base Ball Players. The NAPBBP, often referred to as just the "National Association," is considered the first "major league."[12]

The National Association was poorly designed from the outset. The seeds of its demise were sown at its origins. It seemed as if the originators preferred dysfunction and chaos. Membership by a club in the association required only an annual fee of ten dollars. That was a small price even in 1871 and it meant clubs that were not otherwise well capitalized could afford to join, but their limited finances made it impossible for them to survive a full season. In 1875, for instance, only seven of the 13 teams that started the season as members of the National Association survived to the end. There was leadership in the form of league officers, but they essentially had no authority to enforce rules or discipline players. As historian Tom Melville put it, the National Association was a decentralized organization of autonomous clubs which meant it was unable to muster a "unified front" in the face of corruption from gambling. They also lacked the ability to punish clubs that strayed from Association guidelines or which reinstated players who had been justifiably dismissed for violations of what rules there were.[13]

Two of the rules that were constantly ignored by clubs and players alike were "revolving" and "dissipation," or intemperance. "Revolving" is the term they used for players jumping their contracts with one team to join another. There were Association rules for when players could be recruited by other teams, when contracts expired, when new contracts could be signed and when they could take effect. All were repeatedly ignored. "Dissipation" is the term used for drunkenness. A player could be banished for being drunk in a game or just too hungover to play. According to historian Lee Allen, at times "half the players of the league [were] seldom fit to take the field." Players determined to be guilty were banished by their club, and then another club would sign them, thereby negating the disciplinary purpose of the rule.[14]

But by far the biggest problem the National Association found beyond its grasp, and the one that most disgusted the fans, was the practice of hippodroming. Arguably the worst offender was the Mutual Club of New York. The Mutuals were synonymous with corruption and the title "Mutuals ballplayer" could have been used as a euphemism for gambler. With fans being unable to feel assured that when they paid the price of admission they would see an honestly contested game, attendance dropped. Fans increasingly questioned—doubted, frankly—the integrity of the sport. It was that practice more than anything else that killed the National Association and led to the formation of the league in which Louisville now played. Indeed, when the National League was announced in February 1876, its central objective—the thing its founders professed to be first and foremost among their goals—was to rid the game of the influence and corruption of gamblers.[15] Now, in August of 1877, just 18 months after the League was born, in the League's second season, John Haldeman sat at his desk in the *Courier-Journal* building convinced that the same crooked practice had taken hold of the Louisville Grays. He just could not prove it. Some way, somehow, Haldeman had to get to the truth.

Ultimately, the decision John Haldeman made as to the best way to reveal the truth was to lie. He did not back away from the controversy, he simply fabricated his knowledge of it. He no doubt deceived the public, but his real targets were the players themselves. His goal was to unnerve the wrongdoers—whom he could not yet identify—in the hopes they would reveal themselves. In the end, it worked. The result of Haldeman's success still resonates in Major League Baseball to this day. It would be an over-simplification to assert that players like Shoeless Joe Jackson and Pete Rose remain banned from baseball and from the Hall of Fame as a direct result of John Haldeman and "the Louisville Four" (as they became known). But the Louisville Club, and ultimately the National League, set a precedent in 1877. The National League established that while there are many sins in baseball, the ultimate one, the one that absolutely must be stamped out, is gambling on games. All sports punish gambling on contests in some manner under a given set of conditions. But only in baseball does gambling rise to the level of blasphemy. The goal was announced in 1876 with the establishment of the League; it was declared as a standard in 1877 with the expulsion of the Louisville Four.

CHAPTER ONE

Beginnings

Baseball began in Louisville at least as early as 1858. *The Daily Courier* reported June 30 of that year that the "Star Base Ball Club" had organized. "The invigorating exercises of this association will doubtless prove highly beneficial to those who are closely confined during the business hours of the day." The paper further informed its readers that the "first exercises" of the club would be held July 2 "on the commons adjacent to Kentucky and Fifth streets." A game played June 18, 1858, among the Louisville Base Ball Club was reported in July. According to the *Daily Courier*, it was the eighth contest of the season among the club's members and "compares favorably with games played by old established clubs." Which "old established clubs" the *Daily Courier* is using for comparison is not known. On August 20, the formation of the "Eclipse Base Ball Club" was noted.[1] Not much is known about the first Louisville Base Ball Club, the Star Base Ball Club, the Eclipse Base Ball Club or the one or two others mentioned in 1858, 1859 or 1860. Coverage in the press was minimal and primary sources seldom mention the game at all.

Prior to baseball, there was town ball, a precursor to baseball as we know it. Little is known about how widely played the game was, as it merited mention in the media only upon the death of a player. A coroner's jury held an inquest over the body of Francis Shuck near the corner of Kentucky and Clay streets where, presumably, the 28-year-old had died. According to the report, the jury found that Shuck "was engaged in a game of 'town' ball' and became very warm which caused instant death. The verdict of the jury was that he came to his death from excessive exercise, which produced apoplexy of the brain."[2]

Baseball's origins in Louisville were identical to those clubs elsewhere in that the first clubs were organized as social clubs consisting of players, non-players and women. It was a gentleman's game and players were fined for certain transgressions such as disputing an umpire's decision or cursing during a game or practice. The fines, along with the very position of umpire, were mechanisms by which clubs sought to manage the risk of players becoming excited during a match. Typically, matches between clubs would be arranged through written correspondence and an announcement would be placed in one of the daily papers.

A common inclusion in the announcement was to invite the public to attend such as the one appearing in the *Daily Courier* September 23, 1858: "The public are invited, the ladies particularly." The specific inclusion of women in the announcement was purposeful. As historian Warren Goldstein explains, excitement, or rather, over-excitement, was a major concern of clubs. Women were thought to bring a measure of control and, therefore, were much desired at games. Women were thought to be the "restraining influence on what would otherwise be unregulated passion" of ballplayers and spectators alike. Also, women conferred a certain legitimacy on the sport.[3]

The language used to describe the game and commend it to readers is unfamiliar to us today. An article in the *Daily Journal* referred to baseball as an "admirable and healthy sport" that "will strengthen both the muscular and intellectual man." In another article, the *Daily Journal* encouraged attendance at a game because "these clubs are worthy representatives and fully able to demonstrate the science and beauties of the noble game." Nineteenth-century society had become enthralled with the concept of science and, thus, phrases like "scientific technique" can often be seen in news accounts to describe the play of admired clubs. The *Daily Journal* also referred to it as a "manly game." The term "manly" or "manliness" differentiates the game not from the antonym "feminine," but instead "boyish" or "childishness." Children play at games; men participate in sport. It was part and parcel of the concept and importance of self-control on the ballfield. Goldstein explains that the terms "manly" and "boyish" were "charged words in mid-nineteenth-century America" and that "few words carried so much disdain as 'boyish.'" Newspaper reporters would attack what they deemed "boyish" behavior by players and spectators alike but, as Goldstein notes, it is quite probable that some of the time, the targets of their ire were in fact adult males who, in their estimation, behaved in a child-like manner and, therefore, were labeled "boyish" or "juvenile" as a form of reprimand that would sting most deeply.[4]

* * *

The outbreak of the Civil War in 1861 more or less eliminated the game from newspaper coverage and, undoubtedly to some extent, the ball fields. But the game went on in Louisville and even within the war itself. There are numerous accounts of the game being played by soldiers both in prison camps and on the battlefields themselves. A soldier's often long hours of idleness lends itself naturally seeking entertainment in whatever form is at hand. For many, that meant learning the game of baseball anew or, for others, continuing to play the sport of their pre-war lives. Among the locals who continued playing the game was George Vanvalkenburg. He was in the Union army, stationed near Bowling Green, Kentucky, in January of 1863. He wrote a letter to his wife describing a game of baseball:

> we was playing ball new years day and was having a fine time and enjoying ourselves … when to our surprise there came balls among us that was not so pleasant to play with as the one we had that was made of yarn and covered with leather the balls that was thrown among us was thrown from the muzzle of a ten pounder and was made of a more solid substance than yarn it caused no little excitement among the boys I can tell you and not much less among the officers.…[5]

Some histories put the origins of baseball in Louisville in 1865. Those histories seem to have relied on the work of early 20th-century journalist and baseball historian A.H. Tarvin's *Seventy-Five Years on Louisville Diamonds*. Tarvin, by his own admission, relied on the memories of old timers he interviewed.[6] Remarkably they got a good bit right. But, on some points, they were considerably off.

The Louisville Base Ball club was organized anew in 1865 as the war was winding down. Whether this version was a revival of the first or simply a new club with the same name is unclear. In keeping with the practices of other social clubs, the names of the officers of the club were published in the paper and the club quickly established itself as the pre-eminent baseball club in town. Its chief rival in Louisville was the Olympic Base Ball Club. Both clubs, like their peers in other urban areas, were composed of young men from successful families. Hence, although it may seem odd today, it was almost a given in 1866 that these two clubs among the local clubs would be chosen to take part in the welcoming parade when President Andrew Johnson visited Louisville in September of that year. Most of the time, the young men were themselves already professionals or, in some cases, entrepreneurs. As one historian expressed it, members of early clubs were the 19th-century version of urban "yuppies." However, working class men joined the ranks of baseball players as early as the 1850s.[7]

Officially, the Louisville Club was created by the Kentucky legislature in 1866. In January of 1866 a bill introduced by Sen. William H. Grainger proposed to incorporate the Louisville Base Ball and Skating Park Company. The committee initially tasked with taking up the bill reported it out unfavorably with Mr. Harrison, chairman of the committee, asserting "it would tend to the promoting of dissipation and vice among the young men and women." Senator Grainger countered that he was "personally acquainted" with each of the young men and they "were of the most respectable families in his district; that their only object was to promote healthful amusement in both summer and winter." The bill ultimately passed, and the corporation was born. The name was not in any sense a misnomer. The club conducted baseball in the summer and, in the winter, turned the grounds into a massive ice-skating rink.[8]

Judging from the press, the most popular player on the Louisville Base Ball Club was Theodore Tracy. It may be that Tracy was the first sports star in Louisville. The *Daily Courier* declared his catching was "not to be excelled." The *Daily Journal* bestowed a nickname, "Little Tracy," and declared "there is no better 'catcher' in any club, either in the East or West." Tracy was injured in a game against Cincinnati's Buckeye Club and, consequently, missed the ensuing match against the Cincinnati Club. Louisville's loss was, therefore, attributed in no small part to Tracy's absence. Tracy's popularity was lasting. Decades later in nostalgic articles looking back on the days of amateur baseball in Louisville, it was Tracy the old timers could recall vividly.[9]

The Louisville Club was the first of the local "nines" (a term commonly used at the time interchangeably with "team" or "club") to take on clubs from other cities beginning with the Cumberland Club of Nashville, Tennessee, in 1866. The first match was played July 31, 1866, in Nashville at Ft. Gillem with Louisville the winner 39–23. The re-match took place in Louisville August 16, 1866, with Louisville winning again, this time by the score of 72–11. The series with the Cumberland Club is yet another event for which the date is often misstated. Once again, it is the reliance on Tarvin that causes the error, as he first placed the game in 1865.[10]

There are reasons to conclude the 1866 date is the correct one. The first is newspaper coverage. Neither of the city's two largest newspapers at the time, the *Daily Journal* and the *Daily Courier,* mention a game against a club from Nashville in 1865 but both gave extensive coverage to it in 1866. Moreover, when covering the games in 1866, neither makes reference to there having been a game a year earlier. It was a pattern of both publications when operating separately, and a few years later when merged, to make reference to previous visits by a club from out of town.

A second factor pointing to the games' being exclusively in 1866 is the man who initiated the contests, John Whitby Dickins. Dickins, a native of Great Britain, moved to the United States as a young man to study at the seminary in Boston. He later moved to Brooklyn and taught school while studying law. When the Civil War began he joined the 71st New York militia and was captured at First Manassas. After serving a stint in a couple of Confederate prison camps, he was exchanged and promptly re-joined the army, this time with the 165th New York. He was wounded in 1863, then promoted to sergeant-major and later transferred to the 100th U.S. Colored Troops as a captain. Stationed around Nashville, he was breveted major and then lieutenant colonel for bravery and gallantry displayed at the Battle of Nashville where he finished the war. Although Dickins was not discharged until December 1865, he was able during the year to travel back to England, marry the former Emma Lowe, and then return to the states. Given this history, it is not reasonable to believe the games could have taken place in 1865. It would have been impossible for Dickins to fulfill his responsibilities to the army, travel home to England to be married, organize a local baseball club, and arrange a series of games between the Cumberlands and the Louisvilles, all in the short span of April to September of 1865. Rather than return to Brooklyn once discharged, he accepted a position in Nashville with the Freedmen's Bureau and helped form the Cumberland Base Ball Club.[11]

In 1866 Dickins was invited to Louisville to umpire a game between the Louisvilles and the Olympics "for the Championship of Kentucky." Nine days later he was invited back to umpire the second game (a championship required two out of three). After the Louisville Club secured the championship, Dickins proposed a challenge between his club and Louisville, which was immediately accepted.[12]

* * *

When baseball clubs originated, games were usually intramural affairs. With the opposing players on each nine, and the spectators as well, all being members of the same club, winning and all that goes with it were of little concern. A genteel atmosphere was expected, and the spectators took no particular side. The polite thing to do was to applaud all manner of good play, regardless of who performed it, and to disregard errors. When clubs began to challenge each other, this expectation of non-partisanship among the spectators carried over. This became increasingly difficult for fans to do, especially when one club was local and the opponent was not. On the morning of a game between the Louisville and Cincinnati clubs, the *Daily Courier* felt itself compelled "to make a few suggestions to those who, by their encouraging attendance as spectators, show their lively interest in the manly sport."

> There is one other point on which a few words may as well be said. Of course all the local interest and even prejudice is in favor of our home club, but the slightest tincture of generosity or even justice would dictate an impartial view of the game as far as that is possible, and an impartial distribution of applause for *all good* play. Cheering *bad* play because it is fortunate for the opposite party is in extremely poor taste, and shows an utter want of appreciation of the beauties of the game.[13] [Emphasis in original.]

This idealistic approach to the game was already in disarray among the spectators. In a letter to her brother, a young socialite gives a glimpse into the subtle ways fans were already openly displaying their loyalties at a match. Sally Yandell was the daughter of Dr. Lunsford Pitts Yandell, Sr., who, with colleagues, founded the medical school at the University of Louisville.[14] One of her brothers, David, was also a well-known physician. During the Civil War David was the personal physician to the Confederacy's senior general, Albert Sidney Johnston.[15] On August 7, 1867, Sally wrote to another brother, William, who was at the time studying medicine in Texas. The letter is generally conveying the local gossip and current events in Louisville. But she adds some insight into spectators at baseball games:

> Base Ball is now the fashionable amusement here and most of the gentlemen belong to some club and the girls are strong partisans and most of them sport cockades and badges of some club when on the grounds. Cedar Hill Park is now used for this purpose.[16]

* * *

Aside from the decorum expected of the fans, the game in the 1860s was largely no different from that of today. There were, however, some differences in the rules of play. The pitching rules were different. The pitcher was 45 feet from home but positioned in a box rather than on a mound. The delivery had to be below the waist. That rule did not change until 1884. Also, the batter had the right to demand that pitches be above the waist or below it, and any pitch failing to achieve that (or doing so to excess—e.g., above the chest or below the knees) would be ruled an "unfair pitch." That rule would not change until after the 1886 season.[17]

The game was also significantly more dangerous than today's version. This was due in part to the lack of any protective equipment. Fielders did not wear gloves of any kind and catchers did not wear masks, chest protectors or shin guards. In addition, because medical science had not yet achieved anything close to today's capabilities, fatalities were common. One frequent cause of death was a player being hit in the abdomen by a batted or even thrown ball. "Base ball is a very fine game—a very fine game indeed; but when the ball is addicted to the habit of striking a fellow in the stomach and killing him, as was the case of a young man in Iowa the other day, we, for our part, would much prefer billiards." Perusing 19th-century newspapers reveals perhaps one or two such stories each year. It was not just the stomach. In Henderson, Kentucky, in 1877 a 12-year-old was struck by a ball in the leg, near the knee, fracturing the joint. He died as a result. Then there was the strange case of Peter J. Ward. Around 1876 (the reporter was uncertain), Ward was playing for the Olympic Club in Louisville. He was struck on the side and, though injured somewhat, everyone seemed to think all would soon be forgotten. It was not. Instead, each year around the anniversary of the event, an abscess would form in the spot where he had been struck. The abscess was bad enough it would debilitate him for a couple of days. "These abscesses increased in intensity with each recurring year until the fatal denouement of the present." Ward died April 13, 1883.[18]

* * *

In 1867 the Louisville Club expanded its competition. It began what became a continuing series of matches between clubs in Louisville and those in Cincinnati and Northern Kentucky. The first to appear was the Buckeye Club of Cincinnati who arrived in Louisville to play a game July 2, 1867. The Louisville Club won the game 45–37. A couple of days later, the Louisvilles (clubs did not create nicknames for themselves and were typically referred to in the plural form) boarded a steamship bound for Cincinnati to play the Cincinnati Club on July 4. Cincinnati, already under the management of Harry Wright but still amateur, won the game 60–36.

The big event of the summer was a visit by the National Club of Washington, D.C., on July 17. The National Club was among the first to consist primarily of players recruited to join for the express purpose of playing competitive ball. In 1867, they became the first amateur club to tour west beyond the Alleghanies.[19] Louisville was no match for the Nationals, losing 82–21 with future Hall of Famer George Wright of the visitors contributing three home runs. Whether the Nationals were truly an amateur club in any sense of the word has been questioned. But at the time, the debate was not so much about whether certain teams were paying their players, it centered around whether baseball should be professional at all. "Base ball is not a business," declared the *Daily Journal*, "as soon as it becomes so, it loses its proper and beneficial character, and no longer deserves our support."[20]

Although officially baseball remained an amateur game in 1868, touring by well-known clubs from Eastern cities, mainly New York and Philadelphia, grew more common. Likewise, clubs from New Orleans, St. Louis, Chicago and Iowa would appear from time to time. Following the 1868 season, however, two things changed. Locally, the Louisville Base Ball Club disbanded in a process that began shortly after the season closed. Nationally, there was the NABBP decision to allow clubs to openly pay players.[21]

While the Louisville Club was in charge of the city's baseball fortunes, a junior team formed in 1867 calling itself the Eagle Base Ball Club. Its players consisted of boys ranging in age from 15 to 18. When the Louisville Club's players moved into their professional (non-baseball) lives and the club essentially disbanded, the Eagle Club quickly ascended the ranks as the most prominent team.[22]

The Olympic Club of Washington, D.C., was the first openly professional club to visit Louisville. They faced the newly formed Kentucky Club at Cedar Hill Park July 6, 1869, and won easily, 44–9. The Empire Club of St. Louis, one of the best amateur clubs of the era, visited July 29. After defeating the Kentucky Club 30–28, they remained in town a few days and became the first prominent amateur club the Eagles faced. Despite their youth, the Eagles held up well, losing by a respectable score of 34–25. It would not be the last prominent team the Eagles would challenge. The following year the Eagles opened the 1870 season on April 21 with a game against the still undefeated Cincinnati Red Stockings. The Eagles were not expected to compete, and, in the end, they did just as expected: they lost 94–7. From 1870 through 1874, the Eagle Club, like its predecessor, played against amateur and professional clubs from around the country.[23]

* * *

The center of the baseball universe in Louisville in the 1860s and early 1870s was Cedar Hill Park. The park, which was actually privately owned land made available to the public by its owners, sat on the southside of Ormsby Avenue between Third and Fifth streets, with Fourth Street terminating at that point. Both the Louisville Club of the 1860s and then the Eagles after them called it home. Games against the early professional nines were played there. The *Courier-Journal* described it:

> They are the most beautiful and pleasant grounds in the country, as attested by all visiting clubs. They have, by nature, every quality which the heart of a base-ball player could desire. Water, of the best quality, near at hand, soft, velvety, and never-dying bluegrass, the coolest of summer breezes, and a complete surrounding of shade. They are pleasant not only for the players, but for the visitors. They are a retreat from the cares, the dust, noise, and heat of the city, where one can almost fancy himself in a species of paradise. Stretched out on the soft, green grass, under the sighing cedars, a quiet joy beams from the eye, and a soft tranquility steals over the heart and mind which can only be experienced by those who have escaped a crowded city for a lovely rural spot.[24]

Alfred Victor DuPont, scion of the family's Louisville wing, recognized the value he could realize in a newly constructed, Italian ornate mansion in the city's suburbs. The home stood on 17 acres of land immediately south of Cedar Hill Park. The Rev. Stuart Robinson had recently purchased the land and built the house, but DuPont's offer was apparently generous enough. Among DuPont's holdings in Louisville was the franchise for the passenger rail line on Fourth Street. He devised a plan to increase both the length of his line and the ridership. DuPont's plan was to purchase the home and the land and then petition the City to allow him to extend Fourth Street south. In return he would ask for an extension of his franchise for the rail line. Once that was accomplished, DuPont's brother and his family would occupy the home, and the grounds could be made available to the public as a park. Residents would then pay a fare on DuPont's rail line (both ways) to relax in the park or attend special events (for a fee) thus ultimately netting him a profit for his generosity. It worked. Cedar Hill was no more, and Central Park was born.[25]

* * *

By 1874 there were three tiers of baseball clubs: there were the professional, National Association clubs; there were amateur clubs such as the Eagles; then there were a group of semi-professional clubs consisting both of paid and unpaid talent. Games were commonly played within each tier, and between clubs of different tiers. That, coupled with the financial need of professional clubs to stop along the way to play games for the gate receipts, led to several future Louisville Grays seeing Louisville for the first time long before the formation of the National League.

The Brooklyn Atlantics visited Louisville in 1874 and with them was future Louisville outfielder and manager, Jack Chapman. In October, the Pearls, a National Association club from Philadelphia that finished fourth in the Association that year, took on the Eagles. All nine of the Pearls players who played that day were on a National League roster in 1876. Two of them, Chick Fulmer and George Bechtel, would be on the roster of the Louisville Grays. Another, Bill Craver, would replace Fulmer as the Grays' shortstop in 1877, serve as the team's assistant captain, and become one of "the Louisville Four" as the press subsequently dubbed them. Then there was their pitcher, William Arthur "Candy" Cummings. Cummings is the player most often credited with inventing the curve ball. He would eventually be inducted into the Baseball Hall of Fame in 1939.[26]

While the newspapers focused mostly on games played by gentlemen and the sons of prominent men, other clubs played baseball throughout the city. In 1871 the *Louisville Commercial* was the first local paper to cover a game between black clubs. On September 9, 1871, the *Commercial* reported on a game between the Athletics of Frankfort and the Atlantics of Louisville. The game was played on the grounds of one of the prominent local white clubs, the Falls City, and was well attended. Despite the fact that black and white clubs would not play a reported game against one another in Louisville for another decade, cooperation between them was increasingly frequent in the 1870s. In this case, however, the local club was over-matched as the Frankfort club pounded several home runs in the game and won it 58–33.[27]

The *Courier-Journal* expanded its coverage to black clubs by 1874. "The Globe Base Ball Club, consisting of colored men, has been recently organized in the city." The paper continued: "If they succeed, Louisville may soon see a novelty in a game of base ball between some colored club from abroad and the one now in the city." The Globes would indeed succeed, and the "novelty" would be more than the *Courier-Journal* anticipated. On August 25 the *Courier-Journal* reported that the "Mutuals and the Globe, two city colored clubs, played a game on the Eckford grounds yesterday afternoon." The Globes won 44–18 and, according to the paper, had yet to suffer a loss "by any colored club they have played."[28]

Coverage of African American teams would continue. According to Walter N. Haldeman, coverage of the clubs indicated the preferences of the population of Louisville. In a speech given at the YMCA in January 1878, the senior Haldeman expressed the view that newspapers, rather than inform public opinion, should reflect the interest and views of their public.

> You may be assured of one fact, and that is newspapers will print the kind of matter their readers most desire; and this is why the character of any community may be so readily known and judged by its press. If they delight in bull-fights, or prize-fights, or amusements of a low order and corrupting character, then will reports and discussions of these things most abound in the columns of their papers. If the prevailing appetite is for fairs, concerts, and other amusements conceded to be inoffensive—and I don't know but I should include base-ball in this category—then will references to *them* occupy space commensurate with public requirements.[29]

If one agrees with that sentiment, then the added coverage of including black clubs, albeit to a lesser extent than their white counterparts, indicates the City of Louisville wanted more baseball.

* * *

With the demise of Cedar Hill Park earlier in the decade, the Eagles had to secure new grounds. They did not have to move far. Immediately south of newly opened Central Park was a piece of ground they could use. They enclosed the grounds at the northeast corner at what is now the intersection of Fourth and Magnolia. To increase their revenue needed to maintain their lease, they reverted to a practice of the former Louisville Base Ball Club: in the winter of 1874 they converted the grounds into a massive ice rink.

The work of creating the pond began at the beginning of the fall with the opening set for December 1, 1874. They built a club house, complete with a "red hot stove," and equipped it with an assortment of skates for patrons to rent. They also staffed the club house with "obliging attendants to assist the visitors." A red lantern was hung at the corner of Fourth and Walnut (now Muhammad Ali) each day when the pond was sufficiently frozen. In addition, red flags would be placed on the street cars covering

Walnut and Fourth streets. Theodore Tracy, the first baseball star in Louisville, posted an ad in the *Courier-Journal* letting the readers know that admission to the pond would be 25 cents in the morning and 50 cents after 4:00. Or, if one preferred, a season pass could be purchased for $5.00 for a "Gentleman and Lady" or $4.00 for a "Gentleman or Lady" and $3.00 for those under 14. Tickets were for sale at Tracy's store located at 184 Fourth Street.[30]

The pond measured approximately 400 feet by 500 feet. The club house consisted of a two-story plank house at the entrance "with a commodious sitting room provided with benches and a large stove." The street cars were crowded with those coming and going:

> But at night the scene was most interesting. The place was illuminated by a large chandelier of gas lamps, constructed on a tall pole in the center of the park. The burners were sufficiently large and numerous to shed a mellow light over the entire area of the ice. Several hundred skaters were at one time on the ice together, and the silent, almost noiseless, gliding about of supple forms, faintly reflected by the elevated lights, presented a spectacle wild, weird and peculiar.[31]

In addition to random skating, special events were held at the park. Among the events was a demonstration of "fancy skating" featuring some of the best skaters in town. The skaters "will show how the thing is done on scientific principles." The event of the season was a skating masquerade. It promised to be "the gayest thing on ice." "A number of the first and best young ladies in the city will take part, and some of the costumes are being prepared regardless of expense." But, to alleviate any concerns this might cause, the *Courier-Journal* assured its readers the "management will attend to it that no improper parties are admitted, so that nothing need be feared on that score." In addition to masquerades and demonstrations, there was also a baseball game. The Eagles took on a picked nine in a two-inning affair which the Eagles lost.[32]

* * *

Often, once a club was established in senior status, a new junior version of the club came along. Such was the case in Louisville with the Eagle Club; a Junior Eagle club formed. Among its players was John Haldeman.[33]

John Haldeman was born December 2, 1855, in Peewee Valley, Kentucky. His father, Walter Haldeman, was at the time publisher of the *Daily Courier*. The *Daily Courier* was the city's Democrat-leaning publication and, accordingly, in 1861 Haldeman took editorial positions in favor of the Confederacy. Haldeman was highly critical of President Lincoln and the military effort to hold the Confederate states in the Union. This drew the ire of Federal commanders in Louisville who resolved to arrest the elder

The Eagle Juniors Were "Simon Pures"! ONLY THREE MEMBERS OF THIS FAMOUS AMATEUR TEAM OF 1875 SURVIVE.

The Eagle Juniors of 1874. This copy of the photograph appeared in the *Louisville Evening Post,* February 21, 1922. The handwriting on the photograph is believed to be that of John Haldeman's younger brother, Bruce, who cut it out to send to his son, Walter Haldeman, II. The players appear to be correctly identified in the cutting and are: back row (L to R): Tom Shreve, Louis Davidson and Alex Robinson; middle row: Ormsby Fetter, Joseph Hamilton, John Haldeman and Charles Singleton; seated on the ground (L to R): R.C. Judge and John Morris. During the 1876 and 1877 seasons, Morris occasionally served as a National League umpire in Louisville Grays games including one of the marathon games against the Mutuals in 1876. Credit: The Filson Historical Society, Louisville, Kentucky.

Haldeman in order to silence his criticisms. When his father fled Louisville in 1861 to avoid arrest by federal troops, presumably young John and his siblings went along. They returned in 1865 when the war ended. Other than the family's self-imposed exile in Tennessee and Georgia during the war, John was raised primarily in Louisville. In 1872 he graduated from Louisville's Male High School where his class valedictorian was the 14-year-old son of Jewish immigrants from Eastern Europe by the name of Louis Dembitz Brandeis. From there, Haldeman matriculated to the then-recently re-named Washington & Lee University in Lexington, Virginia.[34]

[21 Feb. 1922]

NAPLES-ON-THE-GULF, FLORIDA

Note from Bruce Haldeman to his son, Walter Haldeman, II. It accompanied the newspaper clipping above and reads: "Tuesday February 21st Dearest Walter: Just a line to enclose this interesting old picture of Uncle Johnnie. He was quite an athlete wasn't he? Am also enclosing a nice little calendar that I thought you might like to have, the Trust Co. having sent me an extra one. I have the most fascinating literature about France Switzerland Italy & Northern Africa—do wish I were within earshot for I'd love to talk it over with you." Walter Haldeman II would later correspond with writer Lee Allen to provide him information about John Haldeman for Allen's book *The National League Story*. Credit: The Filson Historical Society, Louisville, Kentucky.

From school Haldeman wrote his mother often and many of those letters concerned baseball. In 1874 he light-heartedly urged his mother to warn his younger brother, Bruce, that if more letters were not coming his way, "I will not carry him out to any of those big games of base ball the Eagle Juniors are going to play when I get home." The following fall, back at school after a summer with the Eagle Juniors, he informed his mother of his collegiate baseball achievements. "The last game of base ball this year at this place took place yesterday on the VMI grounds. The contestants were the W. & L.W.B. B.C. & the Cadet club of the V.M.I. [Virginia Military Institute—also located in Lexington, Virginia] Score 12 to 5 in our favor. Your humble played first and distinguished himself muchly." Later, he was named captain of the school team for 1874–1875 and promptly set his sights on defeating the University of Virginia "for the grand title of 'Champions of Virginia.'"[35]

Not all his letters were about the game. His mother frequently urged him to become more active in the church. Haldeman finally answered by explaining to his mother where his thoughts resided in the spiritual realm:

I always read over those parts of your letters exhorting me to be a Christian very carefully but I am sorry to say that unless some great change takes place in me I will not become a member of the church for many years. I think a person can be a good Christian without becoming a member of the church and I intend to try and act on the simple little platform of being good myself and doing good to my fellow man. If I were to join the church now I would be simply jumping into something I know nothing about. At my age one is not expected to know much about spiritual doctrine, but after I get well settled down in life and understand the full import of the responsibilities a person has to take upon himself in connecting himself with the church, I will then be better prepared to judge for myself how I shall act—something I am at present positively unable to decide.[36]

During the summers, even prior to college, Haldeman would act as an unofficial correspondent and baseball editor for the *Courier-Journal*. He traveled with the senior Eagle Club reporting their games from around the Commonwealth and beyond. It appears he was in charge of the baseball news generally. His work impressed even his older brother, William, who was working in Texas at the time and following the news from home daily. Yet William, his distance notwithstanding, joined others in Louisville in lamenting the quality of baseball available in his hometown. In a letter to their mother during the Summer of 1874 William wrote: "Pity, ain't it, that Louisville as a supporter of the national game can't rig out anything but a third-rate team? 'but, twas always thus.' Johnnie edits the B.B. column of the CJ very creditably, this in fact being the only creditable part that I can discern that appertains to Base Ball playing in Louisville." In 1875, after completing his studies at Washington & Lee, John Haldeman became the full-time baseball editor of the *Courier-Journal*.[37]

* * *

By 1875 the City of Louisville was like most American cities in that it was experiencing growth in its population and its physical size. Several structures known well to locals already existed such as the courthouse on Jefferson between Fifth and Sixth, City Hall and the Cathedral of the Assumption. The first bridge to span the Ohio River at Louisville had recently opened and new landmarks were coming into existence.

Most of the streets Louisvillians recognize today intersecting Broadway were already in existence by 1875. Not all of them terminated at Ormsby. One block east of Fourth was Third Street that continued about a mile further south past the House of Refuge—a home for wayward children on the grounds now occupied by the University of Louisville's Belknap Campus. In reality, Third Street continued further south, but the Nicholson pavement ended at the House of Refuge. Nicholson blocks as pavement ultimately failed, but at the time, the City of Louisville was experimenting with multiple forms of paving its streets at least in the downtown area and what is now Old Louisville.[38]

About a mile south of that was a piece of ground located practically next to the rail lines operated by the Louisville & Nashville Railroad. The land, about 70 acres, was owned by the uncle of a locally prominent citizen by the name of Meriwether Lewis Clark, Jr., grandson of the explorer William Clark of the "Lewis and Clark" expedition. The younger Clark was married to the former Mary Martin Anderson who, at the time of their elopement, was living with her aunt, Pattie Anderson Ten Broeck, at a farm called Hurstbourne located east of Louisville on Shelbyville Road. Pattie's husband, Richard Ten Broeck, was a well-known breeder and trainer of thoroughbreds and introduced Clark to the sport, including a trip to England to see the English Derby.[39]

Louisville badly needed a first-class venue for thoroughbred racing. The two prior attempts—the Oakland House and Race Course located near Seventh and Magnolia, and later the Woodlawn Race Course east of the city and situated between Westport and Shelbyville roads—had both failed. (Though Woodlawn left behind the oldest continuous trophy awarded, the Woodlawn Vase, which is now awarded each year to the winner of the Preakness Stakes in Baltimore.) Clark set out to establish just such a venue. Clark's uncle, John Churchill, leased the grounds south of the House of Refuge to Clark and his partners and there they organized and constructed the Louisville Jockey Club and Driving Association. To ease access to the venue, Third Street south of the pavement was filled with gravel and Fourth was also extended. In the spring of 1875, with the work complete, they presented the first Kentucky Derby.[40]

Another development Louisvillians of today would recognize is the character of Fourth Street. With the opening of the Louisville Jockey Club, Fourth Street was extended. The *Courier-Journal* observed how retail shopping had coalesced on Fourth and a visitor could enjoy a ride along "as pretty an avenue as exists in the country." In addition to the shopping north of Broadway, there were the homes lining the street in the suburbs south of Broadway, and the visitor could pass by the baseball grounds of the Eagles—"the handsomest in the country"—as well as the new Jockey Club–"the prettiest and most complete in the United States."[41]

* * *

Early in 1875, the management of the Eagles adopted the practices of other regional clubs and began adding hired players to their ranks. The first player to sign a professional contract to play baseball for any Louisville team was Joe Ellick who signed with the Eagles for $900 in April 1875.

Ellick would go on to play a handful of games in the majors over the course of four seasons spanning nine years. Eventually he became an umpire.[42] By the end of the 1875 season, virtually the entire Eagle roster was comprised of paid players.

Having the semi-professional Eagle ball club was a step forward for Louisville. Hosting the first Kentucky Derby which, by all accounts, had gone well for the city, also improved the sports fan's life. In terms of professional spectator sports, there was not much more other than boxing which was highly regulated throughout the country. So in terms of sports as a form of entertainment, Louisville had about as much as any other city. But, for some, it was not enough. A first-rate professional baseball club was wanted.

Word first leaked of the formation of a professional club in Louisville in the summer of 1875. The early rumors were that Nat Hicks, then a catcher with the Mutual Club of New York, would captain the squad. But more important to those involved was that the club be "a first-class one, able to compete closely and successfully with foreign organizations." Success was all important: "unless we can have a good club, it will be better to have none at all." Initially there were two separate groups undertaking the proposition of forming a professional club. A group in the west end of town had already acquired rights on a parcel of ground for just such a purpose. The *Courier-Journal* urged the two to merge as it believed only one professional team could be successful in Louisville.[43]

An organizational meeting was called for August 7, 1875, to be held in the "gentlemen's parlor" at the Galt House. The *Courier-Journal* made clear that the introduction of professional baseball to the city was not merely for sport, but profit as well. A "first-class club" is one that will "pay a dividend to all shareholders." It would also promote the city. "A professional base ball club of high rank not only pays the stockholders, but as has been demonstrated in other cities, helps to bring trade to the city." This, the *Courier-Journal* explained, was due to the fact a professional club "advertises the city all over the country, as with the name of the club is always coupled the name of the city." Stock solicitations began in earnest a few days later with a goal of an initial capitalization of $20,000. The organization took shape quickly and Walter Haldeman was named the club's president. Due to the limitations on the elder Haldeman's time, the day-to-day duties fell to the club's vice-president, Charles E. Chase, a 25-year-old officer and director of his father's wholesale liquor business, E.H. Chase & Co.[44]

Surprisingly little is known about Charles Chase. The first time his name appears in the *Courier-Journal* associated with baseball is when he was named vice-president of the club. His father, E.H. Chase, had an

Receipt for the purchase of stock (at $10.00) in the Louisville Grays in the name of Walter N. Haldeman. Credit: The Filson Historical Society, Louisville, Kentucky.

Receipt for the purchase of stock (at $10.00) in the Louisville Grays in the name of John A. Haldeman. According to Walter Haldeman's biographer, the elder Haldeman paid for both shares of stock. Credit: The Filson Historical Society, Louisville, Kentucky.

established wholesale business in New York through which he purchased bourbon from numerous Kentucky distillers. The beverages would be shipped to New York and, from there, the rest of the country. In 1867 the elder Chase determined this was a foolishly inefficient system and, therefore, established his warehouse and distribution center in Louisville on Third Street near the river. By 1874 the operation had grown to extensive proportions. Charles started his career on Wall Street as the confidential secretary to James Fisk, Jr., then a powerful financier. At some point, he relocated to Louisville to join his father's firm.[45]

What is known, however, is that Chase was no fool. He understood inherently that running a baseball club was not the same as running a wholesale liquor business. There were other issues to consider. To gain a better understanding of the myriad of issues he would face, he began a series of correspondence with William Ambrose Hulbert, president of the Chicago Base Ball Club, seeking his advice on organizing a club and the team. In Hulbert, Chase found a more-than-willing advisor and confidante. "From my store of experience," Hulbert wrote, "I can doubtless furnish many hints and suggestions that will prove of service to you." In Chase, Hulbert found a willing student whose ideas about making baseball more business-like were precisely aligned with his own. Hulbert advised Chase on everything from the structure of the organization ("I would recommend you not to have *more* than five directors"), to the type of players they should target ("Taking the chance is risky, but I want players that go"). Hulbert used his knowledge of players around the Association to inform Chase which ones were trustworthy, and which ones were not ("I think you ought to do much better than to hire Warren White").[46]

Unbeknownst to Chase, and virtually everyone else at the time, Hulbert was already in the process of planning a coup of his own against the National Association. Hulbert made his wealth in the commodities exchange trading coal. "But, being a man of business efficiency and of moral consequence, Hulbert was a total misfit in the financially and ethically bankrupt National Association." Hulbert had become frustrated with the Association's lack of structure and its inability to control the vices among its own. As historian Lee Allen noted, Hulbert's mission was born out of a sense of business rather than altruism. Creating an entirely new model was not enough, however. While he was at it, he wanted to "wreck the men who controlled the game." Physically and mentally, Hulbert was well equipped for the challenge. He was a large man, standing 6'2" and weighing about 215 pounds at a time when the average man was less than 5'10" and 160 pounds.[47] As historian Neil Macdonald described him:

> He was wagon-wide at the shoulders, his massive head supported by a well-muscled neck and topped by a fine crop of hair. His huge body commanded twice the space of an ordinary person. He seemed a stony boulder of a man, an enormous muscular presence whose very appearance ordered attention and respect from any nearby mortal. His awesome physique was augmented by an intellect of superior quality. He was as mentally sharp as he was physically imposing.[48]

In addition to re-making professional baseball, Hulbert set out on a mission to transform his Chicago club into a powerhouse. To accomplish this, he recruited the best pitcher in the National Association, Albert Goodwill "A.G." Spalding, of the Boston Red Stockings. Spalding had grown up in nearby Rockford, Illinois, and Hulbert used that to his advantage to convince Spalding, along with three of his teammates, to commit to playing for Chicago in 1876. With Spalding's assistance, Hulbert also recruited Adrian Anson of the Philadelphia club to make the same commitment. Under National Association rules, contracts for the next season could not be signed prior to a date certain during the current season. Hence, it is questionable whether the signings of Spalding and the others, coming as they did and when they did, would be upheld by the National Association's judiciary committee if Boston or Philadelphia elected to challenge them. But Hulbert did not care—his plan was to gain confederates in the West, then jointly work together to bring in a handful of Eastern clubs, and essentially blow up the National Association.[49]

Charles Chase and Louisville, coming along when they did, fit snugly into Hulbert's plan. In addition to Chase, Hulbert was simultaneously communicating with Charles Fowle of the St. Louis Club and, through A.G. Spalding, John Joyce of the Cincinnati Club. Fowle and Chase seem to have been accepting of the concept of a Western alliance to stand face-to-face with the Eastern clubs. Joyce in Cincinnati was a bit more hesitant. Hulbert emphasized to each that the most important factor was for them to act as one, not as individuals, as otherwise, they would all go down together.[50]

Getting buy-in was not Hulbert's only concern. He also had to determine which Western cities would fit best. First, there was population to consider. Smaller cities traditionally had difficulty adequately supporting their clubs. But even in cities with a population above 75,000, there were issues to consider. The first concern was excluding gamblers from the ball grounds. This was a matter of great importance to Hulbert. His perspective seems to have been that the presence of gambling at the games was ruining baseball's appeal to the middle class and those who just wanted to see an honest game for their money. That could cause a problem in Cincinnati and Louisville. "With wagering a mortal imperative in the Blue Grass country, it amazed some cranks that both Cincinnati and Louisville had followed Hulbert's edict in ordering a copious quantity of police to control betting and keep the gambling community, at least, out of their ballparks." Further complicating matters was Hulbert's plan to forbid alcohol sales at games and to forbid games' being played (even exhibition games) on Sundays. Cincinnati and St. Louis, each with large German populations, would make the prohibition of beer a tough sell. Louisville presented its own problems in that regard. Three of the top directors owned or ran large liquor distributorships. Chase was one, but there were also Thomas H. Sherley of T.H. Sherley & Co. and W.H. Thomas of Newcomb, Buchanan & Co., both of whom sat on the Executive Committee.[51]

Sundays were the biggest problem. The working class tended to work six days a week with Sunday being their only day off. During the week, with games starting mid-afternoon, they had no opportunity to attend. Forbidding Sundays meant excluding a large portion of the population of each city and denying the resultant revenue to the clubs. However, Hulbert saw the connection as running the other way. He, and others, believed that denying the working class a meaningful opportunity to attend would serve to *increase* revenue. Hulbert's goal, and hence, the goal of the National League, was to make the game acceptable to the middle classes which tended to be native-born Protestants. The working classes, which tended to be German, Irish, Catholic and Jewish, were considered undesirable as their rowdy tendencies would offend the middle-class patrons being sought. As Hulbert put it: "The sole purpose of the league, outside of the business aspect, is to make it worthy of the patronage, support, and respect of the best class of people." As one of the owners of the Philadelphia franchise expressed it: "the better class of people will not tolerate the antics of that class … which does not know how to behave itself."[52]

By fall of 1875, Hulbert's plans had advanced sufficiently that a meeting of the group of four clubs seemed appropriate. In a letter to Hulbert, Chase urged that the meeting be held in Louisville.[53] His reasoning was that as Haldeman was the publisher of the largest paper in the state, and was vice-president of the Associated Press, Haldeman could keep a lid on any media leaks. While this was indeed the opinion expressed, the plan failed miserably. The *St. Louis Globe* published in October that there were rumors of the formation of "a Western clique" consisting of Chicago, Cincinnati, Louisville and St. Louis. Before the meeting was even set, the New Haven Club in Connecticut was politicking for inclusion. Moreover, Hulbert's ally, Lewis

William A. Hulbert. Photograph taken probably in the late 1870s or early 1880s. Credit: National Baseball Hall of Fame and Museum, Cooperstown, New York.

Meacham of the *Chicago Tribune*, had already printed an article laying out the entire structure of a new league (no doubt at Hulbert's request). Word of the meeting itself was in the *Courier-Journal* just two days after its adjournment.[54] The substance of the meeting, or at least the details of what was discussed, were not made public by the *Courier-Journal*. It did not need to be, Meacham had already accomplished that. In reality neither the substance nor the conference were ever a secret in any meaningful sense of the word. Later, after the National League was formed, Henry Chadwick, sports editor of *The New York Clipper*, would complain about its having been achieved in secret. But one has to wonder: "secret from whom?"

* * *

The meeting was held at the Louisville Hotel December 16 and 17, 1875, not at the Galt House as has been reported elsewhere. According to A.G. Spalding, who attended the meeting with Hulbert, once the representatives were all assembled Hulbert laid out the ideas he and Spalding had spent the last several months mapping.

> He went over the current history of the game, showed conditions just as they were, declared that gambling in every form must be eradicated at once and forever, and closed with the announcement that it was proposed to organize a National League of Professional Base Ball Clubs, under rules which should protect players and management and reduced the game to a business system such as had never heretofore obtained.

Once agreement was reached in Louisville on what the new League would be, Hulbert and Fowle were deputized by the group to present the plan to four specific Eastern clubs—the Boston Red Stockings, the Hartford Dark Blues, the Mutuals of New York and the Athletics of Philadelphia.[55]

The choice of the four Eastern clubs was by no means at random. New York and Philadelphia, the nation's two largest cities, were a must. But Boston was the key. It was not so much about the city itself, but it was more about the club's manager, Harry Wright. After the original Cincinnati Red Stockings lost their first game ever in 1870, fan support quickly waned, and the club went out of existence in 1871. Wright and his brother George packed their bags and moved to Boston where, with the support of financial backers, they created the Boston Red Stockings. Under Wright's guidance, Boston captured the National Association pennant each of the four years between 1872 and 1875.[56]

Wright's importance to Hulbert went beyond his success in competition. Wright was a potential lynch pin for Hulbert. "Considered by his colleagues as the association's moral pillar, Wright had the potential of being an entire colonnade of morality for any new league." Just as importantly, Wright's support would serve as a badly needed counterweight from the criticism that was certain to come from Chadwick. Although already referred to by some as "the father of baseball," Chadwick was the man Hulbert feared, resented and distrusted most. Chadwick had become increasingly conservative, yet he wielded outsized influence among his peers and the baseball public.[57] Hulbert's thinking appears to have been that if he could create and present the new league without Chadwick's input, then by the time the organization was announced, it would be a *fait accompli* leaving Chadwick nothing to do but complain. That is exactly what ultimately transpired.

Aside from Boston, each of the other three cities presented problems much different than Hulbert had to overcome with Louisville, Cincinnati and St. Louis. Hartford, Connecticut, smallest of the eight, was chosen over New Haven due the fact that while both cities drew well at home, New Haven was box office poison on the road.[58] New York and Philadelphia, despite their importance, presented their own problems. No one wanted anything to do with either the Mutuals or the Athletics. As one historian described it: "The history of the Mutuals was a chronicle of corruption, a team reportedly being in league with gamblers as far back as 1868." As previously mentioned, "the title of ballplayer on the Mutuals was synonymous with gambler."

The club was formed originally in 1857 by members of the New York City Mutual Hook & Ladder Co. No. 1. On paper at least its president was a character by the name of William Cammeyer, owner of the Union Grounds in Brooklyn where they played. However, the real power behind the club was William M. "Boss" Tweed and his corrupt Tammany Hall. Later, after the League was announced, among Henry Chadwick's criticisms was that the League proclaimed itself dedicated to ridding the sport of corruption yet had among its founding members one of the most corrupt clubs ever known.[59] He was, of course, correct and Hulbert never tried to argue otherwise. Hulbert's likely reasoning was that the sizable population of New York simply could not be ignored and the Mutuals were his only viable option.

Philadelphia was a different problem. The club formed originally in 1859 as a townball club and switched to baseball in 1860. By 1876, its president was Col. Thomas Fitzgerald who was at the same time editor of Philadelphia's *City Item* as well as a well-known dramatist and art critic. There were issues between the Athletics and Chicago. The most recent was the Davey Force affair. In 1874 Hulbert signed the star shortstop away from the Athletics. Initially when the Athletics protested the National Association ruled in favor of Chicago. But after the winter meetings and new elections (installing members of the Athletics and their allies onto the league's judiciary committee), the Association reversed itself and awarded Force back to Philadelphia. There were on-going issues as well between Hulbert and Fitzgerald. But Hulbert was by no means alone. Boston's Harry Wright considered the Athletics an unsound and uncooperative organization. Nevertheless, practicalities prevailed in that, as was the situation in New York, there were multiple clubs to choose from among the Philadelphia cohort, but the truth was the Athletics, like the Mutuals, were least bad of a bad lot.[60]

A meeting was called for February 2, 1876, in New York. Prior to the meeting the press was informed of a meeting of the Grand Council of the National Association. The announcement included some puffery, but generally gave the impression that it would be a ho-hum affair to discuss some minor tweaks to the game. Notice was sent to the Eastern teams on January 23, giving them little time to organize a unified front. Chadwick was also given notice, but just one week prior. Upon reading the notice Chadwick decided not to attend. "His decision not to attend the meeting would have a profound effect on the next century of American baseball."[61]

Details of precisely what transpired at the meeting are sketchy at best. According to A.G. Spalding, once all the invited magnates had arrived, Hulbert locked the door and presented his plan. Hulbert explained the cities were chosen based on their population size and that there could only be one club in any city. The reason for both was to monopolize a large population of potential customers. The annual entry fee for the League would be $100, rather than the ten dollars required by the National Association. This would make it more likely that League members would be clubs of financial resources sufficient to see them through the season.

Perhaps most importantly, it would be a league of *clubs*, not players, and each club was to be structured as a business rather than as a cooperative. As A.G. Spalding would later explain, the thinking here was that players had too much say over how the clubs in the National Association were run. Players had the ability to play, but not the ability to manage a business, at least not while they were playing. There had to be a separation between playing and managing. Spalding's explanation was little more than a polite way of saying what management thought of players, at least as a group. As historian Robert Gelzheiser explains: "Owners generally saw themselves as above the players, and they often depicted them as greedy man-children incapable of comprehending the intricacies of their industry or of understanding what was best for them."[62]

Hulbert also decreed that there would be no games played on Sundays by any league team including exhibition games. To control patronage, and to put ticket prices on par with other respectable forms of entertainment such as theater, the admission price to games league-wide was to be 50 cents. The league would be governed by a board of directors with strict enforcement of the rules and, finally, each club was required to eliminate gamblers from entry into the ballparks. The four eastern clubs conceded and on February 4, 1876, the formation of the National League of Professional Base Ball Clubs was announced in the press.[63]

As anticipated, On February 12, 1876, Henry Chadwick penned an article in the *New York Clipper* in which he referred to the new league as "A Startling Coup d'Etat." Chadwick was not opposed to reform. He recognized the need for significant reform with the National Association. His primary objection was the "secret meeting with closed doors and a star-chamber method of attaining the ostensible objects in view." Why was this necessary, he wondered, unless there was "some secret object in view which it was not considered desirable to have made public." Nationally, the reaction of the press was mixed. *The New York Times* merely noted the disappointment of the clubs excluded from the League. The *Courier-Journal* was exuberant: "The National Base Ball League Has Closed the Doors of Admission to Unreliable Clubs" and "The West and the East Have United to Elevate the Standard of the Game."[64]

CHAPTER TWO

The First Season—1876

Prior to any concerns Louisville had with forming a new league, there was the matter of finding players to fill out a professional roster. The first step was to find a field boss, a manager. It was the manager's job to find players, sign them, direct the team through training and during the season, make the travel arrangements, oversee the games, and generally handle the affairs of the club. Louisville considered multiple candidates, but eventually settled on Jack Chapman. Chapman, a native of Brooklyn, New York, had been playing high level baseball since 1862. One of his teammates that year with the Excelsiors of Brooklyn was Jim Creighton, thought by some to have been the first player paid for his services. Chapman was on deck when Creighton belted a home run and at that instant Chapman heard a pop. Creighton assured the young ball player that the sound was his belt snapping. A week or so later Creighton died, most likely the result of a ruptured spleen.[1]

Chapman spent the 1875 season with the St. Louis Brown Stockings of the National Association. He would eventually recruit one of his Browns teammates, Bill Hague, to join him in Louisville. In April of 1875 the Browns visited Louisville

Right: **John C. "Jack" Chapman. Photograph taken probably around 1890. Chapman managed two Louisville teams returning to Louisville toward the end of the 1889 season and led the 1890 Cyclones to the only Major League pennant in Louisville history. Credit: National Baseball Hall of Fame and Museum, Cooperstown, New York.**

to play the Eagles and Chapman was interviewed by the *Courier-Journal*. During the interview he was asked his opinion of professional baseball in Louisville. He conceded he thought the city should have a professional team and expressed surprise it did not already have one. Chapman was highly regarded by other players and owners around the Association and was considered a steady hand.[2]

Chapman was not content with just managing and playing for a baseball club. He had other business interests as well. In January of 1876 he signed a lease for No. 2 Tyler Block intending to "open there one of the finest base-ball emporiums in the West." The Tyler Block was a three-story commercial building which featured a 200-foot-long limestone façade fashioned in a Renaissance Revival manner. It stood along the north side of Jefferson Street between Third and Fourth. Built in 1874, in its 99th year of existence it earned a spot in the National Register of Historic Places. The following year, in 1974, it was summarily razed in favor of what was then a hideous-looking convention center, and now is marginally less so. Leaving aside consideration of the economic impact of a convention center, aesthetically the city lost. In addition to Chapman's baseball store, the space would serve as a headquarters for the Louisville team. In the back portion there was a room measuring 80 feet by 20 feet which was outfitted with billiard tables, writing tables, chairs and sofas, racks for daily papers with "everything calculated to make the members feel at home and contented."[3]

James A. Devlin. Photograph taken in 1876 during his first season with Louisville. Credit: National Baseball Hall of Fame and Museum, Cooperstown, New York.

Prior to his being publicly announced as Louisville's manager, Chapman began writing to players around the Association to begin the recruitment process. Chase assisted somewhat in this process, even going so far as to ask Hulbert to tell four players Louisville might consider, but whom Hulbert had determined to release from his club, "not to make any positive arrangements with any other club until they hear from us." Of the four, three—Warren White, Mike Golden and Paddy Quinn—never signed with Louisville nor any other club in 1876. Of the three, only Mike Golden played more than four major league games after 1875. Golden posted a 3–13 record as a pitcher in 22 games (18 starts) with the Milwaukee Grays in 1878—his last season in the majors. However, of interest to Chapman and among the first targets he identified was the backup pitcher, known in the day as the "change pitcher," for Hulbert's White Stockings, James A. Devlin.[4]

Jim Devlin was born June 6, 1849, in Philadelphia, Pennsylvania. The 1850 Census identified his mother, Agness, as an Irish immigrant. The two lived together with another Irish couple, Patrick and Bridget Dunahue, along with the Dunahues' four children. The Census did not list the Devlins again in 1860 or 1870 so little is known about Devlin's childhood. Based upon the fact that he was only semi-literate as an adult we can deduce that education was not a point of emphasis. He began his major

league career in 1873 with the Philadelphia Whites of the National Association. The following year he was poached by Chicago to play mostly first base and outfield.

Because the rules mandated underhand pitching, most teams used only one pitcher with another player serving as the change pitcher in the event the primary pitcher could not go. In 1875 Chicago's primary pitcher was George Zettlein, but they discovered Devlin had tremendous ability at the craft, so he became the change pitcher that year. In spite of the fact he was on a terrible team, his numbers aside from wins and losses were good. In 28 games (24 of them starts), his record was a meagre 7–16. However, his earned run average was 1.93. He added a .289 batting average and led the White Stockings in runs batted in with 40 in 69 total games played

Charles N. "Pop" Snyder. Photograph taken 1876. Credit: National Baseball Hall of Fame and Museum, Cooperstown, New York.

between pitcher and first base. Louisville signed him to be their primary pitcher and the reviews that followed were universally positive.[5]

To go along with a pitcher, Louisville needed a battery mate to catch. Fairly early on Chapman and Chase set their sights on Charles Nicholas Snyder. Snyder, despite having just turned 21 on October 6, 1875, would be better known by the nickname "Pop" when, as a 27-year-old manager, his players applied the appellation that would stick the rest of his career. Little is known about his youth although it is known he was from Washington, D.C. He began his professional career there playing for the Washington Blue Legs in 1873 before moving to Baltimore in 1874 and Philadelphia in 1875. Eventually he would come to be considered one of the best catchers of the era. Although it was likely unnecessary, even Hulbert took time to encourage Chase to secure Snyder. In a letter written to Chase October 21, 1875, Hulbert inquired as to whether Snyder had signed yet, then followed that up with "I should dislike to have you lose Snyder for I think mighty well of his ability as a catcher and I believe him to be a good man every way." Chase responded at length two days later:

> Snyder has not as yet signed with us, but he has given us his word that he would sign Nov 1st & we have written him that his contract & check for advance money would be forwarded in a few days. I know that the Athletics want him & are using every endeavor to get him, & I sometimes fear that they will be successful. Snyder is undoubtedly a good player & we want him badly, but if he breaks his word with us I can see no remedy save to ventilate him thoroughly through the papers, which I shall take diabolical pleasure in doing. I think it is rather dastardly in the Athletics to try & get him when they know he has given his word to play with us, but I understand that it is in keeping with many other transactions of [illegible].

Hulbert responded two days after that encouraging Chase to call upon Nick Young at the Second Auditor's Office in D.C. Young, who Hulbert described as "square as a dollar," and Hulbert were friends and Young, Hulbert believed, would have a great deal of influence on Snyder's decision. "Mr. Young has probably considerable influence with Snyder as he (Young) brought him out, and has given Snyder great help. I advise you to write to Young. Tell him exactly how you are circumstanced with Snyder. And ask Young to interest himself on your side—I am perfectly certain he will help you." While he was at it, Hulbert also name-dropped another player from the D.C. area—Joe Gerhardt. Both Snyder and Gerhardt eventually signed to play in Louisville.[6]

* * *

Louisville had signed its players before the formation of the National League was announced on February 4. The day after the announcement, the *New York Clipper* included in its weekly publication a short preview of the season which Chadwick declared to be "looked forward to with more eager interest than that of any season in the history of the professional championship." This was not due to the National League. Since the League was not announced prior to the *New York Clipper* going to print, Chadwick would have to wait an additional week to comment on that turn of events. Instead, Chadwick's eager anticipation was due to three factors already known. The first was the rise of the Chicago Club through Hulbert's raids on the Boston and Philadelphia rosters. That movement of personnel made it seem likely that the balance of power might shift. Chadwick lamented that "scarcely a season's play had well get underway before it had been made manifest that the Boston team of the season would almost certainly be the winner of the pennant." Now, after Boston's run of dominance, there was doubt as to whether they could repeat it. "This doubt opens the door to a more even, and, consequently, interesting fight for the pennant than has hitherto marked any season's play."[7]

But Chadwick's second anticipated "event of interest" of the "centennial campaign" was there will be "the first appearance of a regular representative *Southern team* in the professional arena, the new Louisville Club being such organization." [Emphasis in original.] This factor, according to Chadwick, was "beyond doubt." His stated reasoning was that the Louisville Club "is controlled entirely by Southern gentlemen of a Southern city, and it has in its team two or three Southern players." His statement that the roster included "Southern players" was based on those from Baltimore. None of the original signees were from Baltimore. Later, after reviewing the rosters of the four western clubs, Chicago, Louisville, Cincinnati and St. Louis, Chadwick concluded that the two strongest appeared to be Louisville and Chicago.[8]

* * *

Beyond players, Louisville needed suitable grounds. The Eagles' grounds immediately south of Central Park, at the intersection of Fourth and Magnolia, was one option. However, the lay of the ground was such that a basin was formed by an embankment that ran through the outfield and, as a result, water would not adequately drain when meaningful rain fell. The field would be unplayable for days at a time. The Louisville club opted to acquire rights to the parcel adjacent to and immediately south of the Eagles' grounds and rolled the surface flat to prevent ponding of water. The grounds were located at the intersection of present day Fourth and Hill streets. Essentially both grounds together occupied the eastern half of what is now known as St. James Court. A grandstand was constructed for the patrons and work progressed through the winter with a goal of having everything ready for mid–April. The grandstand was positioned closest to the intersection of Fourth and Hill, so home plate was just northwest of it by so many feet.

Several ballpark features familiar today were incorporated into the park and were considered novel improvements. The ladies' area of the grandstand was equipped with seats that had chair backs. A water line was run to the park for the convenience and refreshment of the fans. In some respects, this seems a long overdue upgrade since game were always played in the middle of hot summer afternoons. Such features seem like an after-thought today, but in 1876 it was a considerable step up in luxury. DuPont's Central Passenger Street Railway, which traveled the length of Fourth Street, constructed spurs to the main gate. Another previously unseen fea-ture was added by Western Union. It equipped the park with telegraph lines so that the action could be communicated to the main office down-town and, from there, to other National League cities.[9]

The Louisville Grays, as the media soon dubbed them, made their public debut before about a thousand adoring fans on a disagreeably cold April 1, 1876. It was an exhibition game against a team of amateurs. In addition to Chapman, Devlin, Snyder and Gerhardt, the Grays had also signed Chapman's former teammate in St. Louis, Bill Hague. Hague was a 24-year-old from Philadelphia entering just his second season of major league ball. He started the season as a reserve but would soon be the everyday third baseman. The on-field captain was the shortstop, Charles "Chick" Fulmer. Fulmer was another of the many major leaguers who hailed from Philadelphia and, though just a year older than Hague, was entering his sixth season in the majors. He started his career in 1871 play-ing with the Forest City club of Rockford, Illinois, then played a season with the Mutuals in New York followed by three seasons as a member of the Philadelphia Whites.

Filling out the infield on opening day were Jack Carbine at first and Ed Somerville at second. Carbine would be released soon after season began. He played in only seven games with the team. Somerville would last the entire season, but moved on after the year to play in Canada. In Octo-ber 1877 he suffered what was called by the press a lung hemorrhage (it was probably tuberculosis), and died, making him the first National League player to do so. Chapman occupied left field while Scott Hastings patrolled center. Hastings, a Hillsboro, Ohio, native, was the second oldest on the club behind Chapman and was also entering his sixth major league season having begun his career with Chick Fulmer in the Forest City club before moving to Cleveland, Baltimore, Hartford and finally a year with Hulbert's White Stockings in Chicago. In right was the soon-to-be-troublesome George Bechtel.[10]

Louisville Grays of 1876. Pictured: back row (L to R): Scott Hastings, Jim Devlin, Pop Snyder; middle row (L to R): John Carbine, Bill Hague, Chick Fulmer, Jack Chapman, Joe Gerhardt, Art Allison; reclining (L to R): George Bechtel, Johnny Ryan. Credit: National Baseball Hall of Fame and Museum, Cooperstown, New York.

Meanwhile, as work continued finalizing the ballpark, on April 13, with most of it completed, disaster struck. That evening, a storm suddenly emerged, most likely a tornado, and wreaked havoc, creating "very serious damage to life and property." The path of destruction extended from the area around the ballpark northeastward into what Louisvillians know today as Germantown. A large section of the grandstand was demolished, and the fences surrounding the grounds were laid flat. Homes and businesses along the path were damaged and, in some cases, completely obliterated.[11]

Initial reports appeared in the following morning's papers. When daylight returned, however, it was evident the destruction was worse than initially reported. The section of the grandstand reserved for ladies was destroyed. The clubhouse "is blown so badly out of plumb as to make it unsafe for a large audience." The members' portion of the grandstand, which faced the wind head on, "was lifted up entire, rolled over, and then broken to pieces." Both grandstands were "unroofed," an iron bar bracing the stands was "snapped like a thread" and the "whole place presents a scene of wreck and confusion."[12] Repairing the wrecked ballpark got underway immediately.

* * *

The problems that plagued the National Association were still fresh in everyone's mind. Haldeman was especially keen on the new league and the promises it carried for better baseball in the future. Writing in the *Courier-Journal* on April 23, just two days before the opener, Haldeman expressed his confidence in what was about to begin:

> The managers of the Louisville club have striven hard to secure a list of players in whom are combined the qualities of both skill and honesty, and who are entirely free from the objectionable features of many ball-tossers of the present day. This they have succeeded in doing, and our people will know beforehand that in attending games between our home club and others, they will not be made unwilling witnesses of exhibitions of "hippodroming," sold games, and disgraceful quarrels and "kickings" on the field between a gang of eighteen roughs. The League was formed for the purpose of elevating the standard of the game and to free itself from the men who of late years have brought it almost to the level of a first-class fraud.[13]

One has to wonder if a year and a half later Haldeman recalled writing those words and regretted it.

The Grays opened the 1876 season at home against the Chicago White Stockings on April 25. Damage from the April 13 storm had been remedied in time, or at least sufficiently so, for the game to go on. To accommodate the expected large crowd, DuPont's street rails added seventy-five cars to the line. Haldeman described the rest of the scene patrons could expect to see on opening day:

> The arrangement for accommodating the spectators have been admirably conceived. The stands converging at the entrance gate enable the people to see one another, as well as everything occurring in the field. Of those stands there are two sheltered, one being devoted to the stockholders, with a splendid site for the reporters, while the other is divided into two large compartments, that nearest home-plate being for the ladies. The seats in the stands have comfortable backs and have nothing to obstruct the view. Along the eastern fence have been erected tiers of benches capable of seating an army. Altogether, it is probable that three thousand people could witness the game without being uncomfortably crowded. The dense throng which gathered yesterday not only packed these quarters as closely as sardines, but all the available standing room was occupied, while on the surrounding hills and in the neighboring trees nearly a thousand lookers-on who enjoyed the sport gratuitously.[14]

The Grays' uniforms consisted of white caps, shirts, pants and socks all trimmed in blue. The jersey included an embroidered "L" on the breast and there was a blue stripe around the socks which was roughly three inches wide.[15]

Chicago, with its newly acquired talent of A.G. Spalding, Deacon

White, Cal McVey, Ross Barnes and Adrian Anson (not yet called "Cap") was a heavy favorite to win the inaugural National League pennant.[16] In that regard, they would not disappoint. Ross Barnes would win the batting title with a .429 average, having mastered the fair/foul hit. Unfortunately for Barnes, 1876 was the last year during which the rule would exist. Essentially a fair/foul hit was a ball that landed initially in fair territory, but then rolled foul prior to passing first or third base. He would also lead the League in slugging percentage, on base percentage and total bases. Deacon White would go on to lead the League in RBIs with 60, while teammates Anson, Barnes and Paul Hines would tie for second in that category with 59 while McVey finished fifth with 53. A.G. Spalding would lead all pitchers in wins with 47. On this day, Hulbert's White Stockings were much better than the home-standing Grays and took the opening win 4–0.

The game started well enough. In 1876 and for some time thereafter, a coin toss determined which club had the option of batting first or taking the field to start. Chicago won the toss and chose to have Louisville hit first. Joe Gerhardt was Louisville's leadoff man and he promptly delivered a base hit to center to resounding applause. He moved to second on a ground out by Scott Hastings to short, which was followed by Chapman's groundout to Cap Anson at third. Devlin, batting fourth, had his at bat extended when Anson muffed a foul pop fly. However, Spalding threw the next one by him for the strikeout, leaving Gerhardt stranded. Chicago scored its first two runs on throwing errors by Gerhardt. Its third run was produced by a bases loaded balk by Devlin. The final run came in the seventh with two outs. Ross Barnes hit what Haldeman believed was a clear foul ball which Chapman muffed after a long run. "For some unaccountable reason, the umpire decided it fair, and Barnes took second base."[17] He would score when the next hitter, Cap Anson, hit a line-drive base hit to left.

Optimism remained high in Louisville in spite of the loss. The headlines the next day read simply "Good Enough." The Grays lost the second game to Chicago 10–0 and then lost the series opener against the St. Louis Brown Stockings 6–2 on the 29th. The third loss in as many games began the process of distress with the headline the following day reading "Alas!" The *Commercial* was less constrained in its criticism: "Thus far our home club has done very indifferent work, in fact, no better, if as good, as our amateur clubs did last season."[18] But, the club finally broke through with an 11–0 win over St. Louis on May 3 and the optimism roared back to life. For Devlin it was a masterful game as he held the Browns to just two hits. Grin Bradley, pitching for St. Louis, gave up ten hits in one his worst games during what would otherwise prove to be a career year for him.

Louisville spent the first full month of the season trying to iron out the kinks and figure out which parts fit together best. Chapman employed several lineup changes including moving of Gerhardt off third to first, and inserting Hague in the hot corner. Management also came to realize that the park was situated in such a way that fans could eschew the price of admission simply by watching the game from a hill beyond the left field fence. An awning was erected to resolve that problem and it served a double purpose: not only did it force otherwise freeloading cranks (the 19th-century term for "fans") to abandon their perch, but the club could also use it to sell advertising space.[19]

* * *

The ink had barely dried on reports of Louisville's first victory when the city government nearly wrecked the entire season. On May 4, the lower chamber of Louisville's city council unanimously passed a tax of $500 per year per baseball club. It was designed as a licensing fee to permit the playing of games "by any person, association or club whose business it is to give performances on exhibition of the game of base-ball" if, in so doing, the person, association or club charged an admission price. The language of the ordinance suggested it applied to not only the Grays, but visiting clubs and amateurs as well. *The Courier-Journal* blew a gasket. "DISCREDITABLE!," the headline read. "The Board of Aldermen in a Fit of Legislative Aberration Endeavors to Crush Base Ball in Louisville," was the second headline. The accompanying editorial was no less harsh:

> If the ordinance is adopted by both boards, the result will be either to partially kill base ball in Louisville, or compel the clubs to remove their grounds outside of the city limit. To any fair-minded person, the action of the Board of Aldermen was not only outrageous, but extremely ridiculous, and exhibits the amount of old fogyism that exists among the individuals of that board. It is just such stupidity as this that has given Louisville the unenviable reputation of an overgrown village.[20]

The first reaction came from Jeffersonville, Indiana. There was a suggestion that the Grays move across the river. The Common Council met two weeks later, and the Revision Committee asked that it be relieved of further consideration of the ordinance. That was denied. The same day, in the Board of Alderman, a motion was made to reconsider the ordinance. That motion failed 7–4. Ultimately the Revision Committee proposed an ordinance charging only $25 per annum and limiting it to home clubs. This was approved the following day by the Common Council 10–9.[21]

By now other clubs were learning of the proposal. None of them seem to have taken note of the upper chamber's version making the tax specifically incumbent upon the "owner, proprietor or lessee" of the grounds. In addition, some clubs thought it was $25 per club, *per game*. The *St. Louis Republican* declared that if Louisville expected other clubs to even visit, the Grays would have to foot the bill. The *Cincinnati Enquirer* had the same view. The Board of Aldermen, however, were not done. In June they took the matter up again and rejected the lower fee imposed by the Common Council's version. Instead, they amended their own down to $200 per year. The Revision Committee reported back to the upper chamber recommending it reject the $200 per year fee and reassert its own $25 per year. This the Council did by a vote of 13–6. Being thwarted in its efforts thus far, the Board of Aldermen took one last shot. An ordinance was proposed to direct the sinking fund to levy a fee for baseball games commensurate with the fee charged for other events. This one was rejected outright.[22] It appears that with that last vote, the baseball tax was forever dead.

* * *

Following the May 3 win over St. Louis, the club set out on its first tour of the other cities in the Western half of the League. In the media parlance of the 1870s, anything west of the Allegheny Mountains was "the West." It was common practice, therefore, for the media and the public to think of the League as representing a rivalry between East and West. The first stop on Louisville's western circuit was Cincinnati May 4 and 6th. Louisville split the two-game series against what would turn out to be a woeful Cincinnati Red Stockings club (9–56 on the season). From there they traveled to St. Louis where Grin Bradley shut them out on two successive afternoons May 9 and 11th. For Bradley, it was just two of what would be a league-leading 16 shutouts on the season. Over the course of his nine-year major league career, he had just 33 shut-outs total. Two more losses in Chicago followed May 13 and 16th and then, finally, the Grays found a couple of wins back home against the Cincinnati club on May 18 and 20th. After the second game with the Red Stockings, the Grays again hit the road, this time headed for the four eastern cities.

Haldeman traveled with the team on this first eastern swing. It provided him an opportunity to see how ballparks were set up in the East. His comments on the topic were minimal, but he was at least impressed with the Philadelphia grounds. He wrote his mother about it:

> Tell father for me that if he doesn't get after those directors of the Louisville Club and have them erect a nice stand exclusively for the scorers and reporters in time for those Eastern games after we get home the base ball columns of the CJ will smell of sulphur and brimstone for a long time after. I won't be able to stand any second hand business now after enjoying such ball-reporter's paradise on all the Eastern grounds. On the Athletic grounds in Philadelphia, the place provided for the reporters and scorers is over the ladies stand. Each one of those important personages is provided with a key which unlocks a door leading to their stand and consequently no outsider can get behind them,

whoop and yell, ask them questions without number and otherwise disturb their labors. Be sure and show him this and when I get home I shall of course expect to see my advice acted upon.[23]

The first road series in the east was at Philadelphia. The first two games were competitive, with the Grays taking the opener 3–1 on May 23 followed by a 2–2 tie on the 25th. After that, it got ugly. On the 26th the Grays pounded out 23 hits, with Scott Hastings, a recent addition, and Chick Fulmer each contributing four hits of their own, in a 16–8 win that was never that close. The following day the script was reversed. Louisville managed just eight hits while the Athletics assaulted Devlin for 16 hits and a 9–0 win. By the end of May, the club found itself in New York in the midst of series with the Mutuals and sporting a 6–10 record on the season.

Walter Haldeman, back in Louisville, never lost sight of his son as an employee of the paper. On the day the Grays were shut out by Philadelphia, he managed to write a note to John with a unique mix of editorial, club president, and fatherly advice:

My Dear Johnnie

I intended writing you fully to-day but was too busy, and now—15 mins. of 12—I have time to scratch only a line to be in time for [the] mail. All well at home. Have had only one letter from you. Don't, hereafter, send the dispatch, giving result immediately after close of games, as it is now received here by innings. We were all considerably cut as a result of game to-day, the whitewashing being what hurt us so. Your reports are good, but in the one of today's game you failed to tell how the Athletics made their 5 runs in 8th inning. Go to Mack's *every day* for letters and papers. Tell Chapman to save Devlin and Snyder all he can. They should not be allowed to play in amateur games. You failed to send us report of [the] game. Send reports of result merely of all amateur games, score by innings, and by letter. Of course when any club like the New Havens is played, telegraph it briefly—not full score. May Lord bless you and have you in his keeping. All send love. Write Your mother. Affectionately father. W.N. Haldeman[24]

After taking two of three in Philadelphia at the end of May, the opening game of the series with New York on May 30 resulted in a 7–2 loss. During the game, however, outfielder George Bechtel of the Grays committed three critical fielding errors leading to New York runs. On another play, according to the *New York Times*, his handling of the ball was unusually slow, allowing yet another run to score. It would be another year and a half until the National League would fully come to grips with what happened that day. But, at the time, Jack Chapman just assumed Bechtel was drunk and sent him home under suspension.[25] Louisville managed to salvage the third game of the series 8–1 on June 3 and moved on to Boston. Meanwhile, back in Louisville, Bechtel was discharged by the club for his believed inebriation. Because Bechtel was discharged for intoxication it meant he was officially blacklisted. As a result he was now barred from the League as a whole.

This was not Bechtel's first brush with suspicious play. Bechtel's name is associated with several suspicious games in 1875. Early in the season he was playing for the Philadelphia Centennials who, finding themselves short of cash, sold Bechtel and future Louisville shortstop Bill Craver to the Philadelphia Athletics in the first player transaction in the game's history. Later that year, some of the Athletics' players agreed to sell a game against the Chicago White Stockings. Bechtel was among those suspected. In this instance things took a bizarre turn.

Playing for the White Stockings at the time was Dick Higham, himself a notorious rogue and considered by some to be possibly the most corrupt player in the game's history. Higham learned of the plot to sell the game and wanted a cut of the prize. When this was refused, he and several other Chicago players decided to throw the game themselves to teach the gamblers a lesson. Philadelphia won the game 5–2 in 12 innings, but the game was marred by 21 total errors. In the end, only Higham and Philadelphia's Mike McGeary were positively identified as being involved. At the end of the 1875 season the *Brooklyn Daily Eagle* published its all-star team of rogues. Among the players named to that "team" were Bill Craver and George Bechtel.[26] Just as his problematic behavior did not begin with the Grays in New York in May 1876, it would not end there either.

While the Grays were still in Boston, Jim Devlin received a telegram from Bechtel back in Louisville. In the telegram, Bechtel told Devlin that the two of them could make $500 if the Grays would lose. Devlin refused to cooperate in the scheme but did not report the incident to Chapman. Chapman learned of the telegram when a Boston reporter asked him about it. On June 20, a Philadelphia paper ran with a story claiming that after some investigation, they had determined the telegram was forged. Louisville had not expelled Bechtel for dishonest play. As far as Chapman and the Louisville directors were concerned, the game in New York was still considered to be drunkenness though they had no affirmative proof of that either. The doubt was enough so that when Bechtel re-appeared in Louisville later in July and begged to have his discharge amended to remove the blacklist designation. The Louisville directors agreed. They did so thinking he would finish out the season playing in Jackson, Michigan, in an affiliated league. Instead, he signed with the Mutuals where he lasted just a couple of games before being released outright.[27]

Very little has been written about Bechtel's subsequent release from the Mutuals. The reason is that it likely stemmed not from any nefarious act on his part, but a misunderstanding of the League rules by both Louisville and New York. When Louisville reinstated him, everyone assumed that was the end of the story. It was not. Louisville's rescission of the Bechtel expulsion was ineffectual. Under the League rules he could only be reinstated by the League itself and notice of that fact had to come from the Secretary of League. Hence, his playing for the Mutuals after the fact was in violation of League restrictions. The Mutuals used him under the advice of Al Wright mistakenly believing as Wright told them that Louisville had effectively reinstated his eligibility. When Louisville wrote to League Secretary Nick Young that they wished to do so, management was advised in no uncertain terms that the matter had passed from their jurisdiction.[28] In all probability the Mutuals were advised at the same time and released Bechtel immediately. The Bechtel affair was both an arrow dodged and a foreshadowing of what lay ahead.

* * *

After winning its final game in New York, Louisville took three in a row at Boston. The Boston media was unimpressed with the look of the club. They unanimously disparaged the size of the players as being larger than usual. They also did not care for the uniforms with one calling them "conspicuously hideous" and another called them "dirty white."[29] Devlin had an outstanding series. On June 6 he celebrated his 27th birthday by tossing a three-hit shutout while himself driving in a run in the 3–0 win. Two days later he added two more hits and another RBI while holding the Red Stockings to just four hits in Louisville's 3–1 win. After taking the third game 4–3, Louisville had raised its record on the season to 10–11 and climbed into fourth in the standings. It was the closest they would come to .500 all year.

Following Boston, the team went to Hartford and faced Hartford's Tommy Bond. Bond was one of the top pitchers in the League in 1876, starting 45 games for the eventual second place club and winning 31 of them with a 1.68 earned run average. Against Louisville in the middle of June, he had one of his best weeks. In the first game, played June 13, he pitched a one-hit shutout against the Grays. Two days later on the 15th he allowed ten hits, but just a single run in Hartford's 6–1 win. The third game June 17 was another one-hit shutout.

Hartford completed Louisville's first Eastern swing. Afterward, the two clubs rode the same train to Louisville to resume play at Fourth and Hill. Louisville's Chick Fulmer did not make it all the way to Louisville though as he was compelled to re-route once the train reached Steubenville, Ohio. Word reached him *en route* that his daughter was seriously ill. She died a few days later, making Fulmer one of three players in the League (Cal McVey of Chicago and Cherokee Fisher of Cincinnati the other two), to lose a child during the season.[30]

* * *

In the first game back in Louisville, on June 21, the Grays finally got through against Bond and managed to score five runs. However, six errors led to four unearned runs, giving Hartford five on the day as well. The two clubs played 13 innings before the umpire ended the game due to darkness. The next day, June 22, Bond was back to his old ways allowing just four Louisville hits in a 3–0 victory for Hartford. Louisville got to him again on St. John's Day, June 24, with a 7–2 win. But once again Bond bounced back June 25 and shutout Louisville for a fourth time in seven games. In all, between June 13 and 24th Bond pitched 67 innings against Louisville and allowed just eight earned runs.

Due primarily to Bond, after the sweep of Boston which ended June 10, Louisville managed to win just two of their remaining games in June. Bond alone defeated Louisville five out of six with the one tie. Louisville completed the month with a pair of games at home against Boston. In the first, played June 27, Devlin took a two-hit shutout into the ninth inning. He had also driven in all three of Louisville's runs. But in the ninth Devlin gave up four hits which were exaggerated in effect by Louisville committing three of its five errors in the inning. Boston scored five runs in the frame to win 5–3. In the final game of the month Louisville punished Boston's Joe Josephs with 18 hits, including four by Pop Snyder and three each by Devlin and Gerhardt. Louisville's nine errors in the game kept it close but Louisville won 8–6 to finish the month with a 12–17 record overall.

Josephs, incidentally, was one of at least two players who played under a pseudonym to prevent his family from finding out he was a professional ball player. His actual name was Joe Borden. Later in life, he was rumored to have been among the victims of the Johnstown Flood in 1889. It was not true and *Sporting Life*, the paper that first reported the story, ran a correction June 19, 1889. The other player playing under a pseudonym for the same reason was the Reds' Charley Jones. His real name, which was not revealed until 1887, was Charley Ripley.[31]

Louisville won a pair of early July games over the Mutuals. On July 4, as the city and nation celebrated the country's centennial, some 8,000 fans—about 3,000 of them watching from outside the fence—watched the Grays earn a 4–1 victory. Two days later, amidst the news reaching the local papers that Custer had led his men to slaughter,[32] Louisville picked up a 7–1 win. On the 8th the two teams continued the series and, going to the ninth, it appeared New York was going to get the win as they led 5–1. Louisville rallied, however, and closed the game to 5–3 with two men out and Pop Snyder on second with outfielder Johnny Ryan at first. At that point Snyder attempted to steal third. Mutuals catcher Nat Hicks had him nailed with the throw, but Mutuals third baseman—and future member of "the Louisville Four"—Al Nichols muffed it, allowing Snyder to hustle home and Ryan to move up one bag. Devlin, who was at the plate, then hit a double bringing home Ryan with the tying run. The game remained 5–5 through 15 innings at which point the umpire called the game due to darkness. With no Sunday games allowed, the two clubs returned on Monday to complete the series. However, rather than resume the July 8 game where they left off, they started a new one. This game also went into extra innings with the Mutuals finally prevailing 8–5 in 16 innings. Thus, two games, 31 innings, and just one result.

Louisville completed its homestand with a three-game series against the Athletics. With the Athletics' arrival also came excessive heat, which was blamed for keeping attendance modest. Only four or five hundred attended the first game of the series, a 6–2 win for Louisville. The weather moderated a bit for the second game July 13 and attendance responded accordingly. Louisville won that game too, 11–5, before dropping the series finale 8–5 in front of the largest crowd of the week. The schedule now compelled Louisville to take to the road again traveling to Chicago and St. Louis—two clubs and two locations that had not been kind to the Grays so far.

The first game in Chicago, played July 18, went according to form: a 9–5 Chicago win. It led Haldeman to remark the next day, noting that the two clubs were scheduled to play again on the 20th, that Louisville fans "do not despair of a victory for our side by any manner of means." From Haldeman's point of view, and probably the point of view of many local cranks, the Grays were overmatched by the White Stockings. As it turned out, Haldeman was right: Louisville lost. But no one expected what came. Chicago played the first error-free game in the west in 1876, held Louisville to just four hits, and pounded Devlin mercilessly, winning 18–0.

To this Haldeman remarked that it must be part of the Grays' plan. "Louisville is bound to win one game from Chicago, *ergo*, to accomplish this it is the best plan to run the Chicago men around the bases to such a lively extent in some preceding game, that when a succeeding one comes they will literally be nowhere."[33]

The third game, however, was an even bigger disaster. A common strategy in 19th-century baseball was to pair one pitcher with one catcher. Consequently, when either was disabled from his position, both players had to be swapped out for an entirely new battery. Moreover, because substitutions were not allowed, that meant the new battery had to come from players currently in the game. In the first inning of the third game, played July 22, Pop Snyder was injured behind the plate and could not continue to catch. That caused several moves. First, Snyder was sent to centerfield and the center fielder, Scott Hastings, who was also the "change catcher," was moved behind the plate. That also necessitated moving Devlin out of the box. He was sent to first base, first baseman Joe Gerhardt moved to left field, and leftfielder, Johnny Ryan, came in to pitch.[34] Scoring rules at the time required wild pitches and passed balls to be counted as errors; Ryan and Hastings accumulated 20 of them. That was only slightly over half of the teams' 37 errors for the game. When you add in that Chicago touched up Hastings (mostly) for 31 hits, the 30–7 final is not all that surprising.

Louisville headed to St. Louis where the prospects for the Grays could not have looked worse. Grin Bradley had shut them out twice when they last visited back in May. Moreover, St. Louis had just won three in a row over Hartford—all via the shutout. But, baseball being baseball, in the first game the two teams committed nine errors each and Devlin held the Browns to just four hits as the Grays won 7–4. None of the runs by either team were earned. In the second game St. Louis continued its poor fielding, committing 11 errors to Louisville's four and the Grays won again 4–2—this time, of the six runs scored, only a single St. Louis run was earned. In the third game, played on July 29, Bradley continued his mastery, holding Louisville to one hit and no runs while Louisville muffed 15 chances in the field giving St. Louis seven unearned runs. In the three games, Devlin and Bradley had collectively allowed only a single earned run. With that loss, Louisville finished July where it began—fifth place— only now six games under .500 at 18–24.

In early August, the local press had become jaded if not forlorn. Louisville's first game of the month was on August 1 and ended in a 15–7 loss to Chicago. The *Louisville Commercial* lamented the sense that prevailed among the spectators at the outset that the outcome was predetermined. It opened its report with: "A canvas of the crowd at the base ball game yesterday revealed the fact that none came out to see which club would win, for a victory for Chicago was deemed a certainty." Louisville jumped out to an early 3–0 lead, and the *Commercial* noted of the fans: "the people were so reckless as to think that the Louisvilles might, should, and would at last beat the Invincibles." The *Commercial* continued: "Our boys could not stand the pressure. They are brave enough until they gain an advantage over the Chicagos, but, so much accomplished, they seem to regret their presumption, and, to atone, set about assisting their opponents to the lead."[35]

Nevertheless, four days later in the second game of the series, Louisville finally managed to get its first—and only—win over Chicago in 1876. On Friday night, August 4, 1876, it rained heavily in Louisville. Many thought that would mean no baseball the following day between the Chicago and Louisville clubs as surely the grounds would be unsuitable. Consequently, only about a thousand showed up to witness the game that was indeed played. By game time, "Not a sign of water could be seen anywhere."[36] Louisville lost the toss and Chicago chose to take the field first. Gerhardt led off the game with a base hit to right followed by Devlin's "scorcher" past third which moved Gerhardt to third. Devlin took second on a passed ball which did not scoot away enough to allow Gerhardt to score. Instead, Gerhardt scored on the next play as Hague bounded out to third. Two batters later, Scott Hastings hit a double bringing home Devlin. Louisville led 2–0 after a half inning. Devlin then went to work. He struck out the first two batters in the bottom of the inning and evoked a weak foul out by the third. More strikeouts would follow, and Chicago did not achieve its first base runner until the fourth when Devlin walked Chicago catcher Deacon White. Louisville added two additional runs in the sixth to extend the lead to 4–0.

Chicago shortstop John Peters doubled to right to open the seventh inning. First baseman Cal McVey then singled to right center scoring Peters. McVey stole second base and advanced to third on Cap Anson's groundout to second. When catcher Deacon White grounded to Chick Fulmer at short, McVey broke for the plate. Fulmer attempted to throw him out but was too late and McVey scored while White claimed first. The next batter, centerfielder Paul Hines, grounded sharply to Somerville at second who tagged White then threw out Hines at first for the inning-ending double play. It was the only two hits and runs the White Stockings managed on the day and Louisville prevailed 4–2. Chicago would go on to win the third game 9–2 on August 7.

Grin Bradley and the St. Louis Browns were next, and Bradley continued his career season. In the first game Bradley retired the first 21 hitters and faced taking a perfect game into the eighth inning. In the eighth Pop Snyder reached when a third strike was dropped thus ending any chance for what would have been the League's first perfect game. Nevertheless, the no-hit bid remained intact. Louisville's ninth began with Johnny Ryan striking out looking. Bradley's no-hit bid would go no further. Joe Gerhardt broke up the gem with a sharp line drive to right with one out in the ninth. Bradley retired the next two hitters to preserve the 3–0 shutout. At the time the media gave little credit to pitchers for such an effort. The *Louisville Commercial* remarked that the result was merely the result of "a very dead ball" which, after a few innings, "became so soggy from rolling in the wet grass" hitters were unable to drive it.[37] For the series, Louisville dropped two of three to St. Louis. The rest of August was spent in games against the hapless Cincinnati Reds, with Louisville winning five of the six to run their record to 25–29, though still a distant fifth to the White Stockings.

The highlight for the fans, however, may have been the talk in the stands. On Sunday, August 13, 1876, news broke in the *Courier-Journal* of the August 1 murder of Wild Bill Hickok in the town of Deadwood in the Dakota Territory. According to initial news accounts, the killer was a man named Bill Sutherland who claimed he shot Wild Bill out of revenge for the killing of his brother in Kansas a few years back. Two days later, at the baseball game with Cincinnati, some of the fans would have no doubt discussed it. But at the August 18 game against the Reds, the conversation would have really kicked up. On the 17th the *Courier-Journal* ran a long correspondence from the Dakota Territory by B.D. Porter. According to Porter, the killer's real name was Jack McCall and he told associates in Deadwood he was from Jeffersontown, Kentucky. Jeffersontown is a city within Jefferson County about ten miles as the crow flies from the heart of Louisville. A search of census records and other sources has failed to verify the claim.

The report also told of how the town of Deadwood organized a court (complete with defense counsel) and put McCall on trial. The story of avenging his brother worked as the jury acquitted him. Later that month in Wyoming, McCall boasted that he was the man who killed Wild Bill. A U.S. deputy marshal overheard him and, knowing Deadwood was in Indian Territory, knew that the make-shift court in Deadwood had no jurisdiction. Only the federal district court in the territorial capital of Yankton could decide the case. The marshal arrested McCall and returned him to Yankton on August 29. In December of 1876, McCall was tried again and this time, convicted and sentenced to hang. The sentence was carried out in March 1877. In 1881 McCall's body had to be removed to make way for new construction. It was found at the time that he had been buried with the noose still around his neck.[38]

* * *

Throughout the season, and for several seasons to follow, major league teams scheduled their games days apart to allow sufficient time for the clubs to get in additional games against nearby amateur clubs. They would also stop at various places *en route* to their next League contest. Early in September, while Louisville was on its way to play its last eastern swing, Pop Snyder sprained his ankle in an exhibition game at Harrisburg, Pennsylvania. The injury was bad enough that Snyder would miss the remainder of the season. On hand at that game was a young man from Baltimore by the name of Bill Holbert. He was initially asked to umpire the game, but when Snyder went down, Holbert stepped in to finish the game as Louisville's catcher. Chapman was impressed enough with what he saw, he signed Holbert to a contract to finish the season with the Grays.[39]

Years later, in 1884, Holbert was playing for the New York Metropolitans of the American Association. The Louisville Eclipse were in New York to play series against the Mets. Charles Chase regaled the *Courier-Journal* with the story of Holbert's discovery. Chase told the story of some hayseed barely familiar with the game of baseball that turned out to be a natural phenom. "'Every time I see his name,' said Mr. Chase last night, 'I think of the first time I ever saw him.'" According to Chase's version of events, it occurred in 1877 while the club was in Philadelphia and had an "off day." Chase continued: "we ran out into one of the mining towns in Pennsylvania to play a game with the club there." Chase described "a very rough crowd of spectators present, principally the men who worked in the mines." An issue arose about who would umpire because the Grays had no one with them to act as umpire. Chapman asked the manager of the local club if the local club could select someone. "He said he knew of a man who was somewhat of a ballplayer, and he would get him to act."

It was then that Chase first saw Bill Holbert: "The man was one of the most remarkable specimens I ever saw. His clothes were ragged and dirty, his face covered with coal-dust, and his shaggy brown hair stuck out through the holes in his hat in several places." When Snyder was injured, Chase told Chapman he would have to finish the game to which Chapman demurred. As they were discussing it, Holbert approached them and asked to finish the game behind the plate himself. Chase's response was to laugh, but Chapman shrugged and reminded Chase the game was of no consequence anyway. To Chase's surprise, Holbert played steadily and "finished the remaining five innings without an error or a passed ball." A couple weeks later when the Mets were in Louisville, Holbert corrected the record. At the time Louisville signed him, he had already been playing ball professionally for three years.[40] It was not the last time Chase's memory of the details would fail him.

* * *

September saw the Grays play up and down. The month began with their last eastern swing through the League, and they lost four in a row to start the month—two each at Hartford and Boston. The first game in Hartford on September 5 was a tough loss. Hartford managed just seven hits off Devlin, but four came in the eighth which, when combined with a couple of Louisville errors, led to five runs for the Blues and breaking open what was, up to that point, a 1–1 game. The second game played the following day had a similar feel. Louisville led 2–1 going into the sixth, but then bunched hits coupled with costly errors gave Hartford five unearned runs between the sixth and seven to seize the lead and ultimately win the game 6–3. When the Grays played in Boston September 8, things just got worse. Louisville managed to amass 11 errors in a rain-shortened five-inning game. Boston took the win 6–3. Three days later, the Grays tallied ten hits off Boston starter Foghorn Bradley, but were unable to plate a single run. Boston scored eight off 14 hits.

Baseball being baseball, suddenly everything turned around. The Grays followed the four-game losing streak with a four-game road winning streak—two each in New York and Philadelphia. In the first game in New York on September 12, it was the reverse of what Louisville experienced in Boston and Hartford. This time it was Louisville's turn to come from behind due in large part to the fielding woes of the opponent. New York led 4–2 going into the seventh but coughed up three runs and the lead with all three runs being unearned. Louisville added a run each in the eighth and ninth to win 7–4. The following day, it was a four-run sixth followed by a three-run seventh that gave Louisville the 9–4 win.

From Brooklyn the Grays headed back to Philadelphia for two games with the Athletics. Philadelphia, like New York, was struggling with low attendance and other financial woes. By the time Louisville showed up September 15 it was pretty certain neither the Mutuals nor the Athletics were going to be able to fulfill their commitments to travel west to complete the season. Philadelphia had also decided to make a change in the pitcher's box. Flip Lafferty would make his first, and last, major league pitching appearance. He pitched well allowing just three Louisville hits. But he was poorly served by a defense that committed 12 errors and he was out dueled by Devlin. Devlin pitched a one-hitter with only George Hall managing to get a hit in Louisville's 3–0 win. The next day Louisville closed out its road schedule for the season with a narrow 7–6 win.

A rumor started in Philadelphia after the second game that Devlin had not pitched to win. This prompted an immediate response from Devlin himself. He penned a letter to the editor of the *Philadelphia City Item* to defend himself. In the letter he presumed the person starting the rumor was someone "who has wagered extravagantly, probably that the Louisville would win in two innings—and as they did not in this instance, he feels badly over his loss." The *Courier-Journal* re-printed the letter September 20 and Haldeman immediately joined in Devlin's defense. "There was no necessity in Devlin's writing the above card. Every fair-minded person knows that there is no more honest ball player in the country than Devlin. The only fault which James falls heir to is his quickness of temper, and it is but just to say that he loses temper with himself oftener than he does with his associates."[41]

The Grays embarked on a barnstorming tour after Philadelphia. There were no League games scheduled for more than a week. With confirmation coming that Philadelphia would indeed not be traveling west, Louisville would not play another League game until the 29th. The Eastern barnstorming by the Grays ended September 22 in Pittsburgh. Following the game, several players wished to catch the evening train to start the journey home. Chapman nixed the idea, insisting they wait to take the morning train instead. It was a fortunate choice. The earlier train would have put them on board a train that derailed just east of Columbus, Ohio, killing four and injuring many more.[42]

On the eve of beginning their final homestand, the Grays learned the Mutuals, like Philadelphia, were not going to make the trip west. Due in large part to the poor play of the team, attendance was down in Brooklyn and the Mutuals were broke. In an effort to entice the Mutuals to make the trip anyway, both St. Louis and Chicago offered to guarantee them $400 a game if they would show up. Notwithstanding the fact that the offer was for a substantial sum over what the team could ordinarily expect on the two games in each city, the undertaking was still too much for Mutuals President William Cammeyer. He refused.[43] That left Louisville with only the two games each against Boston and Hartford to close the season.

When League play resumed for the Grays, September 29 at home, they defeated Boston 3–0 to win their fifth consecutive contest. Devlin tossed a four-hitter on an unusually cold late September day. The following day it was still chilly, and the game was played under skies described by Haldeman as "gloomy." Devlin again held Boston to four hits and had two himself, including a double. But Louisville's defense was atrocious as they committed 18 errors, allowing Boston to get away with a 6–5 win.

Louisville closed its season with a pair of bad losses to Hartford, October 4th and 5th. In the first game Candy Cummings baffled seven Louisville hitters leaving them without a hit among them. Only Jimmy Clinton, who had four hits on the day, and Chick Fulmer, who had two of his own, could find the ball. Devlin left the game after the fifth inning due to a twisted ankle, having surrendered just two unearned runs. A 16-year-old local amateur by the name of Frank Pearce finished the game in his only major league appearance. Hartford won the game easily 6–0 as Pearce was victimized by his own defense for two unearned runs in the sixth but allowed two earned runs afterward. *The Louisville Commercial* described the game: "The game throughout was tedious, and so very one sided that even had the weather been bright and warm instead of dark and raw, no considerable enthusiasm would have been aroused at any stage of the proceedings." In the final game, a colder day still, Jimmy Clinton handled the pitching and Louisville was never really in it. Seven unearned runs catapulted Hartford to an 11–0 lead after four and the game ended 11–2. Haldeman described the overall picture: "A small crowd, the Louisville and Hartford players, a trio of half-frozen scorers and reporters and the cold weather to a large extent were the attendants."[44]

Louisville finished its inaugural campaign pretty much where they had been all season: in fifth. Their final 30–36 record was 22 games behind League champion Chicago. They also had three tie games on their ledger. All 30 wins belonged to Devlin, which placed him fourth in the League. Devlin also led the League in innings pitched, with 622; complete games, with 66, and strikeouts with 122. He was second in the League in ERA with a 1.56. Among the players on the Grays with more than 100 at bats, he led the team with a .315 batting average.

Philadelphia and New York missing their final trip west was a serious issue for the League. Clubs not fulfilling scheduled dates was one of the problems that had plagued the National Association. Louisville and the other three Western clubs lost gate receipts because of it. As a consequence, at the League meeting that winter, both Philadelphia and New York were voted out of the League. The League chose not to replace them with other clubs in the New York or Philadelphia markets. The 1877 season would simply be played amongst six clubs, with Hartford moving its home games—but not its name—to the Union grounds in Brooklyn where the Mutuals called home.[45] The League's decision to boot New York and Philadelphia also meant that two dozen major league players were going to be in the market for a new place to play in 1877. Among them were the Athletics' outfielder George Hall and the Mutuals' infielders Bill Craver and Al Nichols.

CHAPTER THREE

The Louisville Four Come Together

Then, as now, the first order of business for a baseball club at the end of a season is to assess its strengths and weaknesses. For the Louisville Grays at the end of 1876, the one area of the club that management felt good about heading into 1877 was the battery of pitcher Jim Devlin and catcher Pop Snyder. Management quickly learned, however, that at least one half of that combination was going to be a problem.[1] Although we will never know, it was a problem that may have, at least in part, sowed the seeds for what was to come.

It was not uncommon for players to seek an advance on their next season's pay. Eventually the League would legislate against it entirely, but in the winter of 1877, it was a matter of management's discretion. Devlin requested an advance. Louisville said no. Devlin went on the warpath. All winter Devlin complained he had been mistreated by Louisville and wanted out. He wrote a series of "cards" to New York and Philadelphia papers. Rumors surfaced that he intended to remain in Philadelphia for the season. Devlin took his grievance to the National League's winter meeting, arguing he should be granted a release from Louisville. A jury composed on Hartford's player/manager, Bob Ferguson, Boston's president Nicholas Appolonio, and St. Louis club secretary Charles Fowle ruled in Louisville's favor and ordered Devlin to remain with the club.[2]

According to the *Chicago Times*, Devlin was publicly stating he would not play for Louisville in 1877. According to the *Chicago Tribune*, the rumor being spread in Philadelphia was that Devlin would stay there and pitch for the Athletics. That rumor was enhanced by one of Devlin's letters. In January he wrote a letter to the *New York Clipper* stating that his contract with Louisville stipulated he would be paid an advance on November 15 which, as of the time of his writing, had not happened. Meanwhile, "I may add that I have received a liberal offer to pitch for the Athletics of my native city." The Athletics, of course, would no longer be playing in the National

League, but the club remained organized and active, albeit at a minor league level. Writing in the *Chicago Tribune*, Meacham dubbed the rumor "too foolish to be true," but admitted it was at least possible. As Devlin saw it, his contract with Louisville was "null and void" allowing him to sign with any semi-professional club he chose. His frustration seems to be with the response he received from the Louisville management. "I have heard nothing from the Louisvilles except a communication from their president a few days since, saying I would have to give them satisfactory guarantees and security before I could get the money due me on Nov. 15."[3]

Most of the rumors were coming from the Philadelphia papers and mostly from the loathsome Al Wright. Wright was the editor who in 1876 jumped to George Bechtel's defense after the telegram from Bechtel to Devlin surfaced asking him to throw a game. Wright claimed he had seen both the telegram and Bechtel's handwriting and the two could not be more dissimilar.[4] (The only plausible explanation for this is that the telegram from Bechtel to Devlin was a Raster Image of a hand-written letter rather than a traditional telegram.) A questionable relationship with the truth was not Wright's only character flaw. He also had a flair for vindictiveness. Wright had been of the belief that St. Louis would oppose the expulsion of the Athletics following the 1876 season. When that failed to materialize and St. Louis voted with the others to expel the Philadelphia Club, Wright started a campaign of lies in his paper against St. Louis with the intent of harming the organization.[5]

Wright also started a rumor—by way of an anonymous letter to William Hulbert in Chicago—that Albert Spalding had been known to sell games. The letter to Hulbert was delivered about the same time the Louisville directors received an anonymous letter in which the writer claimed to have been the person who signed George Bechtel's name to the telegram to Devlin. As it happened, William Cammeyer of the New York Mutuals was in Louisville and the Louisville directors showed him the letter they received, thinking he might have some insight as to who the author might be. Cammeyer, who was aware of the letter to Hulbert, suggested the letter be sent to Chicago so that Hulbert could make a comparison. That was done and Hulbert confirmed the two were from the same hand. To Haldeman, Wright was a "cur among dogs, a brace-dealer among gamblers, a second-rate among Philadelphia sports."[6]

Wright wrote in the *Sunday Mercury* that Devlin would indeed remain in Philadelphia and that the gist of the problem was that Louisville, in an endeavor to keep Devlin from signing last summer to join the Athletics for 1877, re-engaged him "and agreed to pay him a certain sum of money, but failed to pay said money." Then, notwithstanding Devlin's pleas, the League refused to void the contract.[7]

Haldeman responded to the litany of rumors: "Gentlemen (and we refer to the *Times* and *Tribune*), don't allow Devlin to trouble you so far as to attempt to keep a diary of his sayings and doings. The directors of the Louisville Club became pretty well acquainted with the gentleman last summer, and they think they can 'put the screws on him' the coming season in proper style." Henry Chadwick, writing in the *New York Clipper,* eventually weighed in. Chadwick commented that the cards were an attempt to make the public believe that Devlin was the victim, "but those who are acquainted with the facts in the case claim to know otherwise." The silence of the Louisville management throughout the period was, Chadwick believed, the best response.

Eventually Devlin came around: In January, Devlin wrote a letter to someone in Louisville's management (Haldeman does not say who) stating that he was more than willing to play in Louisville this year. Devlin then added he had never done anything that would be a harm to Louisville. Haldeman, as if rolling his eyes, responded again: "If we had the space we would like to publish a few of his very numerous 'cards' which have appeared in several New York and Philadelphia papers...."[8]

It is unlikely Devlin's childish tantrum would have been taken seriously at any time, but his timing in this instance could not have been worse. The country was still undergoing the economic depression that began in 1873. But to add to the tension gripping the country was the still-unsettled presidential election of 1876 between Rutherford B. Hayes, a Republican from Ohio, and Samuel Tilden, a Democrat from New York. Tilden won the popular vote and led in the electoral count 184 to 165. However, to be elected he needed 185 electoral votes and 20 delegates from four states (South Carolina, Louisiana, Florida, and Oregon) were disputed. The controversy was serious enough that northern Democrats—mostly in Ohio, Indiana, and New York—were forming militias. One of the strongest proponents of a militaristic approach was the *Courier-Journal's* own Henry Watterson, who wrote, "it is nonsense to suppose that [Democrats] will quietly yield what they consider the fruits of a hard-earned victory." The possibility of a second Civil War was very much on the minds of the country.[9] This simply was not the time to whine about an advance on one's salary. This was especially true if you were a professional ball player earning roughly twice what the average worker made.

Other ballplayers were likewise probably uninterested as league-wide players faced a new set of conditions eating into their pocketbooks. To aid club finances, the League decreed that players had to pay for certain necessities. Namely, players now had to pay for their uniforms, and they had to chip in a *per diem* for travel. The fee set by the League was $30.00 for the uniforms (not a small sum in 1877) and 50 cents per day to offset the cost of travel. If any thought their complaints could earn them sympathy in the press they were mistaken. Haldeman's reaction to their grumbling was sardonic: "'Tis very sad. They are a much imposed-upon and cruelly down-trodden set. How they manage to live on the mere pittances received for hard work rendered is a conundrum."[10]

* * *

Louisville had legitimate concerns about other roster spots as well. Per Haldeman, Louisville's management was determined to put a better team on the field in 1877. The missing pieces in January 1877 were, in their view, first base, shortstop and two outfield spots. Chick Fulmer was eager to return at short for the Grays, and management was not entirely opposed, but they had misgivings and preferred to look elsewhere if possible. Haldeman noted, "Fulmer has his good points, and then, too, he has his weak ones." His weak points were not in his playing, but in his tendency to run his mouth. "It is not well to have a player in a nine who gives too loose a rein to his tongue, and who causes dissatisfaction among his fellow players by speaking disparagingly of the gentlemen who engage his services and pay him for them." For its part, the *Chicago Tribune* thought Fulmer would stay. The mixed signals coming out of Louisville lent credence to that theory. Initially Louisville had tendered a contract which Fulmer signed. Then management had second thoughts and released him. But now it appeared both sides were ready to sign again. The trouble seems to have been that management was somewhat conflicted: if not Fulmer, who?[11]

While debating internally over the shortstop position, Louisville went ahead and made two commitments to cover other areas of concern by signing outfielder George Shafer and first baseman George Latham. Shafer, whose name is sometimes spelled by historians as "Shaffer," was described by Haldeman as being "a good batsman, a fine base-runner and a hard and diligent worker for the nine in which he plays." Latham was described as a "more than ordinary batsman, and an excellent base-runner." Historically, both are better known by their nicknames. Shafer is best known as Orator Shafer whereas Latham is alternatively known as Jumbo Latham or sometimes Juice Latham. Both earned their appellations. Shafer was a prolific talker. Latham was a large man for the time, hence the name "Jumbo," but he also used prodigious amounts of chewing tobacco thereby earning the moniker "Juice."[12]

Louisville also signed Flip Lafferty to serve as change pitcher and Bill Crowley to act as change catcher. Lafferty had just one appearance in the major leagues prior to 1877 and that was the 3–1 loss he took to Louisville in 1876 while pitching for the Athletics. The day after Lafferty arrived in Louisville, he decided to visit the ballpark and, perhaps, get in a little work. Somewhere along the way he happened upon Lucien Wagner. Wagner was the organizer of the Globe Base Ball club, one of the original and more prominent black clubs in Louisville in the 1870s. The two men strolled down Fourth Street to the ballpark together and Wagner volunteered to serve as Lafferty's catcher for the day's workout. There would not be a black player in the major leagues for another seven years, but Wagner's willingness to assist Lafferty was just one example of the aforementioned growing cooperation between black and white players.[13]

As for Crowley, according to Haldeman he was the regular catcher for the Philadelphia nine in 1875 with Pop Snyder serving as change catcher. Actually, Haldeman got it wrong here. The Philadelphia squad containing both Crowley and Snyder was the Pearls of the old National Association. Referring to the "Philadelphia nine" incorrectly gives the impression that they played for the more noteworthy Athletics. Also, Snyder was the regular catcher with Fergy Malone the change catcher. Crowley played in only nine games, with four of those in the outfield, four at third base and one at first. The same club also included Chick Fulmer and recent Louisville signee, Orator Shafer.[14]

That left two spots unfilled: Louisville still needed a shortstop and another outfielder. In late January word leaked to the public that former Athletics star outfielder George Hall had failed to reach terms with the St. Louis Browns. Three weeks later it was announced he had signed with Louisville. After the announcement Haldeman described Hall as "a brilliant left fielder, a rapid and skillful base-runner, a cracking batter and one of the hardest working men in the profession." His deal called for Louisville to pay him the unheard-of sum of $2,800 per year.[15]

A week prior to signing Hall, the word was Louisville was still toggling between Fulmer and former Mutuals second baseman Bill Craver. With Hall's signing, it was announced Louisville had opted for Craver. Louisville sent him a contract and all that remained was for him to accept the terms. Craver was signed by March 3 leading Haldeman to remark, "Craver is an excellent second baseman, and, in particular of getting at and securing those most troublesome specimens of the fly ball which fall just too short for an outfielder to reach, there are not many of the present-day players who can equal him."[16] Craver would play shortstop for Louisville with Gerhardt moving from first to second and Hague retaining his spot at third. The outfield would consist of Hall, Crowley and Shafer.

As noted in the Prologue, a decade after the fact, club Vice President Charles Chase penned an article telling the story of the Grays scandal of 1877. It is the source for perhaps every history of the club written since. Among the errors was this: "the Louisville league club of 1877 was by many degrees the strongest aggregation of players ever, up to that time at least, brought together in one team, and very early in the season it was considered a foregone conclusion that the Louisvilles would win the pennant." Contrary to the memory of Chase as he expressed it ten years later, the Louisville assemblage was anything but that. Four of the players were National League rookies—more than any other club—though three did have previous time in the National Association. Prior to the season, most of the Western papers picked the Grays to finish fourth or fifth in the League standings.[17]

That is not to say there were not some optimists. One correspondent expressed his expectations thus: "Louisville, I understand, will present a much stronger nine in the field than last season, which should be the means of drawing out large crowds to their games in your beautiful city. Six of their last year's team, so Manager Chapman informs me, have been retained, and several experienced players have been engaged to fill the vacant positions." Pop Snyder expected improvement too. When he arrived back in Louisville in early February he told the *Courier-Journal* he believed the club would be far better both hitting and fielding.

Haldeman, as one might expect, was the most optimistic. After Hall was signed and the prospects for Craver looked nearly certain, Haldeman opined: "Altogether, the prospects for Louisville having a fine team in the field this season looks very favorable." Two weeks later: "Without attempting to overrate the new nine in the least, we believe it is fully fifty percent stronger than the one of last year." O.P. Caylor in the *Cincinnati Enquirer* was among those who were less sanguine on the Grays' chances: "The Louisvilles may be stronger than they were last year, or they may not. That remains to be seen. If they pull together well they may at least defeat the Hartfords of Brooklyn and the St. Louis Club or give the Cincinnatis a close race."[18] Cincinnati won nine games the previous year—no one had to improve at all to "give the Cincinnatis" any kind of race.

* * *

Like many of his 19th-century baseball contemporaries, George Hall was born in England. His date of birth was March 29, 1849, he was christened George William Hall in Stepney, England and was the third of five children brought into this world by George R. and Mary Hall. His father was an engraver and immigrated to the United States a year or so later. Mary and the-then four children soon followed. George grew up in Brooklyn where he learned the game of baseball.[19]

Hall began playing on a club level with the Cambridge Stars (NY) and moved over to the Brooklyn Atlantics in 1870. While with the professional Atlantics, Hall drove in the winning run to hand the Cincinnati Red

Stockings their first ever defeat. In 1871, with the rise of the National Association, Hall played for the Washington Olympics. In 1872 he transferred his talents to the Baltimore Club where his teammates included the notorious Dick Higham along with Bill Craver. Hall and Craver both returned to Baltimore in 1873, but in 1874 Hall signed with the Boston Red Stockings and was part of Boston's third consecutive pennant-winning team. In 1875, he and Craver both signed with the Philadelphia Athletics where one of their teammates was George Bechtel, the same George Bechtel involved in the controversy in 1876 while playing with Louisville and then again after his dismissal. With the origins of the National League in 1876, Hall remained with the Athletics.[20]

During the 1876 season, Hall led the majors with five home runs. He also finished second in the League in Batting Average (.366), on base percentage (.384), slugging percentage (.545) and total bases (146). The League leader in all those categories was Chicago's Ross Barnes. Although not known as a particularly powerful slugger (his home runs were almost all inside the park jobs), during the 1876 season the left-handed-hitting Hall was the only player to hit a ball over the right field fence in Louisville.[21]

When Philadelphia was kicked out of the National League, Hall was free to shop around, and everyone was interested. Once he signed with Louisville, others took note. Mecham in the *Chicago Tribune* admitted his surprise but added: "The *Tribune* does not consider Hall a wonderful fielder, but does call him a great help to a nine on account of his batting. He adds considerably to the Louisville strength where they seem to be most in need, and the engagement is a good thing for both him and the club." St. Louis papers were understandably disappointed as they thought their club was going to secure his services. The *Globe-Democrat* lamented: "Hall was to have played here. He was offered his own price...." The *Republican* was more forgiving: "At least there is a prospect of the sylph-like Hall getting settled. It is semi-officially reported that Louisville has secured his services, and he is at least for the present at peace with all the world. It is probably that his coquetting with St. Louis cost him some 500 dollars. It is but just to say that Louisville has secured a valuable, honest and hard-working, though erratic player." Even Al Wright in the Philadelphia *Sunday Mercury* could say no more than there was not a "more honest player" than Hall.[22]

In March Hall penned a letter to Manager Chapman which the *Courier-Journal* acquired and printed:

> I am delighted with your idea of having Devlin and Lafferty practice while the grounds are not in condition for play. Tell them to put their best licks forward and try to see what they can do this summer, for on them greatly depends the

success of the club. They shall have my humble efforts, and I feel sure all the rest of the players will join with me in doing all in their power to help back up Devlin and strive for the success of Louisville. If we all do our best, play for each other and one and all for the club, there is no telling what may be accomplished. I feel confident we are going to give Louisville a treat this season, in the way of good ball-playing, and knowing how well it will be appreciated gives us a good base to work upon.[23]

His humanity was revealed in April. The season was supposed to open in Cincinnati, but weather interfered. While the players were biding their time at the St. James Hotel, Hall was approached by a friend from Philadelphia by the name of Whitey Richardson. Richardson had recently been signed

George Hall. Photograph taken in 1874 while Hall was with Harry Wright's Boston Red Stockings. Credit: New York Public Library.

to play for the Ludlows of Covington, Kentucky. In fact, he had arrived just in time to play with that club a few days ago when they played an exhibition game against the Grays in Louisville. Richardson came to the St. James to see Hall and other Philadelphians on the team and told them Ben Shott, manager of the Ludlows, had written to him in Philadelphia and offered $50 per month to sign with the Ludlows. Shott had also sent him just enough money to get a one-way ticket from Philadelphia to Cincinnati. Without the benefit of any practice, he was put in to catch a pitcher known to throw a hard ball.

Richardson withstood it for five innings, but then bruised hands forced him to retire. After the game, Shott discharged him and told him he might as well plan to foot it back to Philadelphia. He tearfully told the Louisville players he had not a cent to his name and had had only one meal in the last two days. Hall took it upon himself to see what he could do. He made the rounds and by nightfall had collected between 20 or 30 dollars from the Louisville and Cincinnati players. That seems a small number, but the 1870s was a time when the typical industrial worker earned only about $440 per year. Hence, it was more than enough to get Richardson a few meals, a ticket home and a bit of a surplus.[24]

In May, Hall was named captain of the team.[25] As captain it was his job to direct the club during the course of a game. It was also expected that the captain, and *only* the captain, would express any disputes with the umpire's decision.

* * *

Bill Craver was born William H. Craver to James and Pheba Craver on June 13, 1844, in Troy, New York. His father was a carpenter and young Bill peddled tin as a 16-year-old. In January 1864 Craver enlisted as a private in the Union Army and served in an artillery unit until being mustered out in June 1865.[26]

The baseball club in Troy was sometimes identified with the nearby town of Lansingburgh. Craver began his playing career in 1867 at a time when the club was known as the Union Club of Lansingburgh. By the time the National Association began in 1871, the team was once again identified with Troy. By whatever name, the club was heavily involved with local politicians and gamblers and in 1869 withdrew from a game in Cincinnati over a petty dispute with the umpire. Speculation was, they did so to avoid a loss and

Left: **Bill Craver. Photograph taken some time in the early 1870s. Credit: National Baseball Hall of Fame and Museum, Cooperstown, New York.**

their benefactors, thereby, taking a financial hit on losing bets. Craver later spent time with Boston and Chicago but was dismissed from both teams for suspicious play.[27]

Haldeman assumed the veteran infielder would play second base and, as already noted, was complimentary of his ability on the short fly balls just beyond the infield. Craver's primary shortcoming, according to Haldeman, was his tendency to check out of games mentally from time to time. "If he will only make up his mind to put his whole heart into his work, to play the best he knows how on all occasions, and to provide a potent air-brake for the muscles that move his jaws, his record at the close of the season, we are constrained to say, will make his rather indifferent work on the Mutual team of last season feel heartily ashamed of itself."[28]

The same day Haldeman expressed that opinion, he noted further down that Craver's former manager at Baltimore said of him by letter: "I can only speak of Craver as I found him, and, as I have had occasion to mention before, a hard-working, manageable player. He played under my management one season, and, whatever he may have been before or since, I always found him ready, willing, and cheerfully obedient." Oddly, Haldeman does not name the manager in question. Although Craver only spent two seasons with Baltimore, and managed the team for part of 1872, there were three other managers of the club, Everett Mills, Cal McVey and Tom Carey, during that time period.[29]

While Haldeman assumed Craver would play second, the *Chicago Tribune* had other ideas. It published its "suggestion" to Jack Chapman to play Gerhardt at second and Craver at short. The reason, it said, is that the majority of Craver's errors came from an inability to catch a thrown ball. It noted that last year Mutuals shortstop Jimmy Hallinan had to cover the bag on steals because of that very problem. It concluded by noting Louisville catcher Pop Snyder is a harder thrower than the Mutuals' catcher, Nat Hicks, and thus "needs a good man to face him."[30]

On the same day George Hall was announced as captain of the nine, Craver was named assistant captain and the player in charge of positioning the Louisville infield.[31]

* * *

The club made its public debut April 7 against a team of amateurs assembled for the occasion with John Haldeman being one of them. The term used at the time for an *ad hoc* grouping of players was a "picked nine." The new arrivals, especially Hall and Craver, did not disappoint. Hall hit an inside-the-park home run in his first at-bat. Craver showed off his defensive skills. Juice Latham, despite his large size, displayed a remarkable "fleetness of foot" on the base paths. Later that evening, the players were summoned to the club room where, to their surprise, a feast was given in their honor by the directors of the club. "This was a most unexpected and agreeable surprise, and the amplest justice was done to the elegant and bountiful spread."[32]

The banquet was consumed by speeches and toasts by the directors. Mostly the speeches were to assure the players that they would enjoy the city and its residents. At some point Bill Craver was asked to say a few words to the assembly. "He stated that he came here resolved to do his best for the success of the club, that he felt assured all the other players were impressed with the same idea, and he hoped that when the season closed the individual records of the players and the work of the club as a whole would do credit, not only to the city, but to the players themselves." Following the speeches, Craver, along with Hall and Devlin, "all of whom possess good voices," were asked to perform a song or two "and their efforts were highly appreciated." Afterward, the players prepared a letter addressed to Mr. J.T. Ritchey, who had hosted the evening, and the directors of the club "and other Friends" which the *Courier-Journal* printed the following day:

> Gentlemen: Allow us to thank you for a most pleasant surprise and the many evidences of good will which we received from your hands this evening. If honest, hard work, and a strict obedience to all rules laid down for our guidance will bring forth good results, the success of the Louisville club should be assured, for the attempt on our part shall not be found wanting. Trusting that our Louisville friends will not meet with disappointment in the confidence reposed in us, and that our stay in Louisville may be passed both pleasantly and profitably, we are, very respectfully,

John C. Chapman	Chas. N. Snyder
Jas. A. Devlin	Geo. W. Latham
Jos. J. Gerhardt	Wm. L. Hague
Wm. H. Craver	Geo. W. Hall
Wm. M. Crowley	Geo. Shaffer [sic]
Frank B. Lafferty[33]	

* * *

The regular season was scheduled to begin on May 3 in Cincinnati. Writing from the St. James Hotel in Cincinnati, Haldeman noted that rain had fallen since the previous night and lasted until 3:00 in the afternoon. It was, he said, a "drizzly, provoking rain" the result of which was that the ground was so saturated it would require "a day of warm sunshine to put [the field] in fit condition for a game." A brief clearing on the night of the 4th gave hope a game could be played on the 5th, but the rain quickly returned, and another postponement was endured. Complicating matters were the field itself and the schedule. The field needed time to drain so clear weather on the 6th still did not permit a game.

As for the schedule, Cincinnati was scheduled to play an exhibition in Indianapolis on the 8th so even if a game could be played on the 7th, the Grays would still be sitting idle in Cincinnati for an extra day which did not suit Jack Chapman. As it turned out, the 7th was rained out as well. Chapman, wary of the ever-piling expenses of living on the road without any foreseeable source of revenue, finally gave up and loaded his team back on the train headed for Louisville.[34] Louisville and Cincinnati were already scheduled for a return series in Louisville starting on the tenth, so that would have to serve as the season opener for both clubs.

The season finally opened May 10, 1877, at National League Park in Louisville with Cincinnati taking the game 15–9. Three thousand were in attendance and the "grand stand [*sic*] was resplendent with ladies dressed in the exquisite garniture of spring millinery."[35] Haldeman's comment on the presence of women in the crowd was continuation of the thinking dating back to the 1850s about women providing both a calming and legitimizing role on the game. Such comments would continue in the media for another decade. As for the game itself, it started auspiciously with both clubs plating four runs in the first inning. Louisville would take a 5–4 lead after two, but then Cincinnati erupted for five more in the third, followed by two each in the fourth and fifth, to stake a commanding 13–5 advantage. The game lasted three hours which, for the 1870s, was exceedingly long. It was called after eight innings due to darkness.

In addition to having to take the loss, the day was marred by the actions of two young men, "who move in circles that should make them know how to behave." Though their specific actions are not made clear, it was of "such an unseemly manner as made it necessary for the police to eject them from the stand and grounds." What made the matter even more egregious was that it was committed "in the presence of ladies," making it the first time ever on the Louisville grounds misbehavior was seen being committed in front of women, "and we trust it will be the last." The *Courier-Journal* assured its readers "The offending parties will be rigidly denied admission to the grounds and stand hereafter. The Directors do not intend to permit the slightest disorder on their grounds, and those who attempt it may feel sure they will be summarily dealt with."[36]

The Reds and Grays played another game in Louisville May 12. This time the game was won by Louisville 12–8. Then, in an effort to make up the postponed games, Louisville and Cincinnati returned to the Queen City May 14. A new feature in place for 1877 was that when Louisville played away from home, fans remaining back in the River City could keep up with the game via telegraph. The game was reported inning-by-inning over the telegraph and the results posted on the front windows at both the offices of the *Courier-Journal* on Fourth near Green (Liberty) street and Ritchey's, a wine and liquor distributor on Jefferson near Fourth Street. It was a glorious day in Cincinnati and so the two clubs gave it a go again. This time Louisville won 24–6. The high scoring in all three games was due to the new, official League ball. The League had hoped to generate a bit of excitement by increasing the scoring over the previous season and, therefore, asked their manufacturer to enhance the baseballs. The manufacturer over-shot the mark. The League quietly abandoned the new balls in less than a week.[37]

The Reds and Grays were supposed to play another makeup game in Cincinnati on the 15th. Instead, fans got the first controversy of the season. The way umpire selection worked is that each team had to submit, prior to the season, a list of candidates for approved umpires in their hometown. Other clubs would be allowed to weigh in on the candidates and ultimately the League would approve three in each city. Prior to any given game, the two managers would meet to decide on a mutually acceptable umpire for that day's game. When Louisville arrived at the Cincinnati grounds on the 15th, Cincinnati manager Lip Pike informed Chapman that no League-approved umpires were available, but that a local by the name of Brady could officiate the game. In order to get the game in, Chapman had to consent.[38]

Through the first seven innings Brady made a handful of egregious calls—all of which favored Cincinnati. Notwithstanding the calls, Louisville led 6–5 going to the bottom of the seventh. Devlin opened the frame with a single back up the middle and that was followed by a base hit by Shafer to right. Gerhardt followed by grounding out to the right side of the infield advancing both runners in the process. Craver then singled to right through the legs of Reds right fielder Bob Addy and both runs scored, increasing Louisville's lead to 8–5. A subsequent wild pitch allowed Craver to take third with one out.

Bill Crowley was the next hitter and Brady awarded him a base on balls. The Reds players protested immediately arguing that Crowley still had one more ball to go. As Haldeman put it: "This doubtless may have been true, but it was Brady's business to know whether it was true or not." However, "Brady didn't know what he knew." At that point the Cincinnati players gathered around Brady to argue their point and the Louisville players gathered as well, attempting to argue them down. Through it all, Crowley calmly sat on the bag at first. At one point Brady appealed to the scorers to get their opinion. As the *Cincinnati Commercial* put it, the scorers were clueless: they "didn't seem to know anything about it." Finally, and for no obvious reason, Brady decided the Reds were correct and Crowley was one bad pitch shy of a walk.[39]

With the previous bad calls fresh on his mind, Chapman told Pike he would be okay continuing the game with a qualified umpire, but not with Brady. Haldeman expressed the opinion that Pike was okay with that condition, but Cincinnati owner Josiah "Si" Keck pulled him aside and absolutely forbade it. Brady then strode back to home plate and yelled to Crowley to return to the plate and continue his at bat. Crowley refused to budge and, instead, remained seated on the bag. Brady, having no other choice, declared Crowley out. At that point, Chapman had had enough and ordered his men to leave the grounds which they promptly did. Brady then ruled the game a forfeit to Cincinnati. Haldeman concluded his story with condemnation of Brady. "Brady, thou art a most gorgeous fraud; and in calling you this, we put it very, very mildly."[40]

Ultimately the League determined that since Brady was not a League umpire, the entire game was null and void. This was not done, however, until the Louisville Club formally apologized to Keck for the actions of Chapman. This was necessitated by Keck's demand that Louisville do so or his club would not play Louisville again. That being done, the game was voided and rescheduled for June 16.[41]

* * *

Louisville returned home and promptly split a pair with Hartford. The first game, a 12–2 loss on May 18, started well enough. But in the second inning, with two on and two out, Louisville centerfielder Bill Crowley muffed a routine flyball, allowing both runs to score and opening the flood gates for five unearned runs in the inning. Devlin apparently lost his composure and in the third was shelled for six additional runs. In the second game, played the next day, Louisville built an early lead, eventually stretching it to 9–0, which was enough to overcome five more unearned runs by Hartford late in the contest.

Following Hartford, Louisville was swept in a two-game series with Boston. In the first game Louisville fell victim to Boston pitcher Tommy Bond's three-hit masterpiece as the Red Caps, as they were now known, won easily 5–0. Bond would go on to lead the League in 1877 in wins with 40 and shutouts with six. He also led the League in strikeouts with 170 but picked up none on this day. A day later, on May 22, Boston eked out an 8–7 win. Louisville played without Bill Craver who had injured his groin muscle in a previous tilt. This caused more than a little consternation for Haldeman who commented: "In the games in which he has taken part, he has shown himself a thoroughly capable player, and the nine will realize his absence." Louisville left town, *sans* Craver, for three exhibition games in Evansville, Indiana—all of which Louisville won—then returned to face St. Louis and to learn that Craver's injury was not as bad as originally speculated. He was able to rejoin the lineup.[42]

Once again, Louisville split the two games. The loss came in the first game with St. Louis, 7–4. Haldeman was highly critical, asserting at the outset that the Grays "had presented their opponents with a victory." Fielding was the problem. "It is not pleasant to find fault, but the field work of the Louisville nine in recent contests has been sadly deficient, and to win games there must be some improvement in that direction." It was not, Haldeman argued, that the Browns had been driving the ball thus making some errors excusable. Rather it was effort, or the lack thereof: "when a set of players fall into the school-boy style, and make blunders which only a little care would dispense with, such palpable misplays will not be looked upon with eyes of leniency by those who witness them."

Haldeman saved his harshest criticism for the previously heralded Craver. "And, now, a word as to the field management. If we are informed aright, Craver, as Hall's assistant, is the one appointed to see that the players composing the infield of the Louisville nine occupy their proper positions. These players are under his charge, and he is supposed to do all the talking that has to be done, and to issue all orders." Interestingly, in the same day's column, found in the "General Notes," Haldeman commented on the steadiness with which both Craver and Hague played and concluded that "a set of nine men as cool-headed as [Hague and Craver] are would prove a paying investment to someone anxious to run a nine." After the second game, an 11–6 Louisville win on May 30, it was back to praise. "Both Hall and Craver deserve a word of praise for the skillful manner in which they handled their men."[43]

Louisville closed the month of May with the Chicago White Stockings. Devlin had what Haldeman called his best pitching performance of the season so far, as Louisville won the game 3–1. The win ran the Grays' record to 5–5 on the season, good enough for only fourth place in the six-team League, though just two games out of first. The second game with Chicago, played on June 2, was the first of only two home games Louisville would have in the month of June. Louisville won the game 9–2, and Craver was once again praised for his work in the field. But the real hero of this day was Devlin, who was unhittable after the first inning. With the win placing the team's record at 6–5, they would never again slip below .500 on the season.

Following the short Chicago series, the Grays went on the road and, once again, earned splits. This time it was a pair in St. Louis followed by a pair in Chicago. The first game in St. Louis June 5 was scoreless through seven with Devlin allowing just a single hit up to that point. But a couple of hits in the eighth, aided by untimely errors by Louisville, led to four runs for the Browns on their way to a 6–1 win. Devlin was splendid again on the 7th of June and Louisville needed him to be. Louisville managed only four hits and a single unearned run, but Devlin made it stand pitching a five-hit shutout. In Chicago the Grays took on their old nemesis from 1876, Grin Bradley, who Chicago had acquired in the offseason. This time Louisville was able to string together hits. Louisville overcame a 3–1 deficit in the ninth to send the game into extra innings before finally prevailing 5–4 in thirteen. The next day, however, Bradley held them to just three hits as Chicago won 3–1. Louisville returned home on the 14th for the second of their two June home games. They defeated Cincinnati again, 10–3. This time, Craver was the hitting star going three for four.

* * *

The Cincinnati and Louisville clubs rode up the river to resume their rivalry in the Queen City. Louisville, however, was suddenly without the services of George Hall. Hall was summoned home to Baltimore due to the illness of his wife.[44] The *Courier-Journal* never says what ailment Ms. Hall had, but it must not have been too severe. Hall only missed the one game and rejoined the team in time to begin the series in Brooklyn against Hartford on the 23rd of the month. Nevertheless, Louisville won the game in Cincinnati June 16 by a score of 8–4 in spite of Hall's absence. The story of the game that mattered most in the end, however, was not the play on the field, it was the drama unfolding off the field.

During the game, George Keck, brother of Cincinnati owner Si Keck, told several men gathered around him "the dog's dead." The Reds would not be making their upcoming eastern road trip as Keck was no longer able to take on the financial losses. After that June 16 game, word was released that the Reds were in trouble. It was hoped that a reorganization might be effectuated to place the club in a stronger financial position. Their scheduled eastern tour was postponed pending the outcome of a meeting scheduled for the 18th. The plan, as reported by the Cincinnati press, was for Keck to transfer his ownership to a stock company made up of several prominent local businessmen and created just for the purpose. However, whether Keck would do it was in some doubt. To make matters worse, on Monday the 18th a storm rolled into Cincinnati and blew the roof off the grandstand at the Reds' ballpark which added to Keck's burden another $500–600 from the costs to replace it. At that point in the season, Cincinnati was again woeful at 3–14 and losing money "hand over fist." Keck, a local meatpacker whose business was struggling, could take no more and the club effectively folded.[45]

Unknown to others, but well known to Hulbert as League president, was that as of June 1 Cincinnati had no official standing within the League as Keck had failed to tender the annual fee of $100. Meacham of the *Chicago Tribune*, no doubt at Hulbert's direction, appeared immediately in town and secured the signatures of Jimmy Hallinan and Harry Smith to play out the season with the Whites. Hulbert had decided to take advantage of the situation to benefit the White Stockings as there was no other reason for Meacham to move into Cincinnati so quickly other than to snatch up Hallinan and Smith along with Charley Jones if possible. Notwithstanding his position as League president, Hulbert looked first to how his club could gain. This led to further uncertainty for the group of eight to ten investors ready to take control of the club if Keck could not go forward. Accordingly, the investors delayed action due to the uncertainty as to whether the club could be reinstated in the National League.[46]

The officers of the Louisville Club telegraphed their desire to see Cincinnati reinstated. However, one prominent, unnamed, man in Cincinnati stated the prospects of salvaging the situation were being seriously undermined by the actions of Hulbert trying to sign away the best players for his own club. The prime example was Cincinnati's star slugger, Charley Jones, who was convinced to sign what he believed to be a conditional contract with Chicago. The condition being that if Cincinnati could re-establish the club, Chicago would release him from the contract.[47] After Jones had done so (unknown to others on the Cincinnati Club), the remaining players on the Reds' roster made an agreement with the new organization to play out the season at reduced pay of an unstated percentage and the directors agreed and committed to finalizing the deal with or without the League.

It was at that point Jones informed Cincinnati's new management that he had taken advance money from Meacham on a conditional basis. Jones was sent to return the money and when he came back he advised the Reds that Meacham had refused to take back the money, ignored the condition of the contract, and threatened to have Jones banished if he did not report to Chicago as planned. Two of the stockholders then went to see Meacham themselves and things got ugly. They argued to Meacham that the League itself had been organized in part to prevent just such a thing as this from happening and now here was the president of the League acting dishonorably. Moreover, Hulbert had told the Cincinnati directors that only Louisville objected to their remaining in the League, but Louisville had already been the first to issue a written statement from Charles Chase urging that Cincinnati be kept in. The consensus to that end was unanimous among the League owners.[48]

The stock company finally committed itself, once sufficient assurances were made concerning its players. Cincinnati was still without a pitcher and Louisville was considering loaning them Lafferty. Cincinnati's restoration to the League was not certain, however. On June 23 Jones, Bob Addy, Lip Pike, Will Foley and others signed contracts with the newly organized club. Eventually a resolution was reached on the Jones matter.

He ended up playing two games for the White Stockings before returning to play the balance of the season with Cincinnati.[49]

During the two weeks the drama played itself out in Cincinnati, Louisville made its own trip to the East. Nothing had really changed for Louisville as the club continued to play mediocre, if not uninspired, baseball. They were anything but the title-destined juggernaut Chase described in his narrative a decade later. The Grays managed to take two out of three in Brooklyn against second place Hartford, which moved Louisville to within half a game of second. In the first game, June 23, Louisville had its way with Hartford pitcher Terry Larkin with both Devlin and Hall going two for four with a run scored. Louisville won the game 5–3. The second game, June 25, went 11 innings before Hartford pulled out the 5–4 win. Devlin again had two hits, this time including a double. In the third game June 27 both pitchers were betrayed by their supporting casts with Louisville committing three errors to Hartford's six and neither team scored an earned run. In the end, Louisville won the battle of unearned runs 4–1.

Following their three-game set in New York, Louisville moved on to Boston where they were swept by the first place Red Caps. In the first game, played June 28, again neither team managed to score an earned run. However, this time the Grays came up on the short end of the battle of gifts, 3–1. Hall and Devlin each managed only one hit apiece off Boston ace Tommy Bond while Craver had two. The team as a whole managed just seven hits against ten errors—six by Pop Snyder. Louisville doubled its output of hits in the second game on June 30 with Hall going three for five with a double, Devlin added two hits in four trips and Craver went one for four with the one being a double. Yet, 11 team errors led to four unearned runs as Boston won 9–7. With that the month of June came to an end. Boston led the League with a 13–6 mark with Hartford a full game back at 12–7. Louisville was holding on to third with a record of 12–10, two and a half back of Boston. St. Louis at 11–10 was right on Louisville's heels.

While the club was in Boston, Pop Snyder decided to acquire a recently invented tool for catchers: the mask. When this was reported by Haldeman in July, it was noted "he hasn't mustered up a sufficient amount of heart or cheek, whichever it may be, to introduce it to a Louisville audience yet." Protective equipment was still seen as a sign of weakness. The catcher's mask is believed to have been invented in 1876 or 1877 at Harvard University by the baseball team's captain. Professional players started using it in 1877, but only grudgingly. One of the early experimenters was Louisville's reserve catcher from 1876, Scott Hastings, who was with Cincinnati in 1877. Like most of the early adopters, he only did so after taking a foul ball off the face, determined he did not like it, and quickly discarded it. Most catchers refused to wear it for fear of facing ridicule from fans.

As Chadwick noted of their reticence, and the irony of it all, profes-sional catchers were "Plucky enough to face the dangerous fire of balls from the swift pitcher, they tremble before the remarks of the small boys of the crowd of spectators, and prefer to run the risk of broken cheek bones, dislocated jaws, a smashed nose or blackened eyes, than stand the chaff of the fools in the assemblage."[50] There is no indication that Snyder ever actu-ally wore his in 1877. While Snyder may not have popularized the wearing of the catcher's mask, he is one of the three men often credited with devis-ing the hand signals between catcher and pitcher. It is thought he came up with the practice in 1877. The other two players often credited with invent-ing the practice are Joe Roche, a catcher for the Louisville Eagles in 1875 who is believed to have developed it in 1876 while playing in Binghamton, and James Devlin while he was with Chicago in 1875.[51]

On the way home from the eastern trip, the Grays stopped in Cin-cinnati where the Reds were prepared to resume their season. For reasons that are not clear, when Louisville arrived for the first game July 3, they were without the services of Craver. Having no other players with them on the trip, they drafted Haldeman to play second base with Gerhardt shift-ing to shortstop.[52] Haldeman went hitless in four at bats and committed two errors, but Louisville secured the win nonetheless 6–3. The following day, with both rosters now intact, Cincinnati blew out Louisville 10–1 to, more-or-less, announce their return. However, it was not known whether the game would count in the championship race as the League had sim-ply not bothered to say. Haldeman, for his part, was already back in Lou-isville playing a game for his Louisville Amateurs Club as they lost 18–9 to an amateur club from St. Louis.[53]

Meanwhile, the Reds and Grays headed down the river together for a previously scheduled exhibition game in Louisville. Once again, for rea-sons never made clear, one team was missing a player. Cincinnati slugger Charley Jones failed to make the trip. Cincinnati needed a body and asked Haldeman to suit up for the Reds. O.P. Caylor, the Cincinnati baseball edi-tor, had not made the trip and was, therefore, unaware of the development until it was telegraphed back to Cincinnati just before the game. As he wrote the following day: "it was feared the boys were betrayed." His fear, however, was unfounded. Haldeman, playing centerfield, had two putouts, went one for four at the plate, and drove in the third Reds run in Cincin-nati's 3–1 win. Caylor gave credit where it was due: "But all honor to John" Caylor wrote, "John can always depend on a warm welcome in Cincin-nati when he comes here on account of the work he did for us yesterday." Haldeman used the opportunity to poke fun at himself. "The new $10,000 center-fielder of the Cincinnati Reds appeared with them for the first time yesterday." He continued: "He possibly might command a better salary as foreman in some soup house."[54] Even Meacham at the *Chicago Tribune* had some fun with it:

> Something in the way of a formal protest against J.A. Haldeman of Louisville ought to be drawn up and presented to somebody. It might have been borne that he should continually advertise himself as "Chapman's Unknown" and make himself a conundrum to the press and public, but when he shows up one day as of the Louisville Club, and the next as fielder for the Cincinnatis, he distributes himself too widely, and lays himself open to the charge of revolving.[55]

* * *

On the same day Haldeman was aiding the Reds, the *Courier-Journal* was reporting that third baseman Bill Hague would miss some upcoming games due to a serious boil on his wrist. Two days later, the *Courier-Journal* reported that to replace Hague, the Grays had signed former Mutuals infielder, and currently an infielder with the Allegheny Club of Pittsburgh, Al Nichols. Nichols, like so many others of the period, also hailed originally from England. He was born Alfred Henry Williams and migrated to the United States with his mother, the former Emma Nichols, in 1859. Very little is known about Nichols' early life. He began his professional career in 1875 with the Brooklyn Atlantics where he played in just 32 games. He also played a short portion of that season with Cincinnati. In 1876 he was with the New York Mutuals. After the Mutuals were kicked out of the National League following the 1876 season, Nichols signed with Pittsburgh. Louisville opting to sign Nichols was at the suggestion of George Hall though the connection between the two is not obvious. Nichols arrived in Louisville by July 11 and witnessed a Louisville victory over Boston.[56] The "Louisville Four" was now complete.

Chapter Four

A Myth Is Born

The myth of Louisville's inevitable pennant of 1877 was born in July and was fully formed by August 13. Coming off the two games with Cincinnati on the 3rd and 4th of July, Boston held the lead with a record of 13–7, Hartford was a clear-cut second at 12–8, and Louisville and St. Louis were tied for third with records of 13–11. Louisville had in front of them an opportunity to move up due to the structure of the schedule. Next up for the Grays were Hartford and Boston with both series being played at Fourth and Hill. Louisville's next eight games would be against those two clubs. The Grays took full advantage.

First up was Hartford on the 7th of July. Hartford's Terry Larkin, a 29-game winner on the season, although he would also match Devlin in

leading the League in losses with 25, was no match for the Grays on this day. Louisville pounced on him early with three runs in the first. Louisville did the bulk of its damage in the fifth when, leading 4–1 going in, they batted around and then some, coming out of the inning having increased their lead to 12–1. In all Louisville crushed Larkin for 20 hits with every player in the lineup contributing at least two. Hall and Gerhardt led the way with three each with one of Gerhardt's being a double and two of Hall's being triples. Devlin

Opposite: **Bill Hague. Photograph taken in 1876. It was boils on his wrist that led to the signing of Al Nichols. Credit: National Baseball Hall of Fame and Museum, Cooperstown, New York.**

meanwhile held Hartford to six hits and the Grays won it by a final of 14–4. The win apparently put Haldeman in a good mood. He took the opportunity to promote attendance at games as an oasis in the middle of summer: "Those who wish rest and relaxation during the hot weather should visit the Base Ball Park. The accommodations there are of the finest description—the seats are comfortable, and when it is suffocatingly hot in the city, a pleasant breeze is always felt in the Grand Stand [*sic*]. All this and a fine game of base ball are attractions which ought to be appreciated."[1]

The second game, scheduled for the 9th, was postponed by rain. While the Grays were idled by the rain, Devlin and Snyder met with St. Louis manager George McManus and captain Mike McGeary. This was not uncommon at the time. Teams would often recruit players on another team during the season to lure them to sign for the following season. Both Devlin and Snyder agreed and signed with St. Louis for 1878. Haldeman took the loss of the Louisville battery in stride, calling them "beyond doubt the best pair in the country." However, he did not see them as irreplaceable: "the woods are full of good ballplayers, and the directors will doubtless find satisfactory men to fill the vacant positions." Henry Chadwick saw it much differently, forecasting doom for Louisville's fortunes: "If these engagements have been made, the result may be the practical breaking-up of the Louisville nine; for, though the players may be kept together until the end of the season, the power to discipline is in a measure lost, and the result of their play is likely to show this."[2]

Boston came to town to start a series on the 11th. The series was expected to tell a great deal about where Louisville ranked. Haldeman noted in the *Courier-Journal* that the "nine which has given the Grays more trouble than any other team in the League … are known as Harry Wright's boys from Boston." Indeed, Louisville was winless against Boston on the season having just lost a pair in Boston the previous month, coupled with the two-game sweep Boston put on them in Louisville back in May. Moreover, for Boston's pitcher, Tommy Bond, this was not the only year he was a nemesis for Louisville. While pitching for Hartford the previous year, he kept Louisville's hitters in check holding them on multiple occasions to just a couple of hits. Knowledge of the past, however, did not dampen the enthusiasm of the Louisville fans. Local cranks turned out in big numbers for the first game. Haldeman described the scene: "The grand stand was crowded with ladies, all the other covered stands were filled to overflowing; the uncovered seats on the Fourth-street side had their occupants also, and if ever there was a propitious time for the home-nine to do something desperate and make a good impression, this occasion certainly filled the bill."[3]

Louisville had another offensive eruption. Bill Hague, Joe Gerhardt, George Hall, Orator Shafer and Bill Crowley each had three hits. Every other member of the lineup had at least two excepting Craver who had but one. Devlin added a double as did Snyder, Hague and Gerhardt. Devlin also hit a triple as did Hall and Latham. Louisville attacked Bond with 22 hits in a 14–9 victory. The runs came in bunches. After a scoreless first inning for both clubs, Louisville exploded for six in the second inning. They added single runs in the third and fourth and led 8–0 going to the sixth. Then they ignited again adding five more to their total.

The following day, Louisville did it again. On the 12th they touched up Bond for 18 more hits in an 8–6, ten-inning win for their second in a row over Boston and their third in a row overall. This time Juice Latham and Bill Crowley led the way with three hits apiece while Hall and Devlin were the only two players to have fewer than two. The game was a see-saw affair with Boston taking an early 2–0 lead in the second only for Louisville to take over 3–2 after four. Finally, Boston tied it 6–6 with a run in the eighth to ultimately send the game to an extra frame. In the tenth, Shafer led off with a base hit and two batters later Craver reached on an errant throw. Pop Snyder, who committed seven errors in the game, grounded out to George Wright, but advanced the runners nonetheless.

That brought Crowley to the plate and Bond quickly worked a two-strike count on the Louisville outfielder. For Haldeman this raised the drama: "[T]he males of the audience held their breaths for fear of broken suspenders. We are not a female, and can not, therefore, analyze the feelings of that class of the population, but doubtless some of them partook of the excitement and were as much interested as the most enthusiastic of the enthusiasts."[4] Crowley did not disappoint. He drove the next pitch hard to left, skipping past Boston third baseman, Harry Schafer, driving home both runners.

The win meant Louisville was now in first place for the first time in franchise history. Louisville's record moved to 16–11 on the season (.593) while Boston's was 15–9 (.625). In today's game, that would make Boston first by a half game. But by League rule in 1877, the championship was determined by the number of wins in League games; winning percentage was a tie breaker. As a result, the headline in the *Courier-Journal* the following day was a celebratory "We Ride the Top Wave."[5]

* * *

Following the second Boston game, Louisville had a week off from League competition. As has already been noted, this allowed them to add exhibition dates against amateur and semi-professional clubs. One of the more important such clubs was Indianapolis, which would find itself part of the National League within a year. Indianapolis was led by their star pitching ace, Edward Sylvester Nolan—better known as "The Only Nolan."

The Canadian-born 22-year-old seemed destined for stardom. Louisville first faced him April 16 prior to the start of the season. In that contest, Louisville won 4–2, but Nolan held the Grays to five hits in the game.[6] Twelve Indianapolis errors led to all four Louisville runs.

With Louisville coming off three impressive League games in a row, facing Nolan would not seem to be a large undertaking. However, it was. Nolan held Louisville to two hits while fanning seven as Indianapolis shutout Louisville 3–0. The game went largely unnoticed. The following day the two clubs played again, this time in Louisville. Around 500 spectators showed up for a "dull, insipid, unentertaining and slumber-inviting" game. This time Nolan held Louisville to four hits while fanning five more as Indianapolis won 9–2.[7] Lafferty pitched for Louisville. It was one of the few opportunities he received all year. Again, the result was ignored.

There was no suggestion at the time, and there has been no revelation of any evidence since, to suggest either game was sold. Indeed, as shall be seen later, exhibition games were never suspect. Given Nolan's dominance in the April meeting, not to mention his dominance generally over the next few years, the results in July seem in line. But the games also establish a baseline going forward. With the exception of this one pitching performance by Lafferty, contests between Louisville and Indianapolis were basically even, with both Devlin and Nolan proving difficult for the other club to handle.

* * *

After a week away from League action, Hartford returned to town on the 19th, this time for a three-game set. Louisville resumed its offensive juggernaut, striking for seven runs in the third inning. Larkin did not make it through the inning. Manager Bob Ferguson took over in the box moving Larkin to third. The next batter, George Hall, sent a grounder to Larkin at his new spot and the result was an errant throw which brought in Latham and Hague and allowed Hall to reach third. It was a disastrous inning for Hartford, though they would fight back to make the final a more respectable 10–7. The third game in the series, played July 21, went similarly. Louisville opened with a flurry, doing most of its damage in the first inning, scoring seven. This time it was Ferguson alone who took the abuse. Once again, Hartford was able to crawl its way back to respectability, losing only 11–6.

It was the middle game of the three-game set that was something of a tell. In that game Ferguson held Louisville to ten hits as Hartford handed Louisville its first loss in five games, 8–3. Louisville coupled its mediocre hitting with poor fielding. Every player on the field for Louisville committed at least one error and the team collectively committed twelve.

Haldeman, like many others in the press of the time, often credited luck—good or bad—for the outcome of games. The two most common complaints of the reporters covering games after a loss were bad luck (or good luck blessing the opponent) and the umpire. Only when losses mounted would nefarious forces be blamed. This game was no different. The headline in the following day's paper summed it up with "As Luck Would Have It."[8] Nevertheless, Louisville would not lose again until August.

By the time Boston returned July 23 they had resumed the League lead with a 20–11 record. Since last being in Louisville 11 days before, Boston had won five and lost only two. Louisville, though having played only three games with Hartford during Boston's absence, sat alone in second at 18–12. St. Louis was third at 17–13 and Hartford was fourth at 17–15. The first game between Boston and Louisville was low scoring. Boston managed just six hits off Devlin and, to Louisville's good fortune, none of the hits were enhanced by any of the six Louisville errors. Offensively, Louisville's eight hits were just enough as the Grays won 3–1.

Following the win, Haldeman started counting his chickens. He was looking forward to the next two series: St. Louis and Chicago. "A succession of victories over these nines will establish Louisville's claim to pennant-flyer pretty thoroughly." He also included quotes from the *New York Sportsman* which described Louisville as "the coming champions, apparently."[9] In the second game with Boston, Hall led the way with four hits, including a double, and Bill Hague homered as Louisville overcame an early 2–0 deficit to win 7–4. Louisville was back in first.

Whether Louisville was indeed in first place at any given point was not always clear. The League had still not determined what to do with Cincinnati or its games played both before and after the reorganization. As Haldeman explained it, and for the remainder of the season would repeat over-and-over, what the standings actually were on a particular day depended on Cincinnati games. Haldeman laid out the possibilities each time. On this occasion, he noted, if you counted just the pre-reorganization Reds games, Louisville would lead Boston with a record of 19–11 compared to Boston's 17–12. If, on the other hand, you include all the Cincinnati games played to date, Louisville's record would be 20–12 to Boston's record of 20–13. If all the Cincinnati games were struck from the League records, Louisville would be 15–10 to Boston's 15–12. Since both clubs had games against Cincinnati on the schedule ahead, this was going to sow confusion. The League ultimately would not decide until December, and at that point it had no impact on the final League standings. The decision initially made in December, that the Cincinnati games did not count,[10] would eventually be reversed. Hence, the game in which Haldeman played did not exist in the National League record books until years later.

The Famous Louisville Ball Team of 1877. Several
Members of Which Put a Blot On the National Game

TOP ROW—HALL, SHAFFER, DEVLIN, NICHOLS   MIDDLE ROW—LAFFERTY, GERHARDT, SNYDER, LATHAM, HAGUE   BOTTOM ROW—CRAVER, CROWLEY.

Louisville Grays of 1877. Rarely found photograph of the club, taken some
time after Nichols arrived. The poor quality is due to its only known loca-
tion being from a printing by the *Courier-Journal* in 1910. Unsurprisingly, the
Courier-Journal misidentifies more than half the players shown in one way or
another. In the period since the Grays' scandal, newspaper accounts of it rarely
get any of the facts correct. Pictured: back row (L to R): Orator Shafer, Pop Snyder, Jim Devlin, Al Nichols; middle row (L to R): George Hall, Bill Craver, Joe
Gerhardt, Juice Latham, Bill Hague; reclining (L to R) Flip Lafferty, Bill Crowley. Credit: Society for American Baseball Research (SABR) Pictorial History
Committee.

* * *

Boston departed Louisville for St. Louis, where they would play two
games. Louisville, once again, had a week off. When Boston left, Louisville
was in first by a half game over Boston and a full two games over St. Louis.
The Browns took both games from Boston in the Mound City and then
made their way to the Falls City for a showdown with Louisville on the
31st. Louisville was now in first place by one game over St. Louis and Boston perched just a half game further back. Haldeman set the table:

> Each club has won two games from the other, with half the season finished;
> the home nine is now in the lead in the struggle for the League champion-
> ship of the United States; the St. Louis nine stands next beat, with only a hair's

breadth difference…. The eyes of all other cities in base-balldom are now turned toward the St. Louis and Louisville nines, and when the home organization stands a lively chance of bringing the pennant to this city there should certainly be no apathy in base-ball circles here.[11]

Game one saw Louisville once again come out swinging. On a pleasant afternoon with an enthusiastic crowd on hand, Louisville put up five in the second inning and two more in the third. Hall, Devlin and Snyder led the way with two hits each, but every member of the team tallied at least one hit off St. Louis pitcher Joe Blong. That is all Devlin would need to cruise to a 7–0 shutout win. The second game was much closer. Both clubs struggled to find hits off Devlin and Blong, respectively. For the game, Devlin allowed only six hits while Blong surrendered eight. Of the eight Louisville hits, three belonged to George Hall. Louisville led 1–0 going to the ninth, but in the top half Bill Crowley tripled, Jumbo Latham drove him home with a hit, and Latham himself later scored on Hall's third hit of the day. St. Louis managed to score a run in the ninth to make the final 3–1. Louisville's defense was given credit for winning the game as repeatedly scoring threats by St. Louis were snuffed out by fine defensive plays on Louisville's part.

As much as the series between Louisville and St. Louis was anticipated, in the end what came out of it was controversy. Dan Devinney, one of Louisville's local League-approved umpires, worked both games of the series. On the morning of the second game, he informed one of the Louisville directors that, prior to the first game, St. Louis manager George McManus offered him "$250 if he would work things so as to bring the Browns out on top in both of the games played here." The *Courier-Journal* sent a reporter that evening to meet with Devinney and get his statement. Devinney stated that two years previous, he was employed by the Browns to head up the training regimen of the club. Because of that relationship, on the morning of St. Louis' arrival, Devinney went to the Fourteenth Street station to meet them. McManus walked up to him and asked to meet with him at the hotel later that morning. When Devinney reached the Louisville Hotel, McManus met him in the lobby and invited him to the room. It was there McManus made the offer of money "if I would do the square thing for the Browns."

McManus offered to sweeten the deal further if Devinney would also see to it that St. Louis was well cared for in future games in Louisville. Devinney told the reporter that he was willing to offer a sworn affidavit on the subject. McManus was later found on Main Street and, when asked about Devinney's statement, swore it was false. The *Courier-Journal* reporter then offered the opinion that he believed Devinney for the simple reason that Devinney had no known motivation for making up an accusation of that sort. The story concludes by stating the St. Louis's directorate, which the reporter stated was composed of men of the highest caliber, "owe it to themselves to investigate this matter from beginning to end."[12]

The St. Louis papers erupted the next day with charges of fraud. According to the St. Louis papers, the false allegations against McManus stemmed from the fact that a month earlier the Browns had secured the services of both Devlin and Snyder for 1878. The *Globe-Democrat* asserted that while the allegations against McManus "may cause surprise elsewhere … but will only produce laughter in this city." It continued: "No one in this community will look upon this charge of bribery in any other light than that of a joke." Haldeman was surprised and expressed doubt that the management of the Browns would see the matter quite so cavalierly. Astutely, though, he noted that despite the *Globe-Democrat's* bloviating, "Devinney's statement is still intact." The *New York Clipper* weighed in a week later expressing disbelief that the St. Louis papers would declare the matter a "joke" rather than the very serious accusation it represented.[13]

McManus told a reporter for the *Indianapolis Sentinel* that it was Devinney who approached him. According to McManus, when he reached the hotel, he ran into Devinney in the elevator and the umpire followed him to his room. Once in the room McManus began a bath and Devinney remained and kept talking. It was then he offered up about the two games, "I can fix them for you." McManus responded by saying to Devinney that the latter did not have the nerve to do such a thing and then threatened to call out any unfair decisions going St. Louis' way. Finally, McManus stated he thought the whole thing was the creation of Jack Chapman as revenge for McManus signing Devlin and Snyder.[14]

Eventually, the *Courier-Journal* got around to asking Charles Chase about the affair. According to Chase, prior to the first game he ran into McManus and had a brief conversation with him. At no point during that conversation did McManus express any misgivings about Devinney umpiring the game. Later, during the game when Louisville was in control, McManus came over and sat beside Chase. During the conversation he asked why Louisville did not use Mike Walsh, another local umpire. Chase told McManus the crowd was not fond of Walsh. At that point, McManus nodded at Devinney and said "He's no good; how can he support a wife on what he gets for umpiring one or two games a week? I knew him before he came here, and I know what he is." Chase then offered that McManus' words "nettled" him and he demanded proof. When McManus stated he had none but was just stating his opinion, Chase informed him to keep his opinion to himself. After the game, Chase informed Devinney of what McManus had said. It was then Devinney revealed the contents of his earlier conversation with McManus at the hotel. After the offer was revealed by Devinney, McManus assiduously avoided Louisville management that night and did not appear at all at the ballpark the next day.[15]

Things got even more bizarre later in the month when the *Chicago Tribune* took the very odd position that it was Louisville's responsibility to prove or disprove the charges. "The burden is plainly on Louisville and not on St. Louis; they have made the charge, and if they don't prosecute it, they lay themselves open to the charge of malicious slander." Haldeman responded immediately: "The *Tribune's* position is absurd. The Louisville club advised the St. Louis club of the action of its manager, McManus, here, expressing the belief that Devinney's statement was a true one. If, after this, St. Louis shows no inclination to investigate the matter, and is willing to continue a rascal as its business manager, certainly it is none of Louisville's business to proceed further."[16]

In the end, nothing came of the whole affair other than accusations and threats of lawsuits. But it was not the first time St. Louis' management took the ostrich approach when faced with allegations of wrongdoing of that sort. In 1876, during a series between the Browns and the New York Mutuals, Mike McGeary of the Browns committed five throwing errors which led to all six of the Mutuals' runs and a win. The *New York World* called it "suspicious play." McGeary was one of the players involved in the corruption of a game between Philadelphia and Chicago mentioned earlier in which both clubs attempted to throw the game. He was also called out indirectly prior to the 1876 season by Jack Burdock of the Hartford club who told a reporter for the *New York Clipper* that a player on a Philadelphia club in 1875 offered him $1,000 to "soil" a game between the two. St. Louis suspended McGeary and, according to the *St. Louis Times,* undertook an investigation. The directors of the club met and "decided to sift the charges against McGeary thoroughly." Three days later, in a letter to the *Philadelphia City Item*, St. Louis vice-president C.O. Bishop stated he had "made careful inquiry" and had concluded "there is no evidence, aside from the fielding errors made by him in that game, that McGeary was false to his club, and therefore he is re-instated to-day." Lip Pike, one of the few Browns players never suspected of crooked play, came out and said he thought McGeary sold the game.[17]

* * *

Following St. Louis to town was fifth place Chicago. Haldeman by now was allowing his confidence to get ahead of the facts as he wrote in the *Courier-Journal*, "The coming champions propose this afternoon to show the late champions how to play base-ball." Fortunately, Haldeman's overconfidence did not impact the Grays as, once again, they came to the ballpark ready to hit. Approximately a thousand showed up to see the game "and if heavy hitting was what they went out for, the afternoon sport did not fail to leave a pleasant impression." The Grays knocked Chicago starter Cal McVey out of the box in the third inning on their way to a 15–9 win. Louisville amassed 21 hits on the day, with Hall leading the way going four for six. Devlin, Hague and Crowley each added three hits of their own. Two of Hall's hits were doubles while Hague added a triple and both Shafer and Crowley homered. Haldeman included in his write-up of the game an alleged exchange with Juice Latham: "'Well George, what are we?' And Latham smilingly rejoined, 'The coming champions. Go tell the folks.'" A.G. Spalding said after the game that if Louisville continued to hit the ball as they had been, they would have no trouble capturing the pennant.[18]

Game two was a different story. Louisville would have to face its old nemesis, Grin Bradley. Although 1877 had been nowhere near as successful for Bradley as 1876 had been, Bradley put it together on this day holding Louisville to seven hits and two unearned runs in Chicago's 7–2 win. It stopped Louisville's winning streak at six and constituted the club's second loss in the last twelve games. No alarms were raised by the set back. As Haldeman put it: "considering their numerous brilliant victories no one will grumble at their misfortune."[19] Notwithstanding the loss, Louisville held first place with a record of 23–13. St. Louis was two back at 21–15 and Boston right behind them at 20–15. Hartford was now fading at 17–18.

The Chicago series, like the St. Louis series before it, is best known for the controversy generated over—once again—umpire Dan Devinney. However, unlike the opposing accusations between Devinney and McManus which could never be resolved, this story does not withstand a minimal level of scrutiny. The story concerns the second game between Louisville and Chicago. As noted earlier, prior to a game the two managers would meet to select from the pool of local umpires. Typically, in Louisville, the names of the umpires would be placed in a hat and drawn by the opposing manager. On this particular day, A.G. Spalding of Chicago sent out Cal McVey to do the honors and the name of Dan Devinney was drawn, the game was played, Chicago won 7–2 and, as far as the spectators were aware, that is all that occurred. Neither the *Courier-Journal* nor the *Chicago Tribune* mentions anything out of the ordinary in their respective reports.

The allegations over the August 6 game erupted on the 10th when the *St. Louis Globe-Democrat* repeated a story that first appeared in the *Boston Globe* that Louisville had rigged the umpire selection process to get Devinney. According to the *Boston Globe*, Spalding was annoyed that Devinney's name always seemed to come out of the hat when he drew. In order to change his luck, on this day he sent out McVey to draw. McVey drew a name from the hat and, sure enough, it was Devinney. McVey became upset and demanded to see the other slips of paper in the hat. All of them, as it turned out, bore the name of Devinney. According to historian William Cook, at this point the White Sox became incensed and demanded another umpire be brought to the grounds.[20] The story appears to be mostly true; the controversy is not.

The story becomes suspect at the very outset. When Chicago last played in Louisville May 31 and June 2, Devinney was in fact the umpire in both games and both games were won by Louisville. However, in the first game of the present series, played August 4, Harvey McElwee served as umpire.[21] That game also ended with a Louisville win, and we do not know who did the drawing for any of the three games. Spalding, like most ball players, probably had some superstitions and may have sent McVey to execute the draw as a result of one of them. It could be that McVey had drawn the previous day, McElwee was the result, so Spalding decided to keep the hot hand. But since the end result in all three games was a Chicago loss, that seems doubtful. Moreover, there is no evidence Chicago had a particular issue with Devinney's umpiring.

When this controversy broke out, it was reported that Chicago had been unhappy with Devinney's work in the previous visit made by Chicago at the end of May. The only real indication of that, however, is a report on June 12 that during that series, both Cap Anson and Cal McVey of the White Stockings were so verbally abusive toward Devinney that one of the Louisville directors was compelled to call them out.[22] There is no mention in any of the Chicago papers covering those two games of any complaints about Devinney's decisions. The *Chicago Tribune* concluded about both games that the issue was simply that the White Stockings could not hit. Writing of the May 31 game, Meacham stated, "To sum up the batting, it may be said that there was none on the Chicago side." Regarding the game played June 2, he declared the loss was a "result of loose fielding and scandalously weak hitting."[23] The bottom line is that while we will never know the exact reason Spalding sent out McVey to draw the umpire, it likely had nothing to do with Devinney.

The second part of the controversy has its own set of problems and a history. It was reported that when McVey drew Devinney's name, he demanded to see the other two slips and discovered they too had Devinney's name written on them. This may be true as a matter of fact, but if so, it was the result of a problem about which Spalding would have already been aware. The problem started months earlier. Prior to the season, Louisville Vice-President Charles Chase submitted the names of proposed local umpires to the League for the comment and approval of the other clubs. His list included Devinney along with John Morris, Harvey McElwee and others. The umpires initially selected and approved by the League were Devinney, Morris and Kenneth McDonald. During the season, Jack Chapman notified the League that there was a problem with Louisville's appointed umpires. Namely there was an issue with two of them not being available due to business and other concerns. Consequently, Chapman submitted alternative names for approval. As of August, none of the other clubs had responded leaving Devinney the only umpire officially recognized by the League.[24] That raises questions about how McElwee was allowed to umpire the first game. But it also explains why Devinney's name was the only one in the hat.

Finally, there is the assertion that Chicago demanded another umpire be brought forth. Based on the newspaper accounts of the game, Devinney was the umpire.[25] If Chicago had demanded a new umpire be brought out, their demands were ignored. Moreover, this type of pre-game eruption certainly would have been noticed by those in attendance, yet there is not a single contemporaneous account of it from any of the reporters covering the game. The story strongly implies that something was afoot between Louisville and Devinney. Historian Tom Melville alludes to the story to suggest corruption of the Louisville management.[26] The evidence suggests the entire affair was completely made up by the press.

* * *

Following the 7–2 loss to Chicago, the Grays hit the road, first for a western swing, and then to the East. Haldeman accompanied the team to St. Louis and then to Chicago.[27] The one loss, just their second in 12 games, did nothing to dampen the enthusiasm in Louisville. As the game in St. Louis progressed on August 7, fans stood by anxiously awaiting the results to be posted on the *Courier-Journal's* windows. The game was scoreless through six innings, but St. Louis had broken through and carried a 2–1 lead into the ninth inning. With one out already in the top half of the inning, George Hall doubled to left. Devlin followed with a fly out that failed to advance the runner. The next batter, Orator Shafer, singled to left which brought home Hall to tie the game. Joe Gerhardt then hit a ball into the left centerfield gap that ended up with Shafer scoring and Gerhardt safely on third. Gerhardt ultimately scored on a wild pitch. In the bottom of the ninth Devlin closed it out for the 4–2 win.

The second game was a walkover. Louisville opened with five runs in the first inning and never looked back. In the end the Grays prevailed 10–3. The only downside was that during the game Gerhardt passed out from the heat and had to be replaced by Nichols. The club had now won 12 of its last 14. The press, not just in Louisville, began to get ahead of itself as had Haldeman previously. Even the *New York Herald* began referring to Louisville as "the coming champions."[28]

From St. Louis the Grays proceeded to Chicago. In the first game, played on August 11, Louisville again began slowly and was held scoreless through seven innings. Louisville managed seven hits off Grin Bradley to that point but was unable to push anything across the plate. Chicago, meanwhile, scored single runs in the top half of both the sixth and the eighth to take a 2–0 lead into the bottom of the latter frame. It was then that the Grays' bats came alive. Bill Hague opened the bottom of the eighth with a sharp single to right. Hall followed Hague with a double to left, putting two men on with Devlin coming up. Devlin singled with a line drive to left which fell in allowing Hague to score easily. Hall hesitated at second base and when he broke for third Chicago left fielder Paul Hines saw an opportunity and tried to throw Hall out. However, Hines' throw to Anson was well off the mark allowing Hall to score and Devlin to reach third himself. Orator Shafer hit a bloop single to left which brought in Devlin. Gerhardt grounded to Spalding, playing second base, but the latter's throw to first was too hard to handle for Chicago's first baseman, John Glenn, and everyone was safe. Bill Craver fouled out followed by Pop Snyder grounding to short. Fortunately for Louisville, Chicago's shortstop John Peters muffed the ball, and the bases were loaded. Bill Crowley cleaned it up with a line drive back up the middle scoring both Shafer and Gerhardt.

By the time the inning was over, Louisville had broken through for five runs. But Chicago was not done. Louisville defensive miscues in the top of the ninth allowed three unearned runs to score, tying the game at five. In the bottom of the ninth, Hall led off by fouling out, then Devlin reached on an error. Shafer grounded to A.G. Spalding at second who, in his haste to turn two, fumbled the ball allowing both runners to reach safely. Gerhardt followed with a sharp hit to right, but it was hit too hard to get a man home. With the bases loaded, Bill Craver drove a base hit up the middle, scoring both Devlin and Shafer. Louisville won 7–5. (At the time, games were played through the bottom of the last inning, regardless of the score.)

Two days later the clubs met again and played despite a constant drizzle. It had rained up until game time which diminished the number of spectators on hand as many no doubt expected a postponement. But the rain stopped just before the start, allowing the umpire to call the game to get underway. The drizzle returned in the fourth and continued until the end but, as Haldeman described it, "So anxious were the clubs to get the game off that no official notice of the rain was taken, and the contest went on with the men wet through."[29] An early error by Chicago shortstop John Peters opened the door and Louisville rushed through with six unearned runs in the first. Before the day was over, each team would commit nine errors with Louisville out-hitting Chicago 12–7 to cruise to an 8–2 victory. Of the ten runs, none were earned. The headline the day after the club's 14th win in 16 games read proudly, "Onward and Upward." Louisville would then spend four days making its way East, playing exhibitions along the way. Haldeman, meanwhile, departed the club and headed to Put-In-Bay, Ohio, for a vacation.[30] Afterward, he returned to Louisville. Consequently, he did not witness the upcoming games in Brooklyn and Boston.

By this point in the season, the *Chicago Tribune* considered Louisville a veritable lock for the pennant. The *Tribune* announced with certainty that the Grays would win the pennant. *The St. Louis Times* was equally impressed stating: "Louisville is so far in the lead now in the championship race that there is scarcely any doubt of her winning the pennant." In the *New York Clipper*, Chadwick was hedging his bets:

> That is how the clubs stand up to to-day, Aug. 6. How they will stand by October 6, two months hence, deponent saith not. "But what are the chances?" queries our impatient readers. Well, the chances are that, as things look now, the pennant will "go West," and that "Old Kentuck" will fly the coveted banner at Louisville. That is how things look just at present; but there are so many uncertainties in baseball that it would be very unsafe to bet on this probability.[31]

* * *

The two wins at Chicago, coupled with Boston's two losses at home to Hartford, put Louisville at 27–13 for the season. St. Louis held second, four games back, at 23–17. Boston sat third just a half game behind the Browns at 22–17. The *New York World* opined Louisville needed only to gain a split in the final Eastern swing to secure the flag. Haldeman was of the belief that the upcoming games with Cincinnati would not count, which left Louisville with just 15 League games remaining. To win the pennant, he calculated, they only needed to win seven of those.[32] This, of course, presumed that neither St. Louis nor Boston would win substantially all of their remaining games.

O.P. Caylor in Cincinnati was not as confident about Louisville's pennant chances. "While we recognize [Louisville's] advantageous lead, we also recognize the fact that the Bostons under coming circumstances are by no means distanced."[33] The "coming circumstances" to which Caylor was referring was the schedule. Counting the Cincinnati games, by the time Louisville resumed League play, Louisville and Boston would have, respectively, 20 and 21 games remaining. For Louisville, only six of those would be played at home. For Boston, however, all 21 would be at home. Consider that without the Cincinnati games—that is, assuming only 15 games for each—Boston's maximum win total was 37, meaning Louisville's "magic number" to secure a tie for the pennant was ten games. With Cincinnati included, the number climbed to 16.

Caylor had a point, and it was completely ignored at the time. Since then, historians have continued to ignore it. If Boston pulled off the unthinkable, Louisville had to win 16 of its final 20 games, an .800 winning percentage, just to earn a tie for the pennant. To add to the difficulty, the bulk of those games were away from home. Given that at this point in the season, even with the streak of 14 out of 16 just completed, Louisville's win percentage was only .675. Finishing out winning 16 out of 20 would be phenomenal achievement. But that would only come into play if Boston itself did the impossible. In the numerous histories of the Grays' scandal of 1877, none of them mention what Boston did.

Boston had a slow start to the season, but for the most part they played well in spite of a lop-sided schedule. They opened the year with a scoreless tie at Hartford April 30, then headed west for the entire month of May. Their first two games were a pair of losses at St. Louis May 8 and 10th. But they would not lose another game in May, winning two games each in Chicago, Cincinnati and Louisville. By the end of the month, they were 6–2 and in first place. They opened the month of June with a pair of wins at home against Hartford, then promptly lost two games against Hartford in Brooklyn, each by the identical score of 7–0. The second loss dropped them out of first place by a half game to St. Louis June 12. They spent the rest of the month at home where they won five of seven, including two over Louisville, to finish June with a record of 13–6. That was good enough to hold first place by a game over Hartford and two and half over Louisville.

In July the schedule once again had them spending the entire month on the road, all of it in the Western portion of the circuit. They did not fare as well this time as they had in May, losing nine of the 16 games played including four to Louisville as the Grays were in the early portion of their winning streak. Nevertheless, they retained their hold on first place all the way through until the 7–4 loss at Louisville July 24. By the end of July, the Red Caps found themselves with a 20–15 record and standing third in the League. Only nine of their 35 games played had been at home. By the time Louisville arrived August 17, Boston had added two more wins on the road and two losses at home, all to Hartford.

Boston's record going into the August 17 meeting with Louisville was 22–17 (.564) and did not hint at a miracle. If you consider that their home record up to that point was 7–4 (.636), you would have to consider their finish would be stronger than their overall record. A winning percentage of .636 in 21 games translates into 13.36 wins. If you round up and assume 14 wins, then Boston should end with a record of an estimated 36–24 (.600). With that assumption (and this is counting the Cincinnati games which Haldeman did not), Louisville needed to win just nine games out of its final twenty to secure a tie. That looks quite manageable even if disaster strikes. In baseball, disaster often strikes during the course of a season; and the impossible sometimes happens.

CHAPTER FIVE

Losing the Pennant

On their way to Boston, Louisville stopped off in Buffalo, New York, to pick up some gate receipts as well as a 3–0 win over the local team. After that they traveled to Rochester, New York, for additional gate receipts and a rain-shortened 9–1 win. Meanwhile, the *Hartford Courant* observed that in Louisville's 40 games so far, they had played the same nine men in all but three. In addition, in those 37 games, the batting order was seldom altered. This, the *Courant* believed, was a significant factor in the club's success.[1] For a fan of the game today, such an observation tends to indicate a team that has stayed relatively healthy. Typically, when that occurs, success follows. But success is not guaranteed. Moreover, consistency of names in the batting order does not mean consistency of outcomes on a game-by-game basis or even a week-by-week basis. Looking back through history—even our own personal history as fans of the game—tells us this. Fans and other observers in 1877 had no such history to consult.

The National League was only in its second season, and 1877 was just the seventh season of major league baseball. Prior to that, clubs scheduled games as they could, and the number of games a team played was determined by its desires and opportunities. As a consequence, observers were not accustomed to seeing the hot and cold stretches which naturally occur in an extended season. But it was not just that the seasons were shorter than they are now, rather it was more the competitive imbalance that pre-existed major league ball and continued to pervade throughout the National Association's brief run. If a good team got on a roll, no one noticed. If they went into a slump, they would generally win anyway. Louisville did not have that kind of dominance, but having just won 14 of 16, Haldeman, Chase and others thought they did. By way of illustration, we can compare Louisville's hitting during the just completed 16-game stretch to their stats for the entire season:

Player	Avg Streak	Avg. Season	Difference
Craver	.268	.266	.002
Crowley	.388	.268	.120
Devlin	.295	.268	.027
Gerhardt	.375	.298	.077
Hague	.342	.261	.081
Hall	.444	.331	.113
Latham	.259	.288	-.029
Shafer	.310	.272	.038
Snyder	.319	.259	.060
Team	.332	.276	.056

When a team is busy winning 14 of 16, that is exactly what you would expect to see. Since these stats were compiled from the *Courier-Journal* reports at the time, a way to look at it that might be fairer to contemporaneous observers of that time is to compare the batting averages through July 4, the last loss before the hot streak began, to the averages from the streak itself. The outcome is, as expected, the same:

Player	Avg Streak	Thru 7/4/77	Difference
Craver	.268	.306	-.039
Crowley	.388	.274	.114
Devlin	.295	.218	.077
Gerhardt	.375	.306	.069
Hague	.342	.283	.059
Hall	.444	.365	.079
Latham	.259	.319	-.060
Shafer	.310	.278	.032
Snyder	.319	.240	.079
Team	.332	.284	.048

The expectations that the Grays could or would sustain that level of play were unreasonable. That is obvious to us now. But history tells us that in 1877, even the most astute observers were oblivious to that reality.

* * *

Louisville returned to League play August 17 and found their hitting magic was suddenly gone. Tommy Bond of the Red Caps kept them in check leading Boston to a 6–1 win. The Grays managed just eight hits on the day, but three of those were by Bill Hague. The most notable item was that Devlin struck out four times in five at-bats—something which seldom occurred. The box score printed in the *Courier-Journal* the following day appears below.

Boston	AB	R	1B	PO	A	E
Wright, 2d b	5	0	0	2	1	0
Leonard, l.f.	4	0	0	0	0	0
O'Rourke, c.f.	4	2	3	2	0	0
Murman, 1st b.	5	2	2	6	1	0
Sutton, s.s.	4	1	0	2	2	0
Bond, p.	4	0	2	0	7	1
Morrill, 3d b	4	1	1	4	1	0
Schafer, r.f.	4	0	2	2	0	0
Brown, c	4	0	1	9	2	2
Totals	38	6	11	27	14	3

Louisville	AB	R	1B	PO	A	E
Latham, 1st b	4	0	1	9	0	1
Hague, 3d b	4	0	3	2	0	1
Hall, l.f.	5	1	1	0	0	1
Devlin, p.	5	0	1	1	2	0
Shafer, r.f.	3	0	1	0	0	1
Gerhardt, 2d b	3	0	0	4	5	2
Craver, s.s.	3	0	0	2	4	1
Snyder, c	3	0	0	5	0	0
Crowley, c.f.	3	0	1	3	0	1
Totals	33	1	8	27	11	8

Innings	1	2	3	4	5	6	7	8	9	T
Boston	0	0	0	0	0	1	2	0	3	6
Louisville	0	0	0	1	0	0	0	0	0	1

According to the *Boston Globe*, the game was a "spirited contest to the end" between the Bostons and the "Louisville Giants." Louisville scored first when Hall hit into a fielder's choice forcing Hague at second. Hall then stole second and was driven in by a base hit off the bat of Shafer. Boston's offense was a combination of 11 hits and eight Louisville errors. For Louisville, it was the first of what would become eight consecutive losses. The headline in the *Courier-Journal* the next day was simply "Accidents Will Happen." No one could have known it at the time, but Louisville would not win another game until September 7. For Boston, it was the first win of their final 21 contests. More would follow. The two clubs were supposed to play again the next day, but the game was postponed by rain.[2]

As part of its coverage of the August 17 game, the *Boston Globe* also made note of wagering activity on the game. Prior to the game the clubs were selling evenly in the pools. Despite Hulbert's desire to get gambling out of the game, newspapers at the time frequently reported where the betting pools were selling and to what extent one team was favored over another. As historian Neil Macdonald explained it:

> The press, while condemning the curse of wanton wagering on the integrity of baseball, contributed to its own lack of integrity by publishing the latest odds, mentioning where cranks could place a friendly or unfriendly wager and proudly printing the names of prominent people who were placing bets. National League executives of Hulbertarian hue must have wondered how they'd ever eradicate gambling if it was continually being supported and glorified in the public prints.[3]

From Boston Louisville headed to Brooklyn to take on the Hartfords. By now it was clear to Hartford and the rest of the League that the plan to take advantage of Brooklyn's larger population to enhance the club's fortunes was not working. By season's end the club was in financial ruins. Indeed, as had been the case in 1876, according to baseball historian David Nemec, Hulbert's White Stockings were the only club to turn a profit in 1877.[4]

On the diamond it was a mixed bag. Hartford started the season in good shape. At the end of June, they were 12–7 and tied for first place. But they spent the entire month of July in the West where things went poorly. For the month they were 5–11 which dropped them to 17–18 on the year and into fourth place—four and a half games behind then–first place Louisville. August was looking better for them. They lost their first two games of the month, but by the time Louisville reached town they were riding a four-game winning streak. Still, they remained in fourth place overall and were now six full games behind the Grays.

Hartford, or rather, Brooklyn, is where the Chase narrative actually begins.

> The first of the series were played in Brooklyn, and the morning the first game was to be played I received an anonymous dispatch from Hoboken (the pool

rooms having been driven out of New York, the pool sellers took refuge across the river), stating that something was wrong with the Louisville players, as the gamblers were betting on the Hartfords, and advising me to "watch your men." Presuming that this dispatch was from some "crank," I paid no attention to it, but when I learned that afternoon that our club had been badly defeated, I came to the conclusion that possibly the game might stand investigation.

Chase was eager to see the full reports of the game to see for himself what had gone wrong. Although this was just the second consecutive loss, the impression is its occurrence was heightened by the telegram. Otherwise, why would a loss, even a second consecutive one, evoke such urgency as it did for Chase? He continues: "When the full reports were received that night, I was surprised to find Hague left off and Nichols put in his place at third base, and I also found that it was through errors of Craver, Hall, and Nichols that the game had been lost."[5] And, hence, the legend of the sold pennant begins.

The next day, the pattern was repeated: "Upon the morning the next game was to be played my anonymous correspondent again wired me from Hoboken that the Louisville-Hartford game was to be crooked, and the Louisvilles lose. And lose they did, through errors of Devlin, Hall, and Nichols."[6] As an initial matter, it makes sense that Chase's suspicions would be piqued. Two telegrams, seemingly from nowhere, correctly warned of an unexpected outcome in a game of baseball. But it is worth considering one detail in particular regarding Chase's article: while the two telegrams are presented as having been the catalyst to first arouse suspicion, their first—and only—appearance in the history of events surrounding the 1877 Grays is in Chase's article ten years after the fact. Yet, this is the basic narrative that has followed the 1877 Grays ever since. It is easy to understand why: it explains the otherwise inexplicable.

Chase wanted to know why Nichols was even playing. After the first game he sent a telegram to Jack Chapman to inquire. Chapman replied that "Hall had requested it, giving as a reason that as Nichols was a Brooklyn boy, he naturally wanted to play on his home grounds." That allayed his suspicions at first—it seemed sensible. But after the second Chase had had enough: "It is hardly necessary to say that Manager Chapman was immediately notified not to permit Nichols to participate in any more games."[7]

Chase then states it was at this point the directors of the club knew they had a problem, but the challenge was going to be how to determine who the crooks were. The credit for successfully doing so he gave to John Haldeman, "for as he was a fine player himself, had watched the games closely, and was thoroughly posted in regard to what each player was competent of doing," he detected the actual fraud and confronted the players. Two things about the foregoing: the first is that it conflates events that would not happen until October with the games in Hartford; the second is that it implies Haldeman was an ever vigilant and watchful eye. At least one historian was misled by Chase on this account, as Daniel Ginsburg writes in *The Fix Is In* that Haldeman became suspicious "from watching the play of the Grays." Another historian, William Cook, also appears to have bought in, noting that Haldeman observed at some point during the eastern trip that Devlin was not using his best pitch, the "down-shoot." But the reality is, as will be detailed hereafter, Haldeman was present at none of the eight games on that trip. He was in Louisville the entire time.[8]

The narrative of how the scandal first came to light has been parroted by historians. Daniel Ginsburg directly states, as did Chase, that the first Hartford game was lost "primarily through errors by Hall, Craver, and Nichols." Lee Allen practically quotes Chase, stating, "Chase was surprised to learn that the game had been lost through errors of Hall, Craver, and Nichols." William Cook mentions only the second game in detail but corrects the narrative only to the extent he notes Devlin, while being hit hard on the day, made no errors and that Nichols fielded well.[9] The problem is that Chase, and subsequently those historians who relied on him, was almost one hundred percent wrong.

* * *

We can start with the first game in Hartford played on August 20. The one thing Chase got right was that Hartford won the game—by a score of 5–1. But he states Hague was not in the lineup; Nichols was in his place; and errors by Nichols, Craver and Hall cost Louisville the game.[10] A review of the box score printed in both the *Brooklyn Daily Eagle* on August 21, 1877, and the *Courier-Journal* on August 22, 1877, tells a far different story.

Hartford	AB	R	1B	PO	A	E
Burdock, 2d b	5	2	2	2	3	0
Holdsworth, c.f.	5	0	1	1	0	1
Start, 1st b	4	2	2	15	0	0
Carey, s.s.	4	0	0	1	8	0
Ferguson, 3d b	4	0	2	1	4	1
Cassidy, r.f.	4	0	2	1	0	0
Bass, l.f.	4	1	1	0	0	0
Allison, c.	4	0	0	6	1	1
Larkin, p.	4	0	0	0	2	1
Totals	38	5	10	27	18	4

Louisville	AB	R	1B	PO	A	E
Latham, 1st b	4	0	2	10	2	2
Hague, 3d b	4	0	0	1	1	1
Hall, l.f.	4	0	0	0	0	0
Devlin, p.	4	0	0	1	3	0
Shafer, r.f.	4	0	1	1	2	0
Gerhardt, 2d b	4	0	0	5	5	0
Craver, s.s.	3	0	0	1	3	1
Snyder, c	3	0	0	8	1	2
Crowley, c.f.	3	1	1	0	0	0
Totals	33	1	4	27	17	6

Innings	1	2	3	4	5	6	7	8	9	T
Hartford	1	0	0	0	1	0	1	1	1	5
Louisville	0	0	0	0	0	1	0	0	0	1

According to both papers, Bill Hague played third base, not Al Nichols. George Hall played in the game, was hitless in four at-bats, but was charged with no fielding errors. Craver and Hague each made one error. The story in the *Brooklyn Daily Eagle* tells us Craver's first inning error allowed a run to score, but all Hartford managed in the first was that one run. Hague's error in the fifth also contributed one run to Hartford, making the score at the time 2–0. The box score also tells us how the game was lost—Louisville as a team managed just four hits and Hall worked a base on balls. The two earned runs allowed by Devlin were enough by themselves to lose the game.

Chase gets it similarly right and wrong regarding the August 21 game. Louisville lost that one 7–0 and, according to Chase, it was errors by Devlin, Hall and Nichols that did them in.[11] For starters, when a team is shutout, the fielding is not where the problem lies. But the box score is telling, nonetheless.

Hartford	AB	R	1B	PO	A	E
Burdock, 2d b	5	1	2	4	1	0
Holdsworth, c.f.	5	3	4	2	0	0
Start, 1st b	5	1	3	11	0	0
Carey, s.s.	5	1	1	1	2	0
Ferguson, 3d b	4	0	1	2	4	0

Hartford	AB	R	1B	PO	A	E
Cassidy, r.f.	4	0	2	0	0	0
Taylor, l.f.	4	0	0	1	0	0
Allison, c.	4	0	0	5	2	0
Larkin, p.	4	1	1	1	1	0
Totals	40	7	14	27	10	0

Louisville	AB	R	1B	PO	A	E
Latham, 1st b	4	0	1	13	0	0
Hague, 3d b	4	0	1	1	3	1
Hall, l.f.	4	0	0	0	0	0
Devlin, p.	3	0	2	1	0	0
Shafer, r.f.	3	0	1	0	0	0
Gerhardt, 2d b	3	0	0	3	6	0
Nichols, s.s.	3	0	0	2	7	0
Snyder, c	3	0	0	6	0	2
Crowley, c.f.	3	0	0	1	0	1
Totals	30	0	5	27	16	4

Innings	1	2	3	4	5	6	7	8	9	T
Hartford	1	0	3	0	0	0	3	0	0	7
Louisville	0	0	0	0	0	0	0	0	0	0

Nichols did play in this game. Chapman substituted him for Craver at short. Hall and Devlin played as well, but none of the three were charged with a single error. As for Nichols, the box score shows him with two putouts and seven assists, all without a single miscue. According to the *Brooklyn Daily Eagle*, "Some very pretty fielding was shown by Nichols." According to the *Courier-Journal*, "Nichols bore off the palm in the field." The problem was the same as the day before—no hitting. As a team Louisville had just five hits off Larkin. As far as gambling on the games in Brooklyn, the *Daily Eagle* does not mention it. However, for the second game, according to the *Boston Globe*, Hartford was the favorite at $100 to $75.[12]

Chronologically, the next step in Chase's telling of the story is the benching of Nichols.[13] As we have seen, he played, and was praised for his work, in the second Hartford game. Thereafter, he played in at least three more League games during August and September.[14] He also played in at least nine exhibition games during the same time period.[15] If Chase did in fact order Nichols benched, the record gives no hint as to why he would have done so at the time he says he did. Moreover, the record shows that either the benching was lifted, and we just were not told, or the order was ignored entirely, which is completely out-of-character for someone like Chapman.

Finally, there is the watchful eye of Haldeman. He wasn't there. As noted earlier he went to Ohio after the Chicago series. He then resumed his duties at home in time for the games in Brooklyn. After the first loss the headline in the *Courier-Journal* read simply "!!!–???–!!!." Haldeman explains it later in the Notes: "The first line of the general caption of this morning's ball column is expressive of the feelings of the community yesterday on receiving the news from Brooklyn. The prevalent sentiment can be described only this picturesquely." The next day's headline read "What's The Matter." Haldeman later explained: "The result of the game at Brooklyn yesterday was the occasion of equal surprise and regret here. 'What can the matter be?' was the general exclamation."[16] Both of those explanations, especially the second (note the word "*here*") strongly suggest Haldeman was in Louisville, not Brooklyn. During other games on the road trip, there is even stronger evidence that Haldeman was not in attendance. Those will be addressed as they appear.

* * *

The third game in Brooklyn, played August 23, ended in a 1–1 tie. Once again, the box score tells a tale of futility when it comes to Louisville's offense. Louisville managed only four hits with two of those belonging to Devlin.

Hartford	AB	R	1B	PO	A	E
Burdock, 2d b	4	0	1	2	1	2
Harbridge, c.f.	5	1	2	5	0	0
Start, 1st b	5	0	2	11	0	0
Carey, s.s.	5	0	1	0	6	0
Ferguson, 3d b	4	0	0	2	2	0
Cassidy, r.f.	4	0	2	3	0	0
Taylor, l.f.	5	0	2	1	0	0
Allison, c.	5	0	0	9	0	0
Larkin, p.	4	0	0	0	2	0
Totals	41	1	10	33	11	2

Louisville	AB	R	1B	PO	A	E
Latham, 1st b	5	0	0	13	1	0

Louisville	AB	R	1B	PO	A	E
Hague, 3d b	4	0	0	1	1	0
Hall, l.f.	4	0	0	2	0	0
Devlin, p.	4	0	2	0	2	1
Shafer, r.f.	4	0	0	2	1	0
Gerhardt, 2d b	4	0	0	3	2	0
Craver, s.s.	4	1	1	2	6	0
Snyder, c	4	0	1	8	3	1
Crowley, c.f.	4	0	0	2	0	0
Totals	37	1	4	33	16	2

Innings	1	2	3	4	5	6	7	8	9	10	11	T
Hartford	0	1	0	0	0	0	0	0	0	0	0	1
Louisville	0	0	0	0	1	0	0	0	0	0	0	1

Tie games counted as far as the players' statistics were concerned. They could have come into play at the end of a season to determine the championship, but that never happened. What they did do was necessitate another game. So rather than finishing this one, Louisville would have to return to Brooklyn at the end of the month. Meanwhile, on the same day, Boston defeated Cincinnati for the second time in as many games. Boston would win a third game against the Reds August 24. Boston had now won all four of its games starting its stretch run. When Louisville arrived back in Boston to resume play on the 25th, the standings were:

Louisville	27–16	-
Boston	26–17	1.0
Hartford	23–20	4.0
St. Louis	23–20	4.0
Chicago	20–22	6.5
Cincinnati	8–32	17.5

O.P. Caylor in the *Cincinnati Enquirer* was direct: "Don't bet on the Louisvilles…. We believe the pennant will go to Boston." Following the August 23 tie with Hartford, Haldeman observed the problem was the hitting, or the lack thereof. He called it "one of the eccentricities of base ball that what can be accomplished by a club easily one day becomes an utter impossibility the next." Louisville had hit Larkin well in the past, but in the three games between August 20 and the 23rd, they had managed collectively only 13 hits. Devlin alone had four of them, followed by Juice Latham with three and Orator Shafer with two. Hague, Craver, Snyder and Crowley had one each. The hitting that had thrust them into first place had just as quickly disappeared. Today it is called a "slump." In 1877 there was no concept of the phenomenon. Haldeman observed it and noted its existence—even its frequency. He and others just lacked a developed understanding of it. A string of subpar performances could only be understood as apathy by the players, or something far more sinister: "hippodroming."[17]

Louisville slipped into a tie for first with a tough loss in Boston August 25.

Boston	AB	R	1B	PO	A	E
Wright, 2d b	4	1	1	2	2	1
Leonard, l.f.	3	0	1	0	0	0
O'Rourke, c.f.	4	1	2	2	0	0
White, 1st b.	5	1	2	8	0	0
Sutton, s.s.	4	0	0	0	1	1
Bond, p.	4	0	1	2	8	4
Morrill, 3d b	4	0	0	2	1	0
Schafer, r.f.	4	0	0	1	0	0
Brown, c	3	0	1	10	2	2
Totals	35	3	8	27	14	8

Louisville	AB	R	1B	PO	A	E
Latham, 1st b	4	0	0	12	0	0
Hague, 3d b	4	0	1	3	1	2
Hall, l.f.	4	1	1	1	0	0
Devlin, p.	4	0	2	1	5	2
Shafer, r.f.	4	0	0	1	0	1
Gerhardt, 2d b	4	1	2	3	5	0
Craver, s.s.	3	0	1	1	2	0
Snyder, c	4	0	1	5	1	1
Crowley, c.f.	4	0	0	0	0	0
Totals	35	2	8	27	14	6

Innings	1	2	3	4	5	6	7	8	9	T
Boston	0	0	0	0	0	0	0	1	2	3
Louisville	0	0	0	1	0	0	1	0	0	2

Louisville led 2–0 going to the eighth, and held a 2–1 lead heading to the ninth. In Boston's half, centerfielder Jim O'Rourke walked. The next batter, first baseman Deacon White, lined a shot off Devlin's foot which caromed beyond Joe Gerhardt's grab. O'Rourke did not stop at second but headed for third. Gerhardt attempted to throw him out there, but Hague muffed the throw and White took second on the action. Tommy Bond then bunted, which Latham fielded and attempted to throw out O'Rourke at the plate. It failed and the score was tied with White moving to third. Third baseman John Morrill then hit a sacrifice fly to Hall and White tagged up and came home with the winning run. Neither the *Courier-Journal* nor the *Boston Globe* makes any mention of suspicious play. Louisville did grumble about some calls by the umpire, but the *Globe* assures us it was "as impartial as possible." Haldeman, of course, did not see the game. He was busy that day playing first base and going one for five in his club's 8–2 win over the Red Stockings of New Albany.[18]

In the *New York Clipper*, Henry Chadwick saw Louisville's struggles as part of the charm of baseball. "And herein lies its great attraction. It is the happy combination of chance and skill that characterizes baseball when played in its integrity which gives it the charm it possesses for all classes of the sport-loving community." According to Chadwick, Louisville still had everything in front of them with two more games at Boston and one at Brooklyn to close the month and the road trip. From there they would return home for games with Chicago and St. Louis. The question was whether they had the ability to put the setbacks behind them and take care of the business at hand. "Here, therefore, is a handsome margin to push up in. If they should prove unequal to the task it will not be from a lack of playing skill in the team, but from the want of that harmony and finished effort which is only at the command of thoroughly disciplined nines."[19]

Two days after the 3–2 loss to Boston, Louisville fell to second place as they lost again to the Red Caps on August 27. This time they were never in it, losing 6–0.

Boston	AB	R	1B	PO	A	E
Wright, 2d b	4	0	1	3	2	1
Leonard, l.f.	4	0	1	3	1	1
O'Rourke, c.f.	4	2	1	0	0	0
White, 1st b.	4	1	2	5	1	1
Sutton, s.s.	4	1	3	0	1	0
Bond, p.	5	0	1	0	12	2

Boston	AB	R	1B	PO	A	E
Morrill, 3d b	4	0	0	3	0	0
Schafer, r.f.	4	1	1	2	0	0
Brown, c	3	1	1	11	2	1
Totals	36	6	11	27	19	6

Louisville	AB	R	1B	PO	A	E
Latham, 1st b	4	0	2	9	0	1
Hague, 3d b	4	0	0	2	1	0
Hall, l.f.	3	0	0	3	0	0
Devlin, p.	3	0	0	1	5	0
Shafer, r.f.	4	0	0	2	0	2
Gerhardt, 2d b	3	0	0	4	3	0
Craver, s.s.	3	0	1	1	2	0
Snyder, c	4	0	0	3	4	2
Crowley, c.f.	3	0	0	2	0	1
Totals	31	0	3	27	15	6

Innings	1	2	3	4	5	6	7	8	9	T
Boston	0	0	0	3	0	1	2	0	0	6
Louisville	0	0	0	0	0	0	0	0	0	0

The one stat that stands out in this game is the high number of strike-outs. At the time pitchers were credited with assists for striking out a batter with the catcher (as is true today) recording a putout. Strikeouts were not recorded every game in the box score. But, of those games where the number was included, this one was the highest total on the season. In all, Louisville batters struck out ten times. Their previous high was six and that came in the August 17 loss to Boston. There would also be six recorded in an upcoming game at Cincinnati. For the season Louisville had only 89 strikeouts as a team with 29 of them coming in the eight-game losing streak they were now experiencing. Haldeman, meanwhile, joked that the groundskeeper at the ballpark need not worry about digging a hole for the new flagpole for the pennant.[20]

On the 28th, the Grays lost another heartbreaker, 4–3. Nichols entered the game in the third in relief of Latham who had injured his leg. In two at bats, Nichols contributed a hit. He also had five putouts at first without an error. Louisville overcame a 3–0 deficit at the start to tie the game in the third. Boston got its fourth and final run in the sixth off an error by Gerhardt.

Boston	AB	R	1B	PO	A	E
Wright, 2d b	4	1	1	6	1	0
Leonard, l.f.	5	1	2	1	0	0
O'Rourke, c.f.	4	2	1	3	0	0
White, 1st b.	4	0	1	6	1	0
Sutton, s.s.	5	0	3	0	2	1
Murnane, r.f.	5	0	0	0	0	1
Bond, p.	4	0	2	0	10	1
Morrill, 3d b	3	0	1	0	2	0
Brown, c	3	0	1	11	1	1
Totals	37	4	12	27	17	4

Louisville	AB	R	1B	PO	A	E
Latham, 1st b	2	1	2	4	1	0
Nichols, 1st b.	2	0	1	5	0	0
Hague, 3d b	5	1	1	2	2	0
Hall, l.f.	4	0	1	1	0	0
Devlin, p.	4	1	1	1	2	0
Shafer, r.f.	3	0	0	2	0	0
Gerhardt, 2d b	4	0	0	4	1	1
Craver, s.s.	4	0	1	1	3	0
Snyder, c	4	0	0	6	1	1
Crowley, c.f.	3	0	1	1	0	0
Totals	35	3	8	27	10	2

Innings	1	2	3	4	5	6	7	8	9	T
Boston	3	0	0	0	0	1	0	0	0	4
Louisville	0	0	3	0	0	0	0	0	0	3

Louisville got to Bond early, but from the fourth inning to the end they managed only three scattered hits. Going back to August 17 when Louisville entered the game with a four and a half game lead over Boston, Louisville had failed to win in six consecutive games and Boston had won the same number. Boston now led by two games in the standings.

Louisville still had a game to play in Massachusetts—another exhibition game against the Lowell, Massachusetts, club. This is the first game anyone admitted selling. According to recorded testimony of Hall taken after the season, he and Nichols teamed up to sell this game. Louisville lost the game 7–4, but how exactly Hall and Nichols threw it is unclear.[21]

Lowell	*AB*	*R*	*1B*	*PO*	*A*	*E*
Crane, 2d b	5	2	1	4	5	0
F. Whitney, l.f.	4	1	1	2	0	1
Foley, p.	4	0	1	0	1	2
Stoughton, c.	4	1	1	2	2	1
A Whitney, 3d b	4	0	1	1	2	0
Hawes, c.f.	4	1	2	3	0	0
Piggott, 1st b.	4	1	1	13	0	1
Wright, s.s.	4	1	0	1	2	2
Knight, r.f.	4	0	0	1	2	0
Totals	37	7	8	27	14	7

Louisville	*AB*	*R*	*1B*	*PO*	*A*	*E*
Nichols, s.s.	5	0	0	1	2	1
Hague, 3d b	4	1	1	0	2	0
Hall, l.f.	5	1	2	1	0	0
Devlin, p.	4	1	2	1	1	1
Shafer, 1st b	4	0	1	0	1	1
Gerhardt, 2d b	4	1	1	6	2	2
Lafferty, c.f.	4	0	1	4	0	0
Snyder, r.f.	4	0	0	7	1	3
Crowley, c.	4	0	1	7	0	2
Totals	38	4	9	27	9	10

Innings	1	2	3	4	5	6	7	8	9	T
Lowell	0	0	0	0	0	2	4	1	0	7
Louisville	0	2	0	0	0	0	0	2	0	4

Nichols played short and went zero for five at the plate. But Nichols was a lifetime .172 hitter so he went 0 for 5 many times. No gambler is going to pay a player to do what he will naturally do for free. He did have an error, but he also had two assists. Hall, on the other hand, went two for five with no errors and was lauded for his effort on one defensive play in particular. According to the *Boston Globe's* report on the game, Louisville's demise came in the seventh inning when Louisville "fell off in their fielding, many damaging errors giving the Lowells three unearned runs in the seventh and one in the eighth." In total, Louisville committed ten errors with only Hall, Hague and Flip Lafferty not committing any. The game went mostly unnoticed in Louisville, with the *Courier-Journal* devoting just two sentences and noting only that "Crowley's bad playing at first gave the Lowells four runs."[22] If Hall says he and Nichols sold the game, then one almost has to take him at his word. But there is no way to prove they did so from the objective record.

From Lowell the Grays returned to Brooklyn to make up the tie game with Hartford. Louisville fell behind 5–0 early, then a series of errors by the Dark Blues allowed Louisville to tally three unearned runs in the sixth. It was not enough, however, and the Grays lost 6–3 making it their seventh consecutive League loss. Louisville had more errors in the game than hits (eight versus five) and only two of Hartford's runs were earned.

Hartford	AB	R	1B	PO	A	E
Burdock, 2d b	5	0	1	1	1	0
Harbridge, l.f.	5	1	4	2	1	0
Start, 1st b	4	0	3	11	0	0
Carey, s.s.	4	1	1	3	3	1
Ferguson, 3d b	5	1	2	4	5	2
York, c.f.	5	1	1	2	0	0
Cassidy, r.f.	4	1	1	0	0	1
Allison, c.	4	1	0	3	4	0
Larkin, p.	4	0	1	1	0	1
Totals	40	6	14	27	14	5

Louisville	AB	R	1B	PO	A	E
Latham, 1st b	4	1	1	16	0	1
Hague, 3d b	4	1	0	1	1	0
Hall, l.f.	4	1	1	0	0	0
Devlin, p.	4	0	1	0	0	1
Shafer, r.f.	3	0	0	1	0	3
Gerhardt, 2d b	3	0	1	1	8	1
Craver, s.s.	3	0	1	1	5	0

Louisville	AB	R	1B	PO	A	E
Snyder, c	4	0	0	6	1	2
Crowley, c.f.	3	0	0	1	1	0
Totals	32	3	5	27	16	8

Innings	1	2	3	4	5	6	7	8	9	T
Hartford	1	3	0	1	0	0	0	0	1	6
Louisville	0	0	0	0	0	3	0	0	0	3

The *Brooklyn Daily Eagle* saw the game as confirmation of its opinion that the key to success is the presence of strong leadership on the field. "Even the most casual observer must have seen the difference in the working of the team with Ferguson on the field in command and when he was absent." It continued: "The lack of this great essential of success in a professional nine has made what were otherwise strong teams weak." This is where Louisville came up short, according to the *Eagle*. "The want of this has been the real cause of the defeat of the Louisville."[23] Haldeman saw it differently. "Yesterday's game at Brooklyn closed the last Eastern trip of the Grays in the most disastrous, ignoble and disgusting manner possible." Haldeman then speculated that the reverses may be the result of "dissipating, keeping late hours and having a jolly time generally."[24] A couple of weeks later, writing for the *New York Clipper*, Henry Chadwick seemed to split the two camps. Concerning the losing streak Louisville was undergoing he wrote: "Unaccountable as it may seem, however, it is explainable when the lack of proper discipline, the absence of a competent leader, and the want of harmony in the team are taken into account."

He went on to explain that he was not necessarily calling out personal failings of team captain George Hall and assistant captain Bill Craver. Instead, he blamed the practice of the League of allowing players to sign with other teams during the current season which, he argued, robs the team of an *esprit de corps* necessary to rally from setbacks. He was referring in this instance to the fact that Devlin and Snyder had already signed contracts to play with the Browns in 1878. (Hall would sign to play for St. Louis in 1878 just before the 1877 campaign ended.) This, according to Chadwick, was the crux of the problem. Chadwick's influence remained strong in baseball circles. The following spring the League would end the practice altogether.[25]

Following the game in Brooklyn, the two clubs set out for New Haven, Connecticut, to play an exhibition game. Haldeman began to display frustration and perhaps some suspicion: "To a club which showed itself capable of accomplishing such really excellent work as the Grays did up to two weeks ago, seven successive defeats at the hands of two clubs is something to look at and ponder over." Later, referring to the upcoming exhibition in New Haven, he remarked, "As it is not a regular League game counting in the championship, the Grays may, by some mysterious means, be able to win it." The Grays did win it, 6–4, leading to the headline "But It Doesn't Count."[26] For whatever reason, it never seems to have occurred to Haldeman or others that in exhibition games, there was financial opportunity. They knew wagering on such games was common. But there is little or no evidence it ever dawned on anyone at the time that those were games in which hippodroming might be occurring.

The Grays headed home, but first stopped in Pittsburgh to play two games against Nichols' former teammates. Louisville lost the first game, played September 3, 3–2, with the team collecting only five hits while amassing 14 errors. Hall would later testify that he and Nichols agreed to sell a game in Pittsburgh. The box score shows Nichols going hitless in four at bats and contributing five assists. However, he also tallied four errors in the field. Hall had a single hit and an error as well. Louisville won the next day 3–0. From there they proceeded to Columbus where they lost to the Buckeyes 5–2.

According to their later testimony, both Hall and Devlin admitted that it was in Columbus where Hall first broached the topic of selling games with Devlin. Hall wrote a letter to Devlin and left it on the table in their shared hotel room in Columbus. In the letter, Devlin recalled, Hall wrote "Let us make some money." Devlin later pulled Hall aside and asked him if he meant it. "Yes" was Hall's reply. Hall, who initially testified that it was Devlin who raised the proposition, confirmed Devlin's account the following night when he was recalled to provide additional testimony. Hall confirmed he had a gambling connection in his brother-in-law, Frank Powell, who lived in Brooklyn. However, after Hall and Devlin made their agreement, it was Devlin who telegraphed word to his own connection, a man named James McCloud in New York, to inform him of the plan.[27]

Piecing together what happened next requires some assumptions. The testimony by Devlin and Hall combined with other information Haldeman later revealed does not fit cleanly with the historical record. The team was to make one more stop on the way home—in Cincinnati on September 6. Hall and Devlin understood the game to be a non-league game and it was this one they both testified they agreed to fix together.[28] Louisville lost the game but did so in a peculiar way and under circumstances that are, at best, confusing.

First, the circumstances: Louisville was scheduled to be in Springfield, Ohio, that day but a last-minute change—namely, the disbandment of the Springfield Club—placed them in Cincinnati instead. It is not clear when club became aware of the change. On September 4 the *Courier-Journal* reported Louisville would be in Cincinnati on the 6th and Springfield on the 7th. But on the morning of the 6th, the paper reported the Grays were supposed to be Springfield that day, but the team would go to Cincinnati in hopes of getting another game with the Reds on the 7th.[29] Regardless of how this part came together, it is clear the Grays were in Columbus for only one day, September 5, which is when and where Hall wrote the letter to Devlin, the two later discussed it, they devised a plan and put it in motion.

An additional fact stands out: in Chase's article detailing the story of the scandal, he provides several telegrams the team acquired from Western Union. As will be explained more fully below, the club compelled the players to consent to their incoming and outgoing telegrams to be reviewed by the club. There is no telegram referencing the September 6 game.[30] The importance of this omission is that, according to Chase, the players would telegraph their plans to their gambling connections. How else would gamblers in another city know a given game was to be thrown? Obviously, if Hall and Devlin were unaware that Cincinnati, not Springfield, was in the offing for the next day, no telegram would be sent. But according to their testimony, they were aware and they did send a telegram.

As for the game itself, Louisville lost it, 1–0. Hall was hitless in four at bats, but Devlin, in addition to holding Cincinnati to just four hits, was two for three at the plate. Neither committed an error. The lone run in the game came on a home run by Lip Pike, major league baseball's first Jewish player, in the eighth inning. On the one hand, Pike was the home run king in 1877—with four—but on the other, for his career he only hit five home runs in 733 National League at-bats. If you are going to throw a game, that is a pretty narrow way to do it. As was the case with the game in Lowell, you almost have to take them at their word if they say they threw it. But, also as with the Lowell game, there are no objective data to support their story.

It is possible that Hall and Devlin misspoke as to which Cincinnati game they sold. There is a telegram in the collection of telegrams provided by Chase, dated September 16, which reads: "At Cincinnati to-morrow. Sash." According to Chase, "sash" was the code between Devlin and Hall and their gambling connection which meant the game will be thrown.[31] The problem here is Louisville won on the 17th, 7–2, with Devlin and Hall each going two for four. That is inconsistent with the part of the narrative that says "sash" means they will lose the game. Louisville did lose to Cincinnati 5–0 on the 19th with Devlin and Hall each going hitless. But, as was the case with the 6th, there is no corresponding telegram. In short, while we are almost compelled to believe Devlin and Hall that they conspired to throw a game against Cincinnati, reconciling that with the record is difficult at best. It is quite likely that when Western Union turned over the players' telegrams at the end of October 1877, some were missed. But what has been true to this point, and will continue to be true throughout, is that the objective evidence fails to support the narrative. One other fact that needs to be mentioned here is the September 6 loss *does* count in the League record making it the eighth consecutive loss against National League opponents.

Louisville finally won a League game on September 7 with a 3–2 victory over the Reds. The Grays fell behind 2–0 early but tied the game with a sequence of hits and errors in the fifth. In the bottom of the tenth, with the game still tied at two, Pop Snyder and Bill Crowley both grounded out to short to lead off the frame. Louisville then, finally, got the clutch hits they had been looking for. Juice Latham tripled, and Bill Hague followed with a base hit to bring home the winning run. Haldeman was not there to see this game either. He was, at the same time, helping his Amateurs team gain a 6–3 win over the Mutuals of Louisville.[32] Since reaching Boston on August 17, the Grays were 1–8. Boston during that stretch was now 12–0. The next day, with Haldeman again playing in Louisville with his club, the Grays lost in Cincinnati, 6–2. Boston lost to the White Stockings the same day. The Red Caps would not lose another game in 1877. Though routinely overlooked by historians considering the 1877 scandal, Boston did indeed pull off the unthinkable.

* * *

Haldeman prepared a statistical analysis of the club's eastern misadventures. He reported that in the games against Boston and Hartford, Louisville as a team simply did not hit.[33] In the seven games, Louisville totaled 41 hits. Over half of them, 22, were by three players: Latham (9), Devlin (7) and Hague (6). The other 19 were spread among seven players. Hall and

Opposite: **Harry Wright. Photograph is believed to be from the middle to late 1870s. Wright's Boston Clubs won the NA pennant four consecutive years from 1872 to 1875, and they won the National League Pennant in 1877 and 1878. He later managed Providence for two seasons and then the National League club in Philadelphia that became the Phillies for all or parts of ten seasons. In all, his major league managing career covered 23 seasons. In spite of winning the pennant in six of his first seven seasons in the majors, 1878 would turn out to be his last. Credit: National Baseball Hall of Fame and Museum, Cooperstown, New York.**

Craver each had four; Crowley, Gerhardt and Shafer each had three. Snyder and Nichols (who played in just two of the seven games and had a total of five at bats) each had one. That's the way Haldeman broke it down. But, since he was kind enough to include his tally of at-bats, another way to slice it is that collectively, the Louisville Four were 16 for 68 (.235) while the rest of the club was a collective 25 for 151 (.166). Defensively, the numbers are not much better, but not as bad as you might think. Pop Snyder led the way with ten errors in the seven games. He was followed by Shafer with seven. Latham and Hague each contributed five. That's 27 errors—nearly four a game—by four players. The other six players were Gerhardt (4), Crowley (3), Devlin (3), Craver (2), Hall (1) and Nichols (0). So, of the 40 total errors (one less than the number of hits), the Louisville Four had a combined six. The essence of the argument made by Haldeman, Chase and those that have considered the question since is that the Louisville Four sold the pennant by throwing games toward the end of the season. Yet, statistically, the Louisville Four were collectively less to blame for the losses than their teammates, and that's true both offensively and defensively.

* * *

With the Eastern road swing complete, Louisville had a few days off and filled the 11th with an exhibition match against Haldeman's Amateurs club. The Grays led 4–3 going to the seventh at which point their bats woke up as the Amateurs' fielding broke down. The Grays won the contest 12–7. Concerning the game itself, Haldeman pulled a quote from the prior day's *Evening News* to repeat in the *Courier-Journal*: "It is probable that the Amateurs will not care to defeat a club whom everyone else has beaten, hence a victory may be looked for by the Grays. It will scarcely be profitable to throw the game to the Amateurs, as the pennant does not depend upon it."[34] There is an implicit assumption both in the quote and in Haldeman's choice to re-print it. It assumes gamblers would be focused exclusively on a pennant race rather than an individual wagering opportunity. As has already been seen, exhibition games were sold, and no one noticed it at the time. Haldeman, Chase, and others were focused on the forest while the gamblers were zeroed-in on the trees.

Louisville returned to League play on the 13th of September and promptly split a pair with Cincinnati. In the first game Craver scored two runs and drove in two more, but those were the only four runs the Grays tallied. Louisville led 4–3 going into the eighth, but a pair of unearned runs by Cincinnati in each of the last two frames gave the Reds the 7–4 win. The game really wasn't that close. Louisville only had seven hits in the game, with five coming in the three-run fourth inning. Cincinnati totaled 15 hits on the day. Haldeman did more than hint at his ongoing suspicions. In the

"General Notes" section of his column he stated his thoughts: "Our boys have shown themselves able to defeat this club, and when the one-sided game of yesterday is closely looked at it seems as if there is something crooked going on."[35] The two clubs met again the following day and Louisville's bats finally came alive for an entire game as the Grays pounded Cincinnati's Bobby Mitchell for twenty hits in the 12–6 victory. Nichols played third in place of Hague and his defense was lauded by the *Cincinnati Enquirer* with "his pickups and throwing being remarkable."[36] The game marked the first time since August 13 Louisville had managed double figures in hits.

Following the win over Cincinnati, Haldeman noted that in the last 11 games, Louisville had averaged just 5.55 errors per game. "Nothing the matter with that fielding."[37] He was right, for an era in which players did not wear gloves, that is above-average fielding. Haldeman was looking at the games played dating back to August 21 when the Grays lost 7–0 to Hartford for their third straight defeat. Based on the cumulative stats taken directly from the newspaper box scores, for the entire season, Louisville averaged 6.5 errors per game. Put another way, during the 2–11 slump which includes the eight-game losing streak (August 17 through September 26), Louisville's team fielding percentage was .873. For the entire season it was .869. Al Nichols alone had a fielding average of 1.000. Historian William Cook's statement—that part of the suspicion regarding Louisville's losing streak in August came from their poor fielding—is misplaced given those stats.[38] Fielding was never the problem, the lack of hitting was.

As we did above, we can compare the teams' batting averages during the losing streak with the season as a whole:

Player	Avg Streak	Avg. Season	Difference
Craver	.188	.266	-.078
Crowley	.146	.268	-.122
Devlin	.308	.268	.040
Gerhardt	.125	.298	-.173
Hague	.189	.261	-.073
Hall	.158	.331	-.173
Latham	.298	.288	.010
Shafer	.222	.272	-.050
Snyder	.173	.259	-.086
Team	.203	.276	-.073

That looks like a team losing 11 of 13 games (plus one tie). A couple of things to note: Nichols is not included because all of his at bats came during that stretch of games. But also note that Devlin (along with Latham) actually hit better during those fourteen games. We can also compare the batting averages to what the team did prior to the hot streak in which the Grays hit well as a team. Since that 16-game stretch elevated players' averages, comparing the losing streak to the first part of the season may be a more accurate comparison:

Player	Avg Streak	Thru 7/4/77	Difference
Craver	.188	.306	-.118
Crowley	.146	.274	-.138
Devlin	.308	.218	.090
Gerhardt	.125	.306	-.181
Hague	.189	.283	-.094
Hall	.158	.365	-.207
Latham	.298	.319	-.021
Shafer	.222	.278	-.056
Snyder	.173	.240	-.067
Team	.203	.284	-.081

In this comparison, *only* Devlin was in positive territory. As for his pitching, for the season he had an unadjusted earned run average (ERA) of 1.88 whereas during the slump it was 2.12. That equates to one extra earned run every four games. His walks and hits per inning pitched (WHIP) was 1.14 for the season and 1.22 during the losing streak, which means he allowed one extra base runner every 13 innings. Overall, over the course of the season, the club allowed 4.817 runs per game and during the losing streak just 0.112 more at 4.929 per game. Given Nichols' fielding (recall he had no errors during the losing streak), and Devlin's pitching and hitting during the losing streak, if Devlin and Nichols were part of a vast conspiracy to throw the pennant, they didn't do a very good job.

ㅈ ㅈ ㅐ

Coming off the September 14 win over Cincinnati, Louisville was idle from League play until the 26th. During the 12-day hiatus they played a series of exhibition games, mostly with Cincinnati. But the exhibitions also involved another visit to Indianapolis to play the Blues again. On the 24th, they were man handled 7–3. Devlin was hit hard and Haldeman, for the first time, expressed a level of suspicion over an exhibition game. "It is probable, though not certain, that Devlin pitched in yesterday's game. If he did, nine 'non–Leaguers' hacked away at him for thirteen base hits." It turns out he was correct, as this was one of the games George Hall testified later that he and Devlin sold. It is also another example of an odd way to lose a game. In throwing the game, Hall was two for four at the plate and added a putout and an assist in the field. Devlin's performance looks more in line with an intent to lose. In addition to the 13 hits allowed, he was hitless at the plate. When Louisville returned to League play on the 26th, they lost a 9–6 decision to Chicago in Louisville.[39]

Following the loss to Chicago on the 26th of September, the Grays embarked on a six-game winning streak, matching their season high, with a win over Chicago and two over St. Louis at home, then on the road with two more at St. Louis and one at Chicago. The season finale, however, was a 4–0 loss at Chicago. Louisville finished 35–25. Boston had finished already at 42–18. Louisville was second, seven games back.

* * *

The exact date Al Nichols departed was never reported in the local press or elsewhere. He did not make the final road trip to St. Louis and Chicago. His final game in a Louisville uniform is not even clear. All agree he played in the 3–0 win over Indianapolis on September 25, but there are conflicting reports as to who played second base in the 9–6 loss to Chicago on the 26th. The *Cincinnati Enquirer* lists the second baseman in the Chicago game as being Nichols, whereas the *Courier-Journal* for September 27 says it was Gerhardt. It must have been around that time Nichols went to Charles Chase to seek his release. Whether that was in any way prompted by Haldeman's article of the 27th we cannot be sure. Following the 9–6 loss to Chicago, Haldeman warned his readers: "Before many days there will appear in the *Courier-Journal* a thorough resume of the ups and downs of the Louisville club during the season, from the hands of one who knows whereof he speaks. It will be interesting reading, as soon as it has lain on the ice long enough to cool off."[40] Either way, Chase was willing to grant Nichols his wish, but first wanted to extract some much-needed information from him.

Chase began to interrogate Nichols on the subject of selling games. Nichols denied any knowledge of selling games but confessed that he himself had bet on a few. Chase pressed ahead. Chase demanded that Nichols consent to having any telegrams sent to him while the club was in St. Louis be turned over to Chapman. Nichols chafed at first and refused to consent. He relented, however, when Chase told him that refusal would be taken as a confession. Nichols then had to give a statement to the board. After hearing him confess to betting on games, the directors required Nichols to consent to having Western Union turn over to the club all the telegrams he sent or received while with Louisville. Ultimately, while the

Grays were in St. Louis on their final road trip, Chapman received two telegrams addressed to Nichols. Both were from a known pool seller in New York by the name of P.A. Williams. This was sufficient evidence to confirm in Chase's mind that there was indeed a serious issue with the team.[41] The problem was, Nichols only played in six League games. That left more questions unanswered than answered.

* * *

Chase asserted it was almost a "foregone conclusion" that Louisville would win the pennant and do so "hands down." The club, he said, was "almost invincible." By the middle of the season, all conceded the title was Louisville's to take. Louisville was such a favorite, bettors could not be enticed to wager against them. Chase states Hague being sidelined, and the subsequent hiring of Al Nichols, was the beginning of the downfall.[42] As has been seen, none of that was true. Aside from the one stretch of 14 wins in 16 games, for the season Louisville had a won-loss record of just 21–23. We can look at it another way as well. Louisville's season record was 35–25. The winning stretch of 14–2 and the eight consecutive losses came back-to-back so we could combine them into a single sequence of 14–10. Removing those two extreme stretches of games reduces the season record to 21–15. Using the common denominator in each of those measures reduces the overall season record to 7–5; the combined winning and losing stretches reduces to 7–5 and the remainder reduces to 7–5. Looked at that way, the eight straight losses were merely a reversion to the mean.

It can be seen as well in the batting averages. Previously, the season averages were compared to the averages during the 14–2 streak. It was clear that the team as a whole, and most individual players, hit well above their season average during that stretch. Batting averages from the 2–13 stretch were likewise compared to the season as a whole, and the team and most individual players hit well below their season average. But what if we do with batting averages what we did in the previous paragraph, and compare the combined stretches of 14–2 and 0–8, with the rest of the season? Since those two streaks run consecutively, it is a decent look at a single part of the season when compared to the whole. What we see is as follows.

Player	Avg 7/7–9/6	Season	Difference
Craver	.265	.266	-.001
Crowley	.313	.268	.045
Devlin	.306	.268	.038
Gerhardt	.300	.298	.002
Hague	.284	.261	.023

Player	Avg 7/7–9/6	Season	Difference
Hall	.333	.331	.002
Latham	.259	.288	-.029
Shafer	.252	.272	-.020
Snyder	.245	.259	-.014
Team	.283	.276	.007

Some are a little bit up, some are a little bit down. But the team as a whole is within seven points of its season-long average. Nichols was left out due to the extremely low sample size plus the fact all his at bats were during those 24 games, but his numbers are calculated within the overall team's as are other players like Haldeman who played only one or two games. If you take a selection of any team's season, particularly one in which the overall win/loss record matches that of the entire season, you are probably going to see this sort of proximity in terms of the numbers at least as often as not if not more so.

From the beginning of the season through the July 4 loss at Cincinnati, Louisville was never better than second place in the standings and they held that spot for only three games. They were in third place coming off the July 4 loss. It was then Louisville embarked on the hot streak where they won 14 of their next 16 games. Hague, as you may recall, went out at the very *beginning* of the winning streak and he only missed one game. Nichols, on the other hand, was hired immediately when it was thought Hague would miss several games. The problems started in mid–August—a full month after Nichols arrived. All of this comes from the objective evidence available to anyone who bothers to look. Nevertheless, the flawed Chase narrative has continued to dominate the story.

Coming off the hot streak, the Grays' record was 27–13 (.675). Haldeman discounted the Cincinnati games believing they would not count and, therefore, saw Louisville as having just 15 games remaining of which, he asserted, they needed to win seven to claim the pennant. But Haldeman was assuming Boston would play at roughly the same clip they had played so far. Who wouldn't? When Louisville arrived in Boston August 17, Boston's record was 22–17 (.564). As we now know, Louisville had 20 games remaining, not 15, and they won eight of those 20 games. If you spot Louisville its eight wins, then in order for Boston to earn a tie for the pennant, it had to win 13 of its last 21. That is a winning percentage of .619. No one would bet on that happening. But, to Chase, Louisville threw away the pennant.

As we have already seen, Boston did not win just 13 games down the stretch—they won 20 and lost one. That is an unheard of .952 winning percentage. For Louisville to keep up, it would have had to win 15 of its last 20 (.750)—a full 75 basis points higher than they were playing on the season so far. Moreover, they would have had to accomplish it with the bulk of their games on the road. For some reason, until now, every historian that has written about the scandal of the Louisville Four has ignored what Boston achieved. Louisville didn't lose the pennant: Boston won it. O.P. Caylor saw it coming all the way.

CHAPTER SIX

Investigation and Confession

With the season over, Haldeman was seemingly left with nothing more than his suspicions. By all appearances he was not alone. But despite whatever suspicions there might be, the Louisville directors had voted September 15 to move forward and start getting prepared to field a club in 1878. The Board felt confident in doing so. Financially the club was in good shape. Despite the on-field losses, the Eastern trip had been a good one for them as the club netted a profit of $2,000. According to the *Cincinnati Enquirer* Louisville was one of just three high level clubs to turn a profit in 1877. Part of the reason for Louisville's financial success, according to the *Enquirer,* was that their payroll was among the lowest in the League. Still, they were behind in terms of preparing for 1878. Unlike other clubs, by September of 1877 Louisville had signed only one player, Juice Latham, for 1878.[1] But for Haldeman, 1877 was not yet over.

Haldeman's suspicions first appeared in print with his September 2 comment that the struggles with Hartford and Boston on the Eastern trip "will strike a few as being slightly out of place." However, Haldeman was not the only one. As previously noted, *The Evening News* raised its own suspicions September 11, just before the game with the Amateurs: "It will scarcely be profitable to throw the game to the Amateurs, as the

John Haldeman. This etching is of a photograph taken probably around 1895. Credit: The Filson Historical Society, Louisville, Kentucky.

pennant does not depend upon it, so it is expected that the latter club will accept a defeat." And, as noted last chapter, Henry Chadwick, writing in the *New York Clipper*, attributed Louisville's losing streak to three related factors: "the lack of proper discipline, the absence of a competent leader, and the want of harmony in the team" all of which stems from "the folly of allowing players to be engaged, during an existing season, for service in another club for an ensuing year. It takes all the backbone out of them."[2]

Suspicions began during the season, according to Haldeman, and the losses merely escalated them. But later Haldeman stated that the suspicions were deepened further by:

> the royal style in which some of the players made their appearance on our streets. They were, indeed, princely in their get-up. Craver had a diamond pin and a diamond ring; Nichols had two diamond pins; Snyder had two large diamond solitaires and a new watch and chain; Crowley had a diamond scarf pin; Shaffer [sic] had an eight-diamond cluster breast-pin, and Hague had a diamond ring and diamond stud.

Haldeman goes on to admit that some of the jewelry was "no doubt … obtained honestly," but then circles back immediately to declare that "the bulk of them were from the proceeds of their ill-gotten gains."[3]

Haldeman never said when it was he came up with the idea of dropping hints in his columns suggesting that he knew more than he really did. His thinking was that it might lead to the players outing themselves. That was his plan. There was the comment in September about the Hartford exhibition being of no profit to lose since it did not count in the championship race. His first hint to his readers of his intentions to expose the wrongdoers appeared in the September 27 article that may have frightened Al Nichols into his sudden departure. A couple of days after that piece came out, Haldeman noted that betting in New York and Philadelphia on the September 27 game with Chicago—won by Louisville 9–8—was heavily in favor of the White Stockings. "This looks somewhat strange, but it is one of those things that defy being found out. One may have his own opinions, however."[4]

Suspicions about Devlin seem to have begun by at least October 7. In Haldeman's assessment of the season: "No team in the whole list had a prettier chance to capture the prize than was offered to the Grays of this city." He continued, dropping another hint: "They refused to take it, and how they refused, coupled with other interesting reading will all be given in due time." This is the second time Haldeman vaguely hinted that something was soon to be reported. Barely disguised was that Haldeman was turning his attention to Devlin. In one entry of the General Notes, he laments Snyder's terrible game of the day before, but then proclaims him "decidedly the best catcher in the country" and asserts Louisville regrets losing him. Then he continues: "As for the bull-headed Celt who slings the ball at him from the pitcher's stand—but we forgot, this is Sunday morning."[5] The direct reference to Devlin's Irish heritage was neither accidental nor casual—it was pointed. Haldeman was signaling to his readers reminding them of Devlin's ethnicity as if to say "you know how those people are."

* * *

As usual, after the season the Grays took on extra exhibition games. This year, that mostly meant games in Indianapolis facing, yet again, the Only Nolan. The plan was to face the minor league Blues, and then to play a game against Boston. This time Haldeman planned to attend. In Charles Chase's narrative a decade later, he stated that Haldeman confronted players at his own peril. Most likely he was remembering the conversation that happened here in Indianapolis, though, by Haldeman's telling of it, it was more of an offhand comment by George Hall. Haldeman never says exactly what that comment was. It was after Indianapolis that he confronted Jack Chapman with what he knew, and insisted to other unnamed directors that something must be done by way of investigation, or he would go public. What he saw in Indianapolis that piqued his suspicion was Jim Devlin being on top of his form.[6]

In the first game played against Indianapolis on October 15, Devlin threw a no-hitter as Louisville won 7–0. Louisville's eight hits in the game, including a home run to center by Orator Shafer, were augmented by 15 Indianapolis errors. But Devlin's pitching was the story as Blues hitters were stymied all day just trying to make contact. The next day, Devlin nearly repeated the feat, this time tossing a one-hitter as the Grays won 2–0. Next up was Boston on October 17. Devlin was again masterful, tossing another one-hitter as the Grays again won 2–0. Haldeman now believed he knew who the main culprit was. He had been suspicious of Devlin all along, but he could not prove anything. Now, he was not just suspicious—he was convinced. But he still could not prove the case.[7]

After the Boston game in Indianapolis, all of Haldeman's inhibitions were dropped. Under the headline "Vain Glory," Haldeman described the game as "one of that kind which is not given to a base-ball public more than once in an age." As to Devlin: "Those who have seen Devlin at his best on the Louisville grounds would not have known the man yesterday. His exhibition went beyond the extraordinary—it was simply marvelous." Boston managed to get only three balls beyond the infield. One of them was the club's sole base hit. Even that, credited to George Wright, was, according to Haldeman, more of an error by Shafer than a clean hit. Haldeman's focus was now locked onto Devlin. "Such pitching by the bull-headed Celt through the season would have won Louisville the championship just as sure as beans are not good for dyspeptics. The Celt has completely given himself away in the last three games. But he doesn't know it." Haldeman makes it crystal clear his suspicions have centered on Devlin:

> After the season is over, and all League games have been finished, Devlin jumps into the arena and sports around as gay and lively as the chimpanzee in his native wilds. In making for himself a reputation at this day, the distinguished foreigner smears something over his fair name every time he keeps an opposing nine down to a single hit in a game. You are not politic, Sir James; not politic, sir, by a large jug-full.[8]

Under the October 18 General Notes, Haldeman continues to lay the ground-work for unnerving the guilty. "The *Courier-Journal* scout learned more interesting things about the Grays while at Indianapolis yesterday. It will all make good reading in time, and will not have to be looked at through spectacles to be made distinct and convincing. Wait until the boys get home, so that they, too, may have the benefit of it."[9]

Then, there was silence. No tell-all story was forthcoming. The *Courier-Journal* noted October 23 that Devlin and Snyder had gone to St. Louis to play an exhibition game for the Browns. It later reported that in that game, Devlin once again pitched a one-hitter against Boston.[10] But nothing more would be printed about the losing streak until the expulsions were announced.

* * *

Haldeman's article from Indianapolis, though never followed up in print, likely had an impact on Devlin and Hall. The timing is not clear, but sometime after the article appeared, Devlin called on Chase at the latter's office. We know of this conversation only from Chase, so the accuracy is somewhat in doubt. Chase, according to his article, seized the opportunity to challenge Devlin about the selling of games. Devlin denied it. "He stoutly denied ever having thrown a league game, he acknowledged to having pitched carelessly when playing against outside clubs." Chase was not ready to accept that answer: "I told him that I wanted a full confession, and gave him until 8 p.m. to think over the matter."[11] Unbeknownst to Chase at the time, the altercation had a secondary effect: George Hall was aware of it. Again, all we have to rely upon is Chase's memory of events.

> When I reached my hotel at 6 P.M., I was surprised to find George Hall waiting for me, and he at once opened negotiations by saying: "I know I have been doing very wrong, but, as God is my judge, I have never thrown a league game. If I tell you all I know about this business, will you promise to let me down easy?" Although I had at that time no positive evidence connecting Hall with the selling of games, I thought it the best policy to make him believe otherwise,

and with that end in view I replied that, as I was already fully acquainted with the part he had played in the nefarious business, I could make him no promises. This mode of procedure worked even better than my most sanguine expectations, for, taking it for granted that Devlin had divulged all, and desiring to place himself upon an equal footing with that celebrated pitcher, he commenced to enumerate the games in which he had played crooked, and also told of the part Nichols had taken in acting as a go-between.

When Devlin arrived at the hotel later that night, Chase confronted him with what he now knew. Devlin confessed.[12]

* * *

The Louisville directors summoned the team and compelled each to give testimony on the record. Haldeman never states what specifically caused the directors to summon the meeting, though he does state that "Hall made an admission of crookedness to one of them." That tends to suggest there may be some accuracy to Chase's recounting the story. However, he qualifies that remark by preceding it with "Very soon after, the Directors began their investigation." Whether Chase's confrontation with Devlin was the beginning of the investigation is unclear. The whole point of the investigation, however, is clear: the directors needed to know how far this problem went. The testimonies were taken on the evenings of October 26 and 27. "Their admissions were voluminous, but it is necessary to give only the gist of them, as taken from the club's records." The investigation was conducted by an attorney in Louisville, Asher Caruth, who would later represent Louisville in the U.S. House of Representatives.[13]

George Hall went first:

TESTIMONY OF GEORGE HALL

About three or four weeks after Al. Nichols joined the Louisville club, he made me a proposition to assist in throwing League games, and I said to him, "I'll have nothing to do with any League games." This proposition was made before the club went on its last Eastern trip. He never made the proposition about League games but once. In Pittsburgh he made me a proposition to throw the Allegheny game, and I agreed to it. He promised to divide with me what he received from his friend in New York, who was betting on the games. Nichols and I were to throw the game by playing poorly. While in Chicago, on the club's last western trip, I received a telegram from Nichols, stating that he was $80 in the hole, and asking how he could get out. I told Chapman that this dispatch was from my brother-in-law who lived in Baltimore. I did not reply to the dispatch.

Devlin first made me a proposition in Columbus, Ohio, to throw the game in Cincinnati. He made me the proposition either in the hotel or upon the street. We went to the telegraph office in Columbus and sent a dispatch to a man in New York by the name of McCloud, saying that we would lose the

Cincinnati game. McCloud is a pool seller. The telegraph was signed "D. & H." We received no answer to this telegram. I did not know McCloud. Devlin knew him. McCloud sent Devlin $50 in a letter, and Devlin gave me $25. One of us sent a dispatch to McCloud from Louisville, saying: "We have not heard from you." He then sent the $50 to Devlin; that was the 1 to 0 Cincinnati game. We (Devlin and Hall) telegraphed to McCloud from Louisville that the club would lose the Indianapolis game. I have never received any money for assisting in throwing this game. I think it was the 7 to 3 game. Devlin said he did not want to sign the order to have his telegraphs inspected; said it would ruin him.[14]

Part of Hall's testimony would be contradicted by Devlin. But, as shall be seen, it was later corrected by Hall himself so that the two more-or-less match. What is important to note is that where they agree from the outset is that Devlin handled the communications and the money. This ultimately worked to Hall's detriment beyond the team and League punishment he was about to receive. Devlin was next:

TESTIMONY OF JAMES A. DEVLIN

Was introduced to a man named McCloud in New Yok, who said that when I wanted to make a little money to let him know. Was to use the word "sash" in telegraphing, and he would know what was meant. Hall first made the overture to me to throw games while in Columbus, Ohio. He wrote a letter to me and left it on the table in our room. In the letter he said, "Let us make some money." Can't remember what else was in it. Called Hall one side and asked him if he meant it, and he said "Yes." I proposed to telegraph to McCloud, and we did so. We made a contract to lose the Cincinnati game. McCloud sent me $100 in a letter, and I gave Hall $25 of it. Told him that *McCloud only sent $50*. Helped to throw the game in Indianapolis. Hall was with me in it. Received $100 from McCloud for it. *Did not give any of this to Hall.* Gave it to my wife. Never had anything to do with Nichols. Hall told me that Nichols had approached him, but he never told me that he had thrown any games but those in Cincinnati and Indianapolis. Don't know P.A. Williams. Suspected Craver in one of the Hartford games, and spoke of it to Chapman. Told Hall to-day that we had better make a clean breast of it. [Emphasis in original.]

A decade later, Chase would get this wildly wrong as well. "Of all the money this rascally gang received, and it must have been a large amount, it was proven that Devlin received but $100, for once in the power of Hall and Nichols they forced him to throw games under threats of exposure."[15] Chase completely forgot it was Devlin's own testimony that it was he who handled the money and double-crossed his co-conspirator. Hall testified again the following evening:

GEORGE HALL RECALLED

Since last night I have thought of another game Nichols and I threw. It was with the Lowell Club of Lowell, Massachusetts. He and I agreed to throw it. He did all the telegraphing. Never got a cent from Nichols for the games he and I threw. My brother-in-law has often said "I was a fool for not making money." He has said this for several years past. His talking this way caused a coldness between us. When I was in Brooklyn the last time he asked me if we could not make some money on the games, and I told him I would let him know when we could. He bet on the Allegheny game and lost. Telegraphed him from here about the Indianapolis game. Had a talk with him in June, I think in Brooklyn, about selling games. Have sent two or three telegrams to him—not over three. His name is Frank Powell, and he lives at 865 Fulton street, Brooklyn. Nichols asked me on the last trip if I could not get somebody to work Brooklyn for us. I can't tell you where it was that Nichols first approached me about throwing League games. When I told him that I would have nothing to do with League games, I meant that I would go in with him on outside games. I made the proposition about the Cincinnati game to Devlin. Last night I said he made it to me. I made the proposition in Columbus. Nichols spoke to me in Cincinnati about selling the Cincinnati game, and I said I would see about it. Nichols said: "George, try and get Jim in." He suggested that I should write a letter to Devlin. Devlin was not in the room when I wrote it. In the note to Devlin, I think I said: "Jim, how can we make a stake?" I left the note on the marble-top table in our room at the Burnet House, Cincinnati. When I next saw Devlin he was in the room putting on his ball clothes, and it was there that he said: "George, do you mean it?" And I said: "Yes, Jim." After Devlin accepted the proposition, I told Nichols that Jim was in it. Nichols was not in with us on the Cincinnati game. Think I wrote the letter to Devlin in Columbus, but won't be certain. Think I destroyed the note at the time. Did not take it out of his pocket two or three days afterward and destroy it. Am certain of this. Never got a cent for the Indianapolis game. Devlin said that he had never heard from McCloud about the money for it. Never received but $25 from Devlin.[16]

Orator Shafer also gave testimony. He stated that Nichols told him he was buying pools on games and that if he ever got the chance to make money by selling one, he would do it. Shafer also stated he was approached by a man in New York who was looking for Bill Craver. The man said that a friend of Craver's had taken all the money out of the pool-box and that he (the man) would blow Craver's brains out if he could find him. Joe Gerhardt testified that he also knew McCloud and that he was introduced to him by William Cammeyer, the owner of the New York Mutuals.[17]

The Directors demanded that all the players consent to having their sent and received telegrams released to the Club. Though some were hesitant, all consented with the exception of Craver. Craver's play, according to Haldeman, had been so suspicious in several games "as to amount almost to a conviction" and his management of players in some instances "unmistakably indicated his intention to lose games." In an odd bit of evidence held against Craver, Gerhardt, Shafer and Latham all testified that Craver was the cause of many of their errors as he "rattled" them. The Directors also determined that Craver had violated team and League rules by playing cards late at night and drinking.[18]

The Directors determined that there was no wrongdoing on the part of Shafer, Latham, Crowley or Gerhardt. No evidence was presented against Hague, "although costly errors at important moments and deficient batting provoked comments." There was also no showing of criminality on the part of Snyder, though the fact he committed six errors in one game at the end "caused suspicion and unfavorable remarks." That every guilty player insisted no League games had been sold made no impression on Haldeman: "there is not a man in Louisville who is not thoroughly satisfied that the last games with the Bostons and Hartfords were purposely lost." Moreover, the Directors fully believed that anyone who would sell an Alliance game for $100 "would not hesitate" to sell a League game for the right price.[19]

The following Tuesday night, October 30, 1877, the Directors met to consider the evidence they had heard. A series of resolutions were prepared and adopted:

> *Resolved:* That for selling games, conspiring to sell games, and tampering with players, A.H. Nichols, by a unanimous vote, the ayes and noes being called, be and hereby is expelled from the Louisville club.
> *Resolved:* That W.H. Craver, because of disobedience of positive orders, of general misconduct and of suspicious play, in violation of his contract and the rules of the League, be and hereby is expelled from the Louisville club.
> *Resolved:* That, for selling games, conspiring to sell games, and tampering with players, George Hall be and hereby is expelled from the Louisville club.
> *Resolved:* That, for selling games, conspiring to sell games, and tampering with players, James A. Devlin be, and hereby is, expelled from the Louisville club.
> *Resolved:* That any sums to the credit of players expelled for cause be, and the same are hereby, declared forfeited.[20]

*　*　*

On Wednesday, October 31, 1877, on page four of the *Courier-Journal*, a short, two paragraph, 184 word article appeared:

> A general conviction has existed for some time post in the public ... that there was "crookedness" among some of the players of the Louisville base-ball Club. The popular grasp took such shape that the directors felt it their duty to get at the bottom facts. They have accordingly had frequent meetings during the last two weeks and have diligently pursued their investigations. The developments were startling and, as their result, at a meeting of the directors last night Geo. Hall, Jas. A. Devlin, A.H. Nichols and Wm. H. Craver were, by a unanimous vote, the proof being conclusive, expelled from the club for selling games, disobedience of orders and general misconduct. The directors are still pursuing

their investigations, examining telegraphic dispatches and such other evidence as is within their reach, and it is possible others of the players may yet be involved.

As may well be imagined, the directors felt they had a most unpleasant task to perform, but their duty to the League, to their own club, to themselves and to the integrity of the game left them no alternative.[21]

The reaction was swift and angry in the St. Louis press. The *St. Louis Globe-Democrat* asserted immediately that the expulsions were retaliation for Hall and Devlin signing with St. Louis. "The expulsion of Hall and Devlin from the club, it will doubtless be found after investigation, is due to the fact that they preferred playing in St. Louis to Louisville." The theory was ridiculous on its face as, had that been the case, surely Pop Snyder, who also signed with St. Louis for 1878, would have been included. To its credit, the *Globe-Democrat* admitted that due to the late hour the news had been announced, it did not "permit of much comment." Nevertheless, the paper found the charges of Devlin and Hall surprising. "[Devlin and Hall] have always borne good reputations as honest, reliable men; but as much can not be said of [Nichols and Craver]." The paper also stated it was open to persuasion. It noted that the Browns were about to dismiss two unnamed players for some unstated reason, but "If the Louisville Club can produce as much proof against Devlin and Hall as the St. Louis Club can produce against the two individuals referred to, in its employ, neither Devlin or Hall will ever don the Brown Stocking uniform."[22]

In Cincinnati, the *Commercial*, in contrast to the *Globe-Democrat*, stated that it was a great surprise to see the accusations against Hall and Nichols, but not a surprise at all to read them regarding Devlin and Craver. The *Enquirer's* correspondent in Louisville reported the locals weren't surprised at all:

> Base-Ball people are not astonished at the expulsion of four members of the Louisville Base-ball Club. They have been expecting something of the kind. There is but one impression here and that is that the Louisville Base-ball Club of 1877 could have won the championship pennant easily, if the players had not sold out. Every thing goes to prove this. Their playing in the last few games is evidence of what they could have done. It is probable other players will follow in the footsteps of those already expelled.[23]

The following day, the *Globe-Democrat* took a more mixed approach. It fretted over the future of the national game as a result of the dishonesty of a few men. It also expressed the belief that if the evidence justified expulsion of Devlin and Hall, it surely meant St. Louis would be unable to field a team the following year. The paper expressed the belief that both Louisville and Chicago intended to disband. Additionally, it noted, Hartford was in financial ruin and could not last another season. Those factors, coupled with St. Louis' now-likely demise, would leave just Cincinnati and Boston standing. In that circumstance, baseball would certainly suffer for years to come. However, somewhat optimistically, the *Globe-Democrat* noted that the press release from the Louisville Club mentioned four players being dismissed "for selling games, disobedience of orders and general misconduct" but did not specify who did what. From that, the *Globe-Democrat* concluded, the justification for expelling Devlin and Hall may not exist. It then asserted "it is a notorious fact that the Louisville players have been treated in the most shabby manner, especially as regards money matters, which may have a good deal to do with the expulsions."[24]

The *St. Louis Times* was even more harsh. "The directors of the Louisville are not looked upon by the managers of the St. Louis Club as belonging to a very respectable class of citizens, and they could do nothing that would cause much surprise anywhere." It went on to accuse the Louisville club of being behind on payroll and seeking to punish Devlin and Hall by fabricating a story to deny paying them what was owed.[25] Haldeman responded by calling out the article's author, Dave Reed, personally. According to Haldeman, Reed is "a Philadelphian, and probably a feeling of 'brotherly love' for Hall and Devlin instigated the abusive and slanderous attack on the gentlemen composing the Louisville directory." Haldeman then broadened the aim of his fusillade: "Not to be personal, and to express it as tersely as possible, the *Times* has been guilty of lying most outrageously and premeditatedly."

Haldeman then proceeds to address the "lies" printed by the *Times*, beginning with the statement that the men forming the Louisville directory are not of "a very respectable class of citizens." To this Haldeman argues:

> It is generally conceded that if a man is a rascal and no gentleman, his neighbors will likely be the first to discover it. It makes but little difference, then, what opinions either the St. Louis people or the St. Louis directors have of the gentlemen composing the Louisville directorate. In this city each one of them is looked upon as being a respectable and trustworthy citizen, both in business and private life. As gentlemen, their characters are unassailable. They take an interest in the game of ball, and in the past two years they have drawn liberally on their pockets, merely to see Louisville well represented in this most attractive of summer sports. Not one of them has ever wagered a cent on a game, and they have always tried to impress upon the men they hired the importance of playing honestly, and for the success of the nine of which they formed part.

Haldeman was not finished. In Chapter Four of these pages, there was the story of St. Louis manager George McManus being accused of offering a bribe to umpire Dan Devinney. There was also the story of Mike McGeary of St. Louis being accused in 1876 of selling a game by committing five throwing errors in a game against the Mutuals of New York. In both instances the St. Louis press and management scoffed at the accusations and made no serious attempt to investigate. Now was Haldeman's chance to rip the scab off that wound by drawing a sharp distinction between the actions of the Louisville directors and those of the St. Louis Browns.

> Now when they [the Louisville directors] discover that some of their players have totally disregarded their injunctions, they are abused in round terms for making examples of the guilty ones and saving other organizations from being preyed upon. In this connection it may be remarked that, when St. Louis applies the term "no gentlemen" to other parties, she had better have a care. A club which has had such fine opportunities to investigate—opportunities which had they been seized would have resulted in much good toward purifying the national game—should not open its mouth too wide, merely for the purpose of squalling at its neighbors. But somehow or other the St. Louis club has never been seized with any insane desire to investigate. Ever since St. Louis was first represented in the professional arena its nines have year after year been overrun with notoriously crooked players and marked men.

Haldeman then proceeded to lay out the above-noted stories and one other (also associated with Mike McGeary), and asked and answered his own rhetorical question: "Did St. Louis investigate? Not much."[26]

The *Cincinnati Enquirer's* O.P. Caylor did not see the scandal as necessarily being adverse to baseball's future, but continued that was only if the League did the right thing.

> Now that the first sensation is over, the Devlin-Hall-Nichols *expose* has wore off its wire edge, one can look at the result that must come from it with better judgment. There is scarcely a doubt that all three of the above-named players will be expelled and sent into oblivion by the League Association, at their meeting in Cleveland the 5th of next month. The case against them is self-convicting and there is no escape, and there should be no mercy shown. The League could afford to excuse their faults, but it can not [sic], and will not afford to let the example go by. When players see that such great players as Devlin and Hall are permanently disqualified from playing ball professionally, they will think seriously before accepting a bribe to throw a game.... Cool-headed men admit that the National sport will not suffer from the Louisville crookedness provided the League deal peremptorily and decidedly with Devlin, Hall and Nichols. If they put on no white wash [sic] and carry out the spirit of their rules to the letter the result will be to place base-ball in a more favorable footing than ever.[27]

Still Caylor, like others, was quick to buy in on the story that the players were owed money and, because of that, was conflicted over Louisville's baseball future. "Louisville will raise heaven and earth to put a nine in the field next year, but it is to be hoped, for the general good, that she will not succeed. Players will think twice before engaging to play there after the bad treatment the late team received in the way of back pay."[28]

The *Chicago Tribune* ran a story in which it quoted Devlin as saying the Club owed him $470 and he had not been paid at all since August. The story also claimed the Louisville club was in arrears to several players in the hundreds of dollars. Ultimately, however, Louisville presented its books to the League to show that the players had all been paid.[29]

* * *

On November 3 Haldeman published a long article laying out the entire story including his role and the proof. In an article titled "Cussed Crookedness," Haldeman declared "it is now the *Courier-Journal's* pleasant duty to go deeper into details and to explain to its readers how everything was brought about." He begins by claiming credit for unraveling the conspiracy: "In the first place, this paper modestly asks for its share of the credit in bringing the four unprincipled black-legs to justice." He goes on to explain:

> After the last Eastern tour of the Louisville club, it [the *Courier-Journal*] was satisfied that foul playing had been indulged in. A series of daily paragraphs in its columns charging crooked work, insinuating very strongly that more was known of the doings of the players than had ever been made public, and threatening damaging disclosures at no distant date, all lent their aid in frightening the guilty ones and extorting confessions when the proper time came.

He then confessed: "In reality the *Courier-Journal* had no proof positive against any of the men, but it pretended it had, which served the purpose equally as well." In other words, he lied. This is no small matter. Is it appropriate for a member of the press to lie—directly or by insinuation—in an effort to expose a greater harm? Assuming there are fanciful circumstances which would justify it, where is the line properly drawn? Is the integrity of baseball, or any sport, on the proper side of that line?

Haldeman was unconcerned with such questions. Instead, he partly revealed the beneficial effects of his actions. He informs us that while he was in Indianapolis for the game between the Grays and Boston, "[George] Hall, either unwittingly through ignorance or in the hope of preparing a soft fall for himself on disclosures which he thought bound to come, let out something which acted as a first rate starter to the investigation." The implication Haldeman leaves behind is that Hall was reacting to what Haldeman had been writing in the *Courier-Journal*. However, whether or not that is true cannot be known because the substance of Hall's revelation was never explained.[30]

Whatever Hall said, it was enough for Haldeman to go to Chapman and later at least one director and push them to start an investigation. In an article written for the *New York Clipper* a week after the publication of "Cussed Crookedness," Haldeman tells the readers that after his conversation with Hall, "I told Chapman of it at the time, saying not a word to anyone else in Indianapolis about it; and when I got back to Louisville the circumstance was mentioned to the Louisville directors. I told them that if they failed to investigate now I would take the matter in my own hands, and let the public understand everything I knew about it." It seems odd that Haldeman would feel it necessary to essentially threaten the directors. It is odder still that he would mention it in his piece.[31]

In both "Cussed Crookedness" and his *New York Clipper* article, Haldeman laid out the testimony printed above. But in "Cussed Crookedness," after laying out the testimony and the resolutions adopted by the Board of Directors expelling each of the four players from the Club and, as a consequence, the League, Haldeman took it to the personal level: "There they stand. A noble quartet of 'Lambs.'" It was, for Haldeman, a victory over the chief evil of the game. "The press of the country has been talking 'crooked base-ball' for years, and 'crooked base-ball' has been going on for years, but it simply bordered on an impossibility to obtain sufficient proof against any of the suspected parties." He confessed to the good fortune of the Louisville Club in exposing it. "The Louisville Directors would have found it a hopeless task to have fastened guilt on a single player in their nine had they been dealing with human beings gifted with even an ordinary degree of shrewdness."

The Directors, Haldeman declared, could have had ample suspicion, but nothing more, "had they been dealing with other than the most ignorant of rascals. Had Devlin and Hall locked their jaws, had they refused to answer a single question put to them, or had they worked the thing on a lying ticket all the way through, they could have had a jolly time skipping around on the St. Louis grounds next season." He wasn't done: "Hall and Devlin, however, like two true-blooded numskulls [*sic*], became possessed of the idea that some of their 'secret service' manipulations had been brought to light, and on their first appearance before the directors immediately began squealing worse than two stuck pigs."[32]

Though it was altogether necessary and proper for Haldeman to tell the entire story, the "touchdown dance" at the end was gratuitous at best. However, it was not unusual in the personal journalism of the day, and Haldeman was under the tutelage of one of the masters of that sport, Henry Watterson. Although he ridicules the fears of Hall and Devlin that their scheme had been uncovered, he never seems to couple that with his own efforts, detailed earlier in the piece, to raise or create just such an atmosphere of fear in the hopes of persuading them to do exactly what they did. What Haldeman did in the weeks leading up to the confessions was almost certainly effective. Whether it was ethical is another question. He literally lied to the public through the media in order to pursue an agenda.

Haldeman makes clear that Devlin was suspected early, but Hall was never suspected at all until he confessed. When Hall confessed, "it struck the Louisville directors, and every person interested in the game in this city like a full-grown howling thunderbolt." Chase's statement years later that he had reason to believe Hall was crooked before ever joining the Grays again falls short of accurately portraying events as they really were.[33]

* * *

From the very beginning of the scandal, the case against Bill Craver has never been clear and it remains a question to some. O.P. Caylor believed early on that Craver was likely to be cleared. "It is not probable that a case of guilt can be established against Craver. William has a head on him, some hair on his breast, and a stiff back bone. You'll not catch him putting a club into the League's hands with which to hammer him over the head. Whether guilty or not Craver knows how to look after his interests." Walter Haldeman's biographer cites the elder Haldeman's treatment of Craver, and his later refusal to rescind the ban, as an example of the ways in which he could be "harsh" in his dealings with others.[34]

On November 4, the day after publication of Haldeman's "Cussed Crookedness," a letter to the editor by Bill Craver appeared. Haldeman introduced it rather than simply let it stand on its own. In doing so, he mocked it and its author: "every line of it breathing sweet innocense [*sic*] and virgin purity." Haldeman than conceded the floor, stating "If the publication of it will help the writer's cause he is welcome to it." However, before conceding the floor entirely, he questions Craver's seriousness. "If he wishes a 'complete and searching investigation,' as he says he does, the first thing that will be asked of him is an order which will throw open to inspection his telegrams, both those received and those sent. This he has already refused to do."

Craver's letter begins with an appeal to the character of Walter N. Haldeman:

> Believing that, as the editor of this paper as well as President of the Louisville Base-ball Club, in your efforts to purge that club of those guilty of betraying their positions you would not willingly or knowingly do an act fatal or even prejudicial to any member, I confidently submit the following statement in vindication of my conduct as one of the parties....

Craver then presents a series of statements. The first is that he "unequivocally" denies "any and every allegation or charge preferred" against him.

The second is that he has been denied the opportunity to confront his accusers who alleged any "general misconduct and ... suspicious play" on his part. Third, he denounces the "cowardly attempt of guilty parties ... to identify others as participants in their infamy," stating that such accusations in and of themselves constitute a "feeble foundation" upon which the Board bases its own conclusions "to deprive another member not only of his means to earn a livelihood, but likewise malign his character, blacken his reputation, and prevent any opportunity to allow a fair and impartial investigation."

In the fourth declaration, he states he has appended the statements of Gerhardt and Latham retracting their prior testimony that Craver was the cause of their errors. He follows that with a plea of rights: "[I] appeal to you as a fair-minded man to secure for me that which the humblest citizen, even though like myself a stranger in your midst, has a right to ask and receive." From there he invites the Board to show itself to be better than prior tribunals in history. "If the Board of Directors is not a Star Chamber organization, or a remnant of the paraphernalia of the days of the Inquisition, my demand will be acceded to." The club, apparently, ignored him.[35]

* * *

Days later, the *Boston Globe* took up the task of interviewing the gambler allegedly behind the scandal, James McCloud. McCloud told the paper he had nothing to do with the Louisville games, but stated Hall and Devlin made overtures to him. He said their price was too high and, on the other hand, he would not trust them with his money. McCloud went on to say that "hardly a club played no crooked games." It was, he said, "an easy matter to get a base ball game safe to bet on" and that there was "more roguery among base ball players than among turfmen." His assessment was that he could trust none of them. The *Boston Globe* then repeated the rumor circulating at the time that the final series between Boston and Hartford had been sold to Boston to secure the championship. Of this Harry Wright stated it was absolutely "absurd," given the rivalry between the two clubs. "The Hartfords would be the last club to sell out a game to us, for since we took [pitcher Tommy] Bond away from his nine, [manager Bob] Ferguson has been more anxious that we should be beaten than for any other result."[36]

This notion is worth exploring as it is not trivial. The narrative told for almost 150 years is that the Louisville Four "sold the pennant." This is, to use Harry Wright's term, absurd. To convince a team to sell a game, or even a series, is one thing. All that needs to happen is for the gambler to convince enough players to play in a manner that all but assures his team loses and the other wins. No other cooperation is necessary. But to buy a pennant, the gambler not only has to convince the team in first to lose, but he has to convince the other teams playing against the preferred team to lose as well. In other words, it was not enough for the Grays to lose games—*Boston had to win games.* As has already been seen, Boston won 20 of its last 21 games. Of those games, four were against Louisville, six were against Cincinnati, four were against St. Louis, four against Chicago and three against Hartford. That's the entire National League of 1877!

If you accept the proposition that Louisville "sold the pennant," then you have to accept as well that the entire National League was bought off to secure a flag for Boston. As a practical matter, it is not possible. Note in the prior paragraph McCloud said it is an easy matter to get a game that is "safe to bet on." By that he means it is a sure win for gamblers like him. Fixers do not play "games of chance." They only bet on games in which the outcome is predetermined. Hence, betting on the outcome of the pennant race with 20 games to go is only going to attract them when the outcome is certain and the outcome cannot be certain if there is an uncontrolled variable. In this instance the uncontrolled variable would be Boston winning a sufficient number of games. Even if one believed that with Boston playing their last 21 at home, chances are they would win at a higher clip than they had been all season, that's not enough for the bet to be considered "safe" by McCloud's standards. This is not to say that pulling off such a conspiracy would be impossible. But with all the moving parts that would have to be accounted for and controlled, it seems highly improbable that a man who only makes "safe" bets would undertake the risk.

For its part, the *Boston Globe* was willing to entertain the idea nonetheless. Two days after the story with McCloud and Harry Wright, the *Globe* ran a story from St. Louis suggesting the Browns might disband over the Louisville Four. From the Browns' perspective, replacing Devlin and Hall was seen as a futile proposition as there were no players potentially available with equal abilities. But driving the thoughts of the Browns even more toward disbanding was the fact that "management are disgusted with base ball." According to the dispatch, "those well posted with the inside workings of the club claim that the club purposely lost several games this season they could have won, and that the Bostons, Louisvilles and Hartfords traded games with them for betting purposes." This time players were named in the persons of Joe Blong and Joe Battin who, it was speculated, would soon be expelled. The story went on to assert that "nearly all the clubs belonging to the League Association will be implicated."[37] None of the promised evidence of such wide-ranging hippodroming was ever presented. Even if it had been, it seems more likely what the *Boston Globe* was driving at was a series of individual games being sold for their own profits, and not a vast League-wide conspiracy to fix the pennant. Conflating a series of individual dishonest games into a single organized crime requires an ample imagination and substantial proof. The *Boston Globe* expressed plenty of the former and, ultimately, provided none of the latter.

∗ ∗ ∗

The only question remaining was whether the National League would uphold the expulsions or commute them. In the days of the former National Association, the latter was always the case. But National League President William Hulbert saw the situation as an opportunity. Shortly after the news broke and Haldeman published his full story, Hulbert wrote to Bob Ferguson of the Hartford Club, "The Devlin & Co scandal is opportune. Certainly nothing can be lost to the legitimate game by the conviction and punishment of the thieves and scoundrels who infest it." The upcoming winter meeting presented Hulbert with the platform he needed. "[N]ow it strikes me the exposure and conviction upon their own confession, of the four men named, makes our forthcoming League meeting an excellent time and place to strike an effective blow."[38]

The League magnates, including Charles Chase on behalf of Louisville, assembled at the Kennard House in Cleveland, Ohio, December 4, 1877. In its first order of business, the League Directory ratified the expulsion of the Louisville Four. It also accepted the resignation of the St. Louis Club and determined all games involving Cincinnati in 1877 were a nullity. Finally, it formally awarded the pennant to Boston. The following day, the League Board of Directors recommended acceptance of the application of the Cincinnati Club to join in 1878. It put on ice the application of the Hartford Club. The full League voted that afternoon to accept Cincinnati, Milwaukee and Indianapolis. The full League also accepted the resignation of St. Louis.[39]

The resignation of St. Louis was not a surprise to Hulbert. He had anticipated it a month earlier in the same letter to Ferguson. Hulbert implied it was for financial woes. Others speculated about the scandal about to be revealed involving Blong and Battin. The *Globe-Democrat* joined the afore-mentioned *Boston Globe* in asserting the two would be booted, along with the Louisville Four, for "crookedness."[40] Whether St. Louis resigned to stave off that added embarrassment is not known.

The one surprise from the League meeting was that none of the Louisville Four—not even Craver—appeared at the meeting to appeal the decision of the Louisville Club. According to William Cook, several papers commented on the fact. Craver saw it and felt compelled to respond. He wrote another letter to the editor, this time to *The New York Clipper*:

Troy, N.Y., Dec. 20, 1877

Editor of *The New York Clipper*—Dear Sir

In *The New York Clipper* of the 15th last, you say that none of the expelled players of the Louisville Club made an appeal to the Convention. That is not so, for I sent an appeal to Mr. Young, the secretary of the League, asking him to present it. I had not the means to go to Cleveland; therefore, I could not be present at the Convention to defend myself. I hope you will not be too severe upon me, for I have been dealt unjustly with by the Louisville Club. I wrote to the club before the Convention met, and told them that I would allow them to examine my telegrams, and would submit to anything that was right. They made me no answer. So what am I to do coming season [sic]. It seems hard that I am to be stopped from playing the coming season. It is not justice but still I must abide it. I have an opportunity offered me here in Troy to try and enliven baseball again. They intend to have a good club here in 78, and want me to play with them. The Louisville Club were not satisfied with expelling me, but the [sic] refused me the money that I had honestly earned while in their employ. My record for the season shows that I was not guilty of dishonorable playing. No man worked harder for the success of a club than I did for Louisville the past season. All I ask of you is to assist me in everything that is just and honorable—nothing more.

Yours truly, W.H. Craver.
275 North 3d street, Troy, N.Y.[41]

Immediately below the letter, the *New York Clipper* responded defending the position taken by the Louisville Club. The *New York Clipper* begins by noting it was Craver's refusal to turn over his telegrams, coupled with the accusations of other players, that led the Louisville Directors to expel him:

The facts of the case are plain and simple. Certain charges were made by players of the Louisville team against Craver. The club, after a lengthy examination of the facts and proofs, expelled him. During the trial the officers of the club solicited permission from Craver to examine the telegrams he had received during the season. This he refused to grant. This fact, together with the charges already made, sufficed to prove to them, at least, his guilt as an accessory in the "crooked" work of the season, and he was expelled.

However, the *Clipper* does not stop there. It then makes clear than in its view (more likely Chadwick's view), the expulsion was justified based on Craver's soiled reputation from his past:

There was one circumstance connected with Craver's work in the Mutual nine in 1876 which told very badly against him, and that was his tame submission to a personal attack made on him by a well-known patron of the Brooklyn pool-room. It was stated at the time that Craver dare not have resented the assault, for the reason that the pool patron knew too much. There are certain facts in a professional baseball player's record which are very damaging as collateral evidence, though they may not present direct proof of guilt. The refusal to allow the telegrams to be seen, taken together with his conduct in submitting so tamely to the personal assault in question, are considered as damaging. Mr. Chase of the Louisville Club can throw some light on the matter referred to in Craver's letter.[42]

Craver's letter-writing campaign did not stop there. He wrote additional letters to *The New York Clipper* as well as at least one to Harry Wright. In all of them he returned to the same themes: that he had not been allowed to confront his accusers, let alone cross-examine them on the charges preferred against him. While he may or may not have been aware that the protections afforded the accused in a criminal court are not applicable in the case of a private organization such as the Louisville Base Ball Club, he was certainly cognizant of the principles behind them. In a perfect world he would have had the stronger argument. Craver was old enough by 1877 to know that this is not a perfect world.

* * *

Years later, in his history of baseball, A.G. Spalding reflected on the ouster of the Louisville Four. Some forty years after the events of 1877, and just a couple of years before the "Black Sox" scandal broke, he believed the result of the decisions of the League had proved a great victory by the National League over corruption.

> This, then, was the first great victory won over gambling and the gamblers. It was the direct result of the determination on the part of the founders of the National League to eradicate this evil. Its effect was instantaneous and has lasted from that day to this. It has proven that, under the system of club management introduced at the time the National League was formed, it is possible to control the integrity of the game in every department by the simple exercise of firmness along lines of constant watchfulness and care, and by the inflexible administration of discipline.[43]

As with Haldeman's proclamation in 1876 declaring the honesty and wholesomeness of the Louisville Club, one has to wonder if at some not-too-distant future after publishing those words, Spalding regretted them.

As the year 1877 came to an end, the National League had faced and met the first significant challenge to its credibility. It appeared the only costs it would pay was the loss of a single franchise—St. Louis. Hartford's problems were simply its financial viability. As the sun rose on the morning of January 1, 1878, the National League consisted of Boston, Chicago, Cincinnati, Milwaukee, Indianapolis and Louisville.

CHAPTER SEVEN

Aftermath

Louisville was not kicked out of the National League over the Grays scandal. Occasionally you will see a history of the scandal that says otherwise. It did not happen, nor would it make sense for it to happen. William Hulbert was not a fool. He would not have seen it as in the National League's interest to punish the Louisville organization, which was the victim of the scandal. Louisville suspected there was a problem, sought out evidence, and then took action when it found it. Had Hulbert and the National League expelled Louisville, it would have undermined everything the League stood for. The League's opening statement in February 1876 declared its intent to stamp out corruption in baseball.[1] Kicking out a franchise for taking steps to do just that would have been insane. The message such a move would send to other organizations would have been to bury any evidence of wrongdoing.

The Louisville Grays had every intention of returning in 1878. They fully participated in the League's annual winter meeting. However, their heart was never in it. By February, they still had not signed any players beyond Juice Latham. On the 22nd they released him to allow him to sign with the club in Utica, New York. John Haldeman was writing nothing on the topic of baseball throughout that winter. Finally, it was O.P. Caylor in Cincinnati who said out loud what others were certainly sensing: "It is doubtful whether the Louisville Club will put a nine in the field this season."[2]

Finally, the directors and stockholders met on March 7 to discuss the situation and reach a decision. Once again, as had happened with the announcement of the expulsions, the news was just a short two paragraphs buried on page four of the *Courier-Journal*:

> There was a meeting of the stockholders and directors of the Louisville Base Ball club last evening at which, after a full and free consideration of the situation, it was unanimously resolved to resign the club's membership in the League. It was further resolved that the formation of a strong amateur club be recommended, and that all proper aid and encouragement would be given to it.

> The disgust created in this community by the development of the rascality of last year's players, and the general conviction that dishonest players in other clubs was more the rule than the exception were the causes that prompted the action of the Louisville club in declining to put a nine in the field this season—a season which it is believed will prove disastrous to all the League clubs.[3]

Just 135 words to say that the directors concluded they did not believe they could overcome the public's ill-feelings toward the game. Fielding a team without public support was financially a non-starter.

Truthfully, it was the *Courier-Journal* that led the way in its disgust toward the professional game. Initially, it seemed Haldeman had turned on the game itself, not just the professional ranks. In April, he vented his disdain for the Louisville Four and those who, like them, sought to sell out the game for personal gain. Under the headline "Base Ball. The Game This Season" he wrote:

> Those of the *Courier-Journal* readers who never could see any beauty in the national game, and who complained so vehemently of the space allotted in these columns to a record of the sport during the past two seasons, need not be alarmed at this caption. We do not intend to allow them to be violently bored this season. Base ball in Louisville is one of the lost arts. Its most ardent admirers are those most disgusted at the game. Last year Louisville gathered together the strongest and best club the country had ever produced. They were wonderful batters and magnificent fielders, and they were able to win the championship with scarce an effort. Indeed, they had already won it, and, at the close of the season, with but about a dozen games to play, they shamefully sold out. The best and most trusted players were discovered to be rascals. They sunk principle and pride in their club for a few dishonest dollars. They cheated their directors and stockholders right under their very eyes. And not one of them would have ever been discovered but for the cowardice of one whose guilty conscience made him believe his rascality was discovered, and who confessed his own crimes and exposed his associates. This experience satisfied the Louisville directors that detection of crookedness in base-ball playing was next to an impossibility, and they determined not to put a nine in the field this season, as trusting to the honor of players did not promise good results. All this as introductory to the remark that while our base-ball department is not absolutely abolished, we yet propose to keep such of our readers as may be interested in the game posted as to the results of the matches played between prominent clubs abroad and the amateur game at home.[4]

Haldeman knew the game itself was in little danger. In fact, he would continue playing it himself. A few days after his tirade, he admitted as much.

> After all there is a prospect that the interest in the national game will not be permitted to die out entirely in Louisville and that we will have some lively games during the season. They will be chiefly between home clubs, but we may also expect occasional visits from the League and Alliance clubs.[5]

By May 4, Haldeman (and the *Courier-Journal*) had come back around to fully embracing the sport:

> The future welfare of the game depends in a great measure upon those who play it merely for recreation and the healthy exercise it gives. Professional base ball has seen its best day. A heavy majority among its representatives are ignorant, uneducated, vicious men, whose moral faculties might all be bundled together and placed under a bucket from Liliput [sic], with plenty of room to spare. Such men as these are not the ones to make the national game still remain the national game. Intellectual ball playing will in the end hold its own against all contestants, and we trust the support given this season to the amateur fraternity of Louisville by those of our citizens who enjoy the game will abundantly exemplify it in this section of the country.[6]

Nevertheless, true to Haldeman's previous words, baseball barely dotted the pages of the *Courier-Journal*. Throughout 1878, then again in 1879 and 1880, the *Courier-Journal* reported the scores of National League games, but little else. Even the amateur games played in the city were given very little coverage. It was not until 1881 that the *Courier-Journal* realized the enthusiasm for the game had returned (assuming it had ever waned). While the National League still received little more than daily reports on the scores of games, local games appeared more prominently.

* * *

The seeds of Louisville's future in baseball had already been sown. A group of teenage boys in the West End, organized by businessman and baseball enthusiast John Reccius, announced their formal organization as the Eclipse Club in March of 1877.[7] The players ranged in age from 14 to 17, thereby classifying them initially as a "junior" club. Five of their original nine, Louis Rogers "Pete" Browning, Fred Pfeffer, William "Chicken" Wolf and two of Reccius' sons, John and Phil, would all go on to major league careers in just a few years. Two younger players who would join them between 1878 and 1881, Monk Cline and Hub Collins, would do likewise. By 1881 the club was playing semi-professionally throughout the region.

In 1882, the Eclipse Club, along with a new version of the Cincinnati Reds, a revitalized St. Louis Browns and a newly reorganized Allegheny Club of Pittsburgh became the inaugural members of a new, rival major league, the American Association. Soon joining them in that first season was a reorganized Athletics Club in Philadelphia and a club in Baltimore known as the Orioles. Of the eight original National League clubs in 1876, only two, the Boston Red Stockings and the Chicago White Stockings, survive to this day. The Boston club eventually became the Atlanta Braves and the White Stockings remained in Chicago and eventually came to be known as the Cubs. By contrast, of the original six in the American

Association, three, Cincinnati, St. Louis and Pittsburgh, remain. All of them still play in their original cities with only the Reds retaining their initial nickname. Three other current organizations saw their beginnings in 1883. The Dodgers originated in Brooklyn as part of the American Association, while the Giants and Phillies began play in New York and Philadelphia respectively as part of the National League.

The Eclipse Club had success in the American Association. Several times they challenged for the pennant, only to swoon toward the end of the season much like the Grays in 1877. In 1889, due to several factors, not the least of which was terrible management, they fielded one of the worst team in the history of baseball and set a record that stands to this day—26 consecutive losses. They also became the first team to go on strike. By mid-season the Association stepped in and forced team owner Mordecai Davidson to sell the club. It wasn't enough to save the season for the Colonels, as they were known by then. Instead, they became the first team to lose more than 100 games in a season, finishing with a record of 27–111. At the tail end of the season, management turned to an old friend, Jack Chapman, and convinced him to return to Louisville to manage the club going forward.

In 1890, again due to a host of outside factors, Louisville turned it completely around and won the American Association pennant with a record of 88–44. During the season, because of a massive tornado that struck Louisville in March, the club was dubbed the Cyclones. A post-season series between the winners of the National League and American Association first occurred in 1884 and was played each year through 1890. It was known then, as now, as the World Series. Louisville faced Brooklyn, who had moved over to the National League during the immediately preceding off-season, and the two played to a 3–3 tie in what would turn out to be the last of the pre–1903 World Series. The last game of the Series was not played due to frightfully cold conditions. Today, in the main pavilion at Louisville's Slugger Field, there is a display showing all the pennants won by Louisville franchises throughout the years—except one. There is no banner for the lone major league flag won by a club in Louisville, that of the Louisville Cyclones of 1890.

Following the 1891 season, the American Association and the National League merged into a single 12-team circuit which included Louisville. The Louisville Colonels competed in the National League through 1899, though they never finished in the top half of the standings. The League decided to contract to just eight clubs in 1900. Seeing the handwriting on the wall, Louisville's president at the time, Barney Dreyfuss, acquired an ownership interest in the Pittsburgh Pirates. He then negotiated the sale of Louisville's best players—Honus Wagner, Rube Waddell,

Deacon Phillipe and manager/outfielder Fred Clarke—to Pittsburgh. The Pirates, as they had been known since 1892, would win the National League pennant in 1903 and participate in the first of the modern World Series. In fact, the winning pitcher in game one of that series was Deacon Phillipe who defeated Cy Young of the Boston Pilgrims. For the City of Louisville, however, major league baseball was now a thing of the past. Louisville is the last city in the United States to lose a major league franchise and never get one back.

Louisville tried, but failed, to gain a spot in Ban Johnson's newly organized American League in 1901. However, Louisville acquired a franchise in the reorganized American Association which was by then one of the minor league circuits. With the exception of ten years starting in the early 1970s, Louisville has had a minor league franchise just about every year since. Louisville was also home to one of the last Negro League teams, the Buckeyes, in the early 1950s. In 1964 Charlie Finley, owner of the Kansas City Athletics, agreed to move his team to Louisville. However, the deal was nixed by the other American League owners, as they felt Finley was being unfair to Kansas City.[8] Given the current business model of Major League Baseball, it seems unlikely Louisville will ever get another team in the majors. The proximity of Cincinnati, and the small population size of both cities, make having two franchises 90 miles apart impractical.

* * *

William Hulbert was not the first president of the National League of Base Ball Clubs. In an act of political deftness, in February 1876 at the meeting in New York, he nominated for that position Morgan Bulkeley, president of the Hartford Club. Bulkeley was himself an impressive businessman, serving on the board of directors for Aetna Insurance and being one of the organizers of the U.S. Bank of Hartford. Making him president of the new League had a public relations benefit, but it also served as a bit of a sop to the Eastern clubs that one of their own would be in charge. Bulkeley stepped down from the role at the end of the 1876 season to further both his fortune and his political career. He would eventually serve as Hartford's mayor, then governor of Connecticut and, finally, Connecticut's United States senator.[9]

Hulbert assumed the position of League president in 1877 though, in reality, he had been the driving force in the League all along. Following the Grays' scandal, he helped usher in the reserve clause in 1879 which had the effect of binding players to their teams almost for life even though their contracts were for only one year at a time. Under the clause, which at first was just an agreement among the owners and only later part of the players' contracts, any player under contract with a club was the property of that club until the club released him. No other organization in the League or in any of the Alliance leagues could sign him. The intended impact of the rule was to hold down salaries by preventing teams from bidding against one another for a player's services. The rule would last in one form or another until the 1970s. In April of 1882, Hulbert, who had been ill for a few weeks, died somewhat suddenly of heart failure at the age of 49. He is buried in Chicago's Graceland Cemetery.[10]

* * *

With the dissolution of the Browns, Pop Snyder had to find a new home. He did all right for himself, landing in Boston where he helped Harry Wright and the Red Caps win another pennant in 1878. Snyder eventually spent time in Cincinnati and Cleveland before wrapping up his career in his hometown of Washington, D.C., where he appeared in just eight games in 1891. He died in Washington October 29, 1924, at the age of 70. Joe Gerhardt was almost as fortunate, playing 1878 in Cincinnati where the Reds finished second in the League race. He was under contract with the Detroit Wolverines in 1882 when the American Association formed. He wanted to return to Louisville at that point but a release could not be arranged. After sitting out the 1882 season, Gerhardt was able to return to Louisville and played two years with the Eclipse. He returned again in 1891 for just two games with the Colonels before hanging it up for good. He died March 11, 1922, in Middletown, New York, at the age of 67 and was buried in his hometown of Washington, D.C. Bill Hague, whose boils triggered the hiring of Al Nichols, played just two more seasons of major league ball, both with the Providence Grays, in 1878 and 1879. He died November 21, 1898, at the age of 46 in his hometown of Philadelphia. Orator Shafer continued his career in 1878 with the Indianapolis club, newly part of the National League. He played for several different clubs in the majors through 1890 finishing his career with the Philadelphia Athletics. He died January 22, 1922, at the age of 70 in his hometown of Philadelphia.

Juice Latham spent the next four season in the minors before finally getting back to the majors in 1882 with the newly organized Philadelphia Athletics of the American Association. He returned to Louisville in 1883 and spent two years reunited with Gerhardt as part of the Eclipse Club. Latham's final season in major league baseball was 1884. He died May 26, 1914, at the age of 61 in his hometown of Utica, New York. Bill Crowley also was unable to remain at the top level in 1878, but returned in 1879 with Buffalo of the National League. After bouncing around the League a couple of times, he ended his career back in Buffalo in 1885. Crowley died July 14, 1891, at the age of 34 in Gloucester, New Jersey, and is buried nearby in Bellmawr, New Jersey.

Jack Chapman managed a few National League clubs after Louisville. He was in Milwaukee for part of 1878. In 1882 he took over the Worcester Ruby Legs at the end of the season. In 1883 and 1884 he guided the Detroit Wolverines and in 1885 he took over the Buffalo Bisons early in the season. Prior to the Louisville Cyclones' 1890 season, Chapman had never piloted a major league team to a winning record. His final stint was the first half of the 1892 season with Louisville, after which he became the club's business manager.

In 1905 after Chapman had left the game entirely behind, he returned to Brooklyn where the *Brooklyn Daily Eagle* decided to interview him at length about his memories of the game. According to the story, Chapman was then "as great a baseball fan now as he ever was." He recounted a story from his days with the Brooklyn Atlantics in 1868 when the club traveled to Louisville to play the Eagles. In re-telling the story, Chapman exhibited the same flaw in memory that befell Charles Chase in his magazine article in the 1880s. According to Chapman's telling of the story in 1905, the day after the game between the Atlantics and the Eagles, the Atlantics had all but decided to travel to Cincinnati on the large steamer *Patrick Rogers*, and the manager and secretary were on their way to purchase the tickets. Before they could do so, a committee of local business leaders met them and persuaded them to remain over as it was the committee's intent to have a banquet that night in their honor. It turned out to be a good choice as "the Brooklyn boys were treated handsomely that night by their Kentucky friends." The next morning, they discovered the choice had been fortunate in more ways than one. They learned en route to Cincinnati on the early train that the *Patrick Rogers* had burned the night before, and many lives were lost both by drowning and being burned to death.[11]

It is a good story of death narrowly averted by the Grace of God. In all probability it did not happen—at least not the way Chapman recalled. The Atlantics, with Chapman, did in fact play in Louisville on July 2, 1868, against the Louisville Base Ball Club of Theodore Tracy and John Dickins. The Atlantics were one of the premier clubs in the country at the time, having only recently been proclaimed as the "national champions" (a somewhat dubious and purely subjective title as used at the time). The *Daily Journal* declared the game would be "a contest of giants, well worth seeing." It was not. The Atlantics crushed their hosts, 66–11, with Chapman himself scoring nine of Brooklyn's runs. The Atlantics left after the game on the mail boat headed for Cincinnati.[12] The mail boat did not burn that night, and neither did the *Patrick Rogers*.

The Atlantics and Jack Chapman returned to Louisville for a match with the Eagles six years later. In a game played August 1, 1874, the Atlantics again prevailed, but this time by a more modest 12–8 score. Chapman managed to score only a single run. As the Mutuals of New York had just been in Louisville, and were playing at that point in Chicago, an effort was underway for them to return to Louisville to play an exhibition game against the Atlantics on the Eagles' grounds at Fourth and Magnolia on August 3. For reasons not stated, the game did not happen.[13] The *Courier-Journal* never reported on the departure of the Atlantics from Louisville. It also never reported on any festivities hosted by the Eagles for the benefit of the Atlantics. Such events were common in the 1860s when the Atlantics first visited, but far less so by 1874 when they returned. So, it is possible that the Atlantics stuck around in Louisville for four days after their game with the Eagles. But given the financial constraints of clubs, the likelier scenario is that they left on the 3rd when it was clear the game with the Mutuals (and the gate receipts they would have earned) would not come to fruition.

At 3:00 p.m. on August 4, 1874, the *Patrick Rogers* was scheduled to get underway from the docks at the foot of Third Street in Louisville. On board were about 60 passengers along with a herd of sheep, some cattle, "a large lot of tobacco" and the mail. The boat had been built in Cincinnati about two years earlier and was a large side-wheel steamer "with a splendid cabin, and was a model of beauty and speed." At 7:00 a.m. on the 5th, Captain C.T. David wired in that the ship had burned to the waterline at Aurora, Indiana, about 26 miles below Cincinnati. The initial report stated, "Passengers and crew principally safe." Locally, rumors spread quickly of a disaster with as many as 50 to 100 lives being lost. Captain Frank Carter was trying to obtain information with little success until 9:40 a.m. when an officer on the steamer sent a telegram giving the names of six passengers confirmed to have been saved and the names of three crewmen currently missing. As the day wore on, more news trickled in with names of passengers and crew whose status had been confirmed. But, with no manifest to use as a reference, confusion and fear reigned. In the end, a majority of the passengers and crew survived though several were seriously burned. By the 6th of August, only eight were confirmed dead, but 11 were still missing and presumed to have drowned.[14] In all likelihood, given the proximity in time and place, Chapman read the story of the *Patrick Rogers* and, over the years, conflated the memories into a single, near-death experience.

In the same interview with the *Brooklyn Daily Eagle* Chapman also recounted other narrow escapes he experienced with the Louisville club. He told the story of the decision to take a later train, much to the disappointment of the team, only to later discover the train they would have been on had they taken the earlier departure was involved in a wreck along the road in Ohio. The only problem with the story is that he placed the affair as being in 1877 when in fact it was 1876. He recalled the time in 1890, just before the season, the club was attending a show at the Buckingham Theater when a horrific cyclone hit the city killing hundreds. The theater was just three blocks from the path of destruction. (The Buckingham was on Jefferson, between Third and Fourth.) The 1877 scandal is never discussed in the interview though he does mention Charles Chase.[15]

Jack Chapman died June 10, 1916, at the age of 73, still in his hometown of Brooklyn, New York.

* * *

Charles Chase's 1880s account of what happened in 1877 was by no means intended to mislead. His only fault is a flaw shared by all, which is an imperfect memory, especially of events distant in time. As was true of Jack Chapman's story of the *Patrick Rogers*, research has shown that our brains can develop false memories. Academic research has developed a concept called "fuzzy trace theory" to help measure and explain the phenomenon. Subjects are often given a list of words that fit a specific category such as household furniture or farm animals and then asked to recall them. Their recitation of the list from memory will lead them to include words that, while they fit the given category, were not on the list they were initially given. Yet, the subjects will confidently insist they were. The phrase "fuzzy trace theory" was coined by researchers Charles Brainerd and Valerie Reyna. As Professor Reyna explained to *Business Insider* in 2017: "It's a really powerful, psychological phenomenon. A reality mismatch. It's not 'I can't remember,' which is forgetting, but 'I remember vividly something that didn't happen.' So fuzzy trace theory was the first theory applied to explain that." The explanation applies not just to words, but further experiments demonstrate it applies to a broader pattern of memories which can be separated into two types of memory: verbatim and gist. In verbatim memory, precise details are recalled. But with gist, it is more of a recollection of the overall concept of what happened.[16]

Ten years after the fact Chase vividly recalled the concept of what happened: Devlin, Hall, Nichols and Craver were expelled from baseball after they confessed to selling games. Telegrams later confirmed the wrong-doing and John Haldeman, a ballplayer himself, was instrumental in uncovering the truth. It was in his description of the details that the cart came off the rails. We will never know, for instance, whether the two telegrams he claimed to have received just before the Hartford games were in fact what he recalled them being. The telegrams were not preserved, though some obtained from the players obviously were, as he included them in his article. It is notable that in Haldeman's recounting of events in the *Courier-Journal* on November 3, 1877, he never mentions those two telegrams. It is inconceivable that Chase would not have told the other directors and Haldeman about them. As noted already in these pages, certain assertions by Chase can be dismissed based on the historic, objective record. Some, such as the telegrams and the confrontations of Hall and Devlin, cannot. The fault lies not with Chase for having the same shaky memory shared by us all, it lies with historians who failed to verify the facts against the record.

Charles Chase lived out the rest of his life in Louisville, mostly tending to his father's liquor business which he later inherited. There is no indication he had any further endeavors in managing a baseball club. Instead, he and wife Julia contented themselves with the work and social life of a prominent businessman. There is no hint they ever sought out any publicity although from time to time one or both of them would be mentioned in the society pages of the *Courier-Journal* as attending some social function or theatrical performance. They were residing at the Galt House on November 28, 1882, when Julia died. Julia Chase had been ill for several years prior to her passing. Nevertheless, according to her friends, she was "always evincing a spirit of Christian resignation which refused to look at the dark side of life, being hopeful to the last."[17] She was just 28.

Chase eventually re-married the former Carrie French of Evansville, Indiana, and he and his second wife maintained an existence similar to that he had shown before. Aside from the occasional social mentions, Chase was an active leader in various trade associations, working to lobby government at all levels on matters of interest to the liquor trade. His public comments were limited. There were the misstatements he made in the 1880s concerning Louisville's discovery of Bill Holbert in 1876. There was, of course, the one article he wrote which has been much discussed herein. In a bit of irony, in 1886 he commented on efforts in New York to eliminate wagering on horse racing. He was opposed to such efforts because "If they stop pooling at the tracks they stop racing. If they stop racing they ruin the thoroughbred interests, and that would be a severe blow to Kentucky, for a thoroughbred is only good for racing."[18]

In 1892, Chase joined with several other local businessmen (including Haldeman's older brother, William), in signing a letter endorsing the idea of organizing a charity baseball game for the benefit of then business manager for the Colonels, Jack Chapman. Chase was the only former officer or director from the Grays to participate. Chapman's response to the offer was customary for the time. He wrote a letter of acceptance addressed to Chase and a handful of other signatories and had it published in the next day's *Courier-Journal*. "The undersigned gratefully accepts your kind offer to lend your aid in arranging a base ball game for his benefit, a proposition especially gratifying and all the more appreciated because so unexpected."

Just above Chapman's letter was a letter signed by the then-current members of the Colonels offering their services to the game. The game went off with success and raised around $900 for Chapman—a tidy sum for the time.[19]

Chase disposed of his business interest and retired in 1918, no doubt due in large part to the passage of the Eighteenth Amendment to the U.S. Constitution banning the manufacture or sale of alcohol. In 1920, while visiting Baltimore with his wife, Chase died suddenly on March 25. His body was returned to Louisville where he is interred at Cave Hill Cemetery. The short obituary that appeared mentioned he was survived by both his wife and a son, Edward, from his first marriage. It also noted that he and his wife then resided at the Weissinger-Gaulbert Apartments, one building of which still stands today at Third and Broadway. The obituary noted that in his youth he had served as the confidential secretary to one of the most prominent figures on Wall Street and that he left that position to come to Louisville to join his father's business. There is, however, no mention of his involvement with the Louisville Grays and the scandal of 1877.[20]

* * *

The Louisville Four never played major league baseball again. As for Al Nichols, little is known about his life prior to baseball and little is known about it after baseball. William Cook, in *The Louisville Grays Scandal of 1877*, states Nichols did play minor league ball at some point after 1877. Nichols made several attempts to be reinstated by the National League, all to no avail. It was rumored at one point Nichols was playing amateur ball on Long Island. But even that was too much for the *Brooklyn Daily Eagle*, which protested that not even in the amateur ranks should he ever be allowed to play. Nichols made one last effort at reinstatement in 1887 but was rebuffed with little discussion. In the 1880s he was married and raised a family. He worked at various jobs throughout the remainder of his life. According to his great-great-granddaughter, he spent the rest of his life feeling remorseful about his actions while with Louisville. He died in Richmond Hill, New York, on June 18, 1936,[21] His death went unreported in the press. Ironically, Nichols was the last surviving member of the 1877 team. Between the 1876 and 1877 teams, only Chick Fulmer, the captain and shortstop of the 1876 club, who died in 1940, outlived him.

Like Nichols, Craver sought reinstatement several times and was denied. Eventually Craver gave up on trying to return to baseball. He became a police officer in his hometown of Troy, New York, where he died in 1901 at the age of 57. In reporting his passing, the *Louisville Evening Post* got almost everything wrong. It began by referring to him as "the ringleader of the Craver-Hall-Devlin conspiracy" and informs its readers that "all *three* players were blacklisted for life." It then recounts his career, stating he and the other two joined the "Louisville Browns" in "1879" and sold games until they were caught by club president Zach Phelps (president of the Eclipse for part of the 1880s) and, in the end, cost the club the "American Association pennant." The *Louisville Times* came closer. It at least got the year right. But both papers essentially just pasted large portions of an Associated Press release and stated Louisville was playing in the American Association. Both also omit Nichols and overstate Craver's proven involvement.[22] The *Courier-Journal* ignored the story altogether.

George Hall also sought reinstatement. In 1878, Bob Ferguson had been hired by William Hulbert to manage the White Stockings. Ferguson needed a solid hitter, so he approached Hulbert about reinstating Hall, who was among the best hitters in the game. Hulbert steadfastly refused to even consider it and so that was the end of that discussion. Hall himself also entered petitions in 1879 and 1880 seeking reinstatement by the League. Along with the others, his was denied. With the denial in 1880, the League passed a resolution banning any future consideration of appeals from any of the Louisville Four. The banishment was now permanent.[23]

Hall took up the same profession as his father: engraver. Later he became a clerk at a New York art museum. He died of heart trouble June 11, 1923, at the age of 74.[24] As happened with Nichols, George Hall's passing brought not a single mention in any newspapers. In the nearly 46 years that had passed between the Grays' scandal and Hall's death, the country had been through a lot. There were multiple economic depressions, the Spanish-American War, the Philippine insurrection and, of course, World War I. Baseball had experienced expansion and then contraction of the National League, a new rival league in the American League, and the rise of stars like Ty Cobb and Babe Ruth among others. There was the "Black Sox" scandal of 1919 which broke in the media nearly a year after the fact just as tragedy struck the game on another field. On August 16, 1920, Kentucky-born Carl Mays of the New York Yankees struck Kentucky-born Ray Chapman of the Cleveland Indians on the temple with a vicious fastball, causing Chapman's death hours later. The Grays were, so it seems, virtually forgotten. Still, Hall, like Devlin, might have someday earned a plaque in Cooperstown but for his actions in 1877.

For James Devlin, a barely literate man with no discernible skills beyond baseball, banishment from the game may have been the hardest. In 1878 he pitched for a Canadian club which ultimately failed to pay him, leaving him and his family, once again, in desperate circumstances. He never did give up trying to gain a pardon from the National League. He appealed for reinstatement each year between 1878 and 1882. The *Cincinnati Enquirer* quickly tired of his efforts: "Jim Devlin still keeps petitioning for reinstatement. He had better employ his time at any thing else—even at trying to teach a dog how to talk."[25] In 1879 there was a report of his playing in a pick-up game in Philadelphia against a strong nine and, reportedly, he was dominant. The *Louisville Evening Post* was led to comment: "He has still some cunning in his right arm."[26]

Being banned from the National League also meant banishment from the affiliated leagues under the national agreement. Those leagues had to honor the National League's contracts and its blacklist. Failure to do so would jeopardize their relationship with the League which brought them exhibition games and required the League to reciprocally honor their player contracts. Early in 1879 Devlin tried to obtain a waiver from the International League in what the *Enquirer* dubbed a "pitiable plea." "For Devlin personally we have the profoundest sympathy; for Devlin morally we have none at all."[27] After being denied the endorsement of the Judiciary Committee, Devlin appealed to the open convention:

> Gentlemen, what can I do to prove to you that I regret my crooked action with the Louisville Nine. I have suffered poverty; been obliged to beg; seen my wife and child want for something to eat; been living on charity, and I thought that I would come to Utica to this Convention as my last hope. I am sorry that I did wrong. I want just one more chance. I think I have repented of my crooked work, and don't, for God's sake, refuse to give a man a chance to redeem himself.[28]

His appeal was denied. In 1880 there were reports Devlin was playing in San Francisco. In 1882 when the Louisville Eclipse Club was preparing to join the American Association, Devlin wrote to the directors begging for a chance to pitch for free to prove himself as a man and a ball player. The club declined the offer.[29]

A.G. Spalding related a story he witnessed as William Hulbert's righthand man with the White Stockings. Hulbert had been friends with Devlin since the pitcher played for him in Chicago. Since Hulbert was the man in charge of the League, Devlin sought his assistance. Devlin appeared in poor condition on a cold day in Chicago. Spalding described the meeting:

> The situation, as he kneeled there in abject humiliation, was beyond the realm of pathos. It was a scene of heartrending tragedy. Devlin was in tears, Hulbert was in tears…. I heard Devlin's plea to have the stigma removed from his name. I heard him entreat, not on his own account, he acknowledged himself unworthy of consideration, but for the sake of his wife and child. I beheld the agony of humiliation depicted on his features as he confessed his guilt and begged for mercy.
> I saw the great bulk of Hulbert's frame tremble with the emotion he vainly sought to stifle. I saw the president's hand steal into his pocket as if seeking

to conceal his intended act from the other hand. I saw him take a $50 bill and press it into the palm of the prostrate player. And then I heard him say, as he fairly writhed with the pain his own words caused him, "That's what I think of you, personally; but, damn you, Devlin, you are dishonest; you have sold a game, and I can't trust you. Now go; and let me never see your face again; for your act will not be condoned so long as I live."[30]

Devlin appealed to Harry Wright, perhaps the most influential man in baseball. The letter, reproduced here, is unedited from its original form:

Phila Feb 24th 1878

Mr. Harry Wright

Dear Sir

as I am Deprived from Playing this year I though I woed write you to see if you Coed do anything for me in the way of looking after your ground or anything in the way of work I Don't Know what I am to do I have tried hard to get work of any Kind But I Canot get it do you Know of anyway that you think I coed get to Play again I Can asure you Harry that I was not Treated right and if Ever I Can see you to tell you the Case you will say I am not to Blame I am living from hand to mouth all winter I have not got a Stitch of Clothing or has my wife and child You Don't Know how I am Situated for I Know if you did you woed do Something for me I am honest Harry you need not Be afraid the Louisville People made me what I am to day a Begger I trust you will not Say anything to anyone about the Contents of this to any one if you can do me this favor By letting me take care of the ground or anything of that Kind I Beg of you to do it and god will reward you if I Don't or let me Know if you have any ide of how I coed get Back I am Dumb Harry I don't Know how to go about it So I Trust you will answear this and do all you Can for me So I will Close by Sending you & Geo and all the Boys my very Best wishes hoping to hear from you Soon

I am yours Trouly
James A. Devlin
No 908 Atherton St
Phila Pa[31]

Harry Wright never responded.

Eventually Devlin took a job as a police officer in his hometown of Philadelphia. He served in that position for roughly a year, until tuberculosis struck. Jim Devlin died October 11, 1883, at the age of 34. Following his death, his superior officer stated that Devlin had served nobly and with honor and that he would be greatly missed by his fellow officers.[32]

Devlin's passing, so soon after the scandal, did not go without notice. It is interesting, and perhaps telling, to see the various editorial choices made in how he was remembered. *The Pittsburgh Post-Gazette* called him an "expert" at baseball from a very young age. Of the 1877 scandal, it said: "Owing, *it is said*, to a misunderstanding with the management of the club, he resolved to 'sell out,' and the championship went to another club" [emphasis supplied]. The *Boston Globe* led with the scandal in announcing his death and stated the "ringleader" of the four was Craver. His hometown paper, the *Philadelphia Inquirer*, made no mention of the scandal and noted only, "He was at one time connected with the Chicago and St. Louis clubs." It completely ignored any association he had with the Louisville club. In Louisville, the *Evening Post* noted his death and the fact he had played for Louisville in 1876 and 1877. It did not mention the scandal. The *Louisville Times* did not mention his death at all. The *Courier-Journal* simply reprinted a piece from an unnamed Chicago paper, but first introduced the story by noting Devlin's expulsion and stated it was believed it was due mainly to the influence of Hall.[33]

Perhaps the most nuanced approach to Devlin's passing was that of *The New York Clipper*. It gave a brief history of his amateur and professional career, concluding that he had pitched "effectively" for Louisville in 1876 and 1877. It then states Devlin was expelled by Louisville "on a charge of having 'sold' certain exhibition games." *The New York Clipper* continues: "His sin was a peculiar one, and he suffered sufficiently in after years to atone for any injury done anyone else." The article then repeats the allegation that Louisville owed Devlin back pay and states he was in a financial hole as a result. Leaving unsaid, but clearly implied, that his actions were the result of that, it states "he was ignorant that he was doing any wrong."

Next the article reports: "One of the directors of the old Louisville Club circulated a petition recently, which was signed by all the members of the directory, asking for Devlin's reinstatement. [Chick] Fulmer of the Cincinnati Club consented to present the petition at the annual meeting of the League." However, as Devlin had just died, "it is not worthwhile to present the document, and it has been filed away."[34]

This *New York Clipper* article appears to be the only place this petition favoring reinstatement has been reported. It is not mentioned in any of the histories of the Grays consulted for this work. Its existence, if accurate, may explain, or be explained by, Chase's account of Devlin in his article. In language quoted above, Chase sees Devlin as a victim of Hall and Nichols: "it was proven that Devlin received but $100, for once in the power of Hall and Nichols they forced him to throw games under threats of exposure."[35] By 1883 Chase had apparently come to the conclusion in his own mind—his memory—that Chase was a child-like follower, and not the double-crossing man his own testimony revealed. In the memory of Chase, and judging from the above, Chadwick as well, Devlin's ignorance of his own wrongdoing warranted forgiveness and compassion.

* * *

Baseball historian David Nemec speculates that Haldeman's motive for exposing the scandal stemmed from his own resentment toward Jack

Chapman for not giving him a fair chance to play regularly on the team. That seems unlikely. During the era several players played under assumed names to prevent their families from discovering they were playing ball for a living. Being a professional ballplayer was seen as being lower class. According to Walter Haldeman's biographer, however, it was he who forbade his son from even trying out for the team. Walter Haldeman thought it beneath the dignity of man with John's education and upbringing.[36] The most likely explanation is that exposing the scandal was Haldeman's job as a reporter. The zeal with which he approached the task may well have been fueled by a strong sense of righteous indignation. After all, the victim of the scandal was *his* team in every imaginable respect: stockholder, son of the president, beat reporter, and part-time player.

Haldeman continued playing baseball after the scandal and he continued with the *Courier-Journal*. He also continued to be a fan of the professional version of the game. In 1886 he accepted the position of official scorer for the Eclipse Club. But it was in 1884 and 1885 that he faced perhaps the best and worst of times in his life making the scandal of 1877 pale by comparison. The *Courier-Journal* decided it needed to compete for the afternoon daily market and launched the *Louisville Times*. Haldeman was soon thereafter made the business manager of the paper. However, in the spring his wife of just a few years, Lollie, took ill and died in May. Haldeman was left a widower with a four-year-old daughter, Adelaide. Three months later, while he and his daughter were relaxing at Crab Orchard Springs, Kentucky, Adelaide became violently ill and died the same day. Haldeman remarried two years later to the former Annie Buchanan, and the two produced three more daughters: Jean, Bessie and Isabel.[37]

In 1899, at the age of 44, Haldeman became ill with cerebritis, an inflammation of the brain typically caused by a bacterial infection. The condition worsened to the point that he and Annie went to Hot Springs, Arkansas, hoping the baths would have a curative effect. In the 19th century, bacteria were not understood. There was no concept that a pathogen causes illnesses such as cerebritis or tuberculosis. The prescribed cure was often a retreat to warm climates or the invigorating effects of natural warm baths. Once at Hot Springs, Haldeman was too ill to partake in the baths, so he and Annie returned to Louisville during a sweltering hot August. Travelling under those conditions worsened his illness. Shortly after midnight September 17, 1899, John Haldeman died at his home on the northeast corner of Fourth and York. One of his obituaries noted his time with the celebrated Eagles of the early 1870s but made no mention of his role in exposing the Louisville Four. Similarly, the *Chicago Tribune* noted his passing, as did the *New York Times*, but both acknowledged only his role as newspaper man without mentioning his role in exposing the scandal.[38]

* * *

In *The Louisville Grays Scandal of 1877*, historian William Cook notes that Haldeman has apparently never been considered for the J.G. Taylor Spink Award given by the Baseball Hall of Fame. The award is intended for "meritorious contributions to baseball writing." Part of the reason for snubbing Haldeman may be because that part of the story is seldom told. When Lee Allen was putting together his book *100 Years of Baseball*, he was completely unaware of Haldeman's contribution.[39] A large part of the reason Haldeman was lost was that his own employer—the very megaphone he was able to use—the *Courier-Journal*, seldom mentions it.

Between 1878 and 2023, there have been at least seven accounts of the scandal reported in the *Courier-Journal*. Only one mentions John Haldeman. The first one was an article appearing August 19, 1887, when there were rumors about similar behavior among the Washington club of that year. Just ten years removed from the actual events, the *Courier-Journal* managed to get almost every single fact wrong:

> In 1877 the Louisville Club, which had belonged to the National League, had the championship won, but some of the players were bribed by pool sellers to throw the games, and through this intentional loss the Bostons won the pennant by two games, the Louisvilles coming out second. The great strength of the Louisvilles was their celebrated battery, Devlin and Snyder, which was much the strongest in the country. A club then had only one battery, curves being unknown, and Devlin pitched in every game of the season. The sell-out was exposed by the *Courier-Journal*, which obtained the telegraphic correspondence between the players and the bribers. The League officials sat in judgment upon the case, and four men were found guilty, namely, Devlin, pitcher; Snyder, catcher; Hale, left field; Craver, short stop. Joe Gerhardt, the second baseman, did not escape without suspicion, and retired temporarily from baseball. The others were blacklisted, and none of them except Snyder, who is now the catcher of the Clevelands, ever succeeded in having the blacklist raised. Devlin became a street car driver in Philadelphia, and died two years ago. He was an ignorant man, and was led into it by Craver, the short stop and Captain of the club, a shrewd fellow, who planned the fraud. The men received ridiculously small sums for their treachery, throwing games for $10 apiece, but their severe punishment has ever since been a warning to any player who was disposed to sell the chances of his club.[40]

Other than the year it occurred, there is hardly a single fact in that paragraph which is correct.

Three years later, a brief mention on August 31, 1890, gets it mostly correct but lumps George Bechtel in with the other four and fails to mention Haldeman. In a December 18, 1910, story, the *Courier-Journal* ran a piece quoting at length from Alfred H. Spink's account of the scandal in his recently released book, *The National Game*. Spink, the founder and publisher of *The Sporting News* from St. Louis, merely mimics Chase's erroneous account from the 1880s. An historical piece appearing April 17, 1938, got the names of the four players correct but missed the year by ten, stating the scandal occurred in 1887. Once again, the story neglected to mention Haldeman. John Haldeman finally appeared as the answer to a trivia question posed by the late baseball journalist/historian A.H. Tarvin in the September 6, 1951, edition of the paper. The *Courier-Journal* next explored the story April 5, 1959, but Haldeman is not there. A November 10, 1968, *Courier-Journal Centennial* piece gives credit for breaking the scandal to Haldeman—*Walter* Haldeman. Then on the centennial of the events, *Courier-Journal* sportswriter Jim Bolus wrote a long piece which got the story substantially correct, including due credit for John Haldeman. Finally, in 2000 in a piece presenting a brief history of professional baseball in Louisville, there is this: "1877—Louisville is eventually replaced in the National League after a player's wife tells the manager about a plot to throw a series of games." As with the first look back in 1887, not one word is correct beyond the year. It is said that journalists write the first draft of history. That may be true, but they are lousy historians. To go back to Cook's observation, it is no wonder Haldeman has been overlooked. His own paper set the trend.[41]

* * *

The punishment of the Louisville Four set the tone for Major League Baseball on how it was going to deal with recurrences of the problems left over from the old National Association. Hippodroming, as it was called, was not the only issue Hulbert and the League wanted to stamp out, but it was the core one. Drug and alcohol use were a problem then as they are now. But the reality is that only marginal players, or those whose abuse of a substance is so bad as to render them unable to function, have suffered the ultimate consequences. The problem of players jumping contracts was fixed for the time with the reserve clause put in place in 1879. But gambling on baseball could not be tolerated by the League. The Grays scandal was not the last instance of the practice appearing, but it established a precedent, nonetheless. It is more likely than not that the Louisville Four did not throw any League games, and one can argue that since they only sold exhibition games the punishment exceeded the crime. But that wasn't the point. Public perception of the integrity of the game was the overriding concern. The harsh punishment of the Louisville Four was not so much about punishing a wrong as it was a deterrence of future misconduct.

Gambling on baseball by players or managers is, in essence, the original sin. It is the one act which cannot be overlooked, let alone forgiven. It seems unlikely that will ever change. Players like Shoeless Joe Jackson and Pete Rose will most likely always be on the same side of the fence as Jim Devlin, George Hall, Bill Craver and Al Nichols: that is, outside the baseball fraternity.

Chapter Notes

Prologue

1. "As a Matter of Course" *The Louisville Courier-Journal*, August 9, 1877, p. 4. ProQuest Historical Newspapers: *The Louisville Courier-Journal* (1869–1922); "The Championship," *Chicago Tribune*, August 12, 1877, p. 7.

2. "Baseball: Crooked Play," *New York Clipper*, November 10, 1877, p. 2; *Haldeman Family Papers, 1843–1985*, Filson Historical Society, Louisville, KY., Mss A H159, Correspondence Vol. 25, Letter from John A. Haldeman to Elizabeth Haldeman, June 6, 1876; and see: "The Same Old Story," *The Louisville Courier-Journal*, July 4, 1877, p. 2. ProQuest Historical Newspapers: *The Louisville Courier-Journal (1869–1922)*; "Good!" *The Louisville Courier-Journal*, July 6, 1877, p. 4. ProQuest Historical Newspapers: *The Louisville Courier-Journal (1869–1922)*; Cusick, Dennis Charles, "Gentleman of the Press: The Life and Times of Walter Newman Haldeman," Masters Thesis, University of Louisville, 1987, at 120; Chicago Cubs, 41D, Box 1, Correspondence 187 876, Abakanowicz Research Center, Chicago History Museum, Chicago, Illinois: Letter from Chas. E. Chase to W.A. Hulbert, October 23, 1875.

3. Allen, Lee, *The National League Story* (New York: Putnam, 1961), at 3.

4. Palmer, Harry Clay, J.A. Fynes, Frank Richter, W.I. Harris, et al., eds., *Athletic Sports in America, England and Australia* (Philadelphia: Hubbard Bros., 1889), at 69.

5. Goldstein, Warren, *Playing for Keeps: A History of Early Baseball* (Ithaca: Cornell University Press, 1989), at 10–14 and 17–20; Melville, Tom, *Early Baseball and the Rise of the National League* (Jefferson, NC: McFarland, 2001), at 9–11; Seymour, Harold, and Dorothy Seymour Mills, *Baseball—The Early Years* (New York: Oxford University Press, 1960), at 15–22.

6. Goldstein, *Playing for Keeps*, at 17–20; Melville, *Early Baseball*, at 12–15; see: e.g., Isenberg, Nancy, *White Trash. The 400-Year Untold History of Class in America* (New York: Penguin Books, 2016) and Kleber, John E., Mary Jean Kinsman, Thomas D. Clark, Clyde F. Crews, George H. Yater, eds., *The Encyclopedia of Louisville* (Louisville: The University Press of Kentucky, 2001), at 97, "Bloody Monday."

7. Seymour and Mills, *Baseball*, at 13–14.

8. Wright, Marshall D., *The National Association of Base Ball Players, 1857–1870* (Jefferson, NC: McFarland, 2000), at 7.

9. Goldstein, *Playing for Keeps*, at 70.

10. Morris, Peter, William J. Ryczek, Jan Finkel, Leonard Levin and Richard Malatzky, eds., *Baseball Pioneers, 1850–1870: The Clubs and Players Who Spread the Sport Nationwide* (Jefferson, NC: McFarland, 2014), at 272–273; Seymour and Mills, *Baseball*, at 52.

11. Wright, *The National Association*, at 238–239.

12. Morris, et al., *Baseball Pioneers*, at 147; Wright, *The National Association*, at 254 and 308; Wilbert, Warren N., *Opening Pitch: Professional Baseball's Inaugural Season* (Lanham, MD: Roman & Littlefield, 2007).

13. See: e.g., Allen, *The National League*, at 1–3; Macdonald, Neil W., *The League That Lasted* (Jefferson, NC: McFarland, 2004), at 2–4; Melville, *Early*

Baseball, at 59–60; and Seymour and Mills, *Baseball*, at 75.

14. Allen, *The National League*, at 1–3; Macdonald, *League That Lasted*, at 2–6.

15. Seymour and Mills, *Baseball*, at 75; Macdonald, *League That Lasted*, at 4–6; Allen, *The National League*, at 3; Cook, William, *The Louisville Grays Scandal of 1877* (Jefferson, NC: McFarland, 2005), at 35; "Shut Out," *The Louisville Courier-Journal*, February 6, 1876, p. 4. ProQuest Historical Newspapers: *The Louisville Courier-Journal (1869–1922)*.

Chapter One

1. [No Title], *Daily Courier*, June 30, 1858, p. 2. ProQuest Historical Newspapers: *Louisville Courier-Journal (1851–1868)*; "Local Matters. Game Played by Louisville Base Ball Club," *Daily Courier*, July 15, 1858, p. 2. ProQuest Historical Newspapers: *Louisville Courier-Journal (1851–1868)*; "Eclipse Base Ball Club," *Daily Courier*, August 20, 1858, p. 2. ProQuest Historical Newspapers: *Louisville Courier-Journal (1851–1868)*.

2. [No Title], *Daily Courier*, February 24, 1857, p. 3. ProQuest Historical Newspapers: *The Louisville Courier-Journal (1851–1868)*.

3. Goldstein, *Playing for Keeps*, at 32, 34, 38–39; "Base Ball Match," *Daily Courier*, September 23, 1858, p. 2. ProQuest Historical Newspapers: *The Louisville Courier-Journal (1851–1868)*.

4. "Base Ball," *The Louisville Daily Journal*, April 4, 1866, p. 3. ProQuest Historical Newspapers: *The Louisville Courier-Journal (1839–1968)*; "Base Ball," *The Louisville Daily Journal*, May 8, 1867, p. 2. ProQuest Historical Newspapers: *The Louisville Courier-Journal (1839–1868)*; "Base Ball Match To-day," *The Louisville Daily Journal*, May 24, 1867, p. 2. ProQuest Historical Newspapers: *The Louisville Courier-Journal (1839–1868)*; Goldstein, *Playing for Keeps*, at 43.

5. *George W. Vanvalkenburgh Papers, 1861–1907*, Filson Historical Society, Louisville, KY, Mss A V284 2, Correspondence January 1863–March 1863.

6. See: e.g., Jewell, Anne, *Baseball in Louisville* (Charleston, SC: Arcadia Publishing, 2006); Tarvin, A.H., *Seventy-Five*

Years on Louisville Diamonds (Schumann Publications, 1940) and "The City's First Baseball Game" (Work is unpaginated).

7. [No Title], *Daily Union Press*, April 14, 1865, p. 3; "The Presidential Visit," *Daily Courier*, September 11, 1866, p. 1. ProQuest Historical Newspapers: *Louisville Courier-Journal (1851–1868)*; Alexander, Charles C. *Our Game: An American Baseball History* (New York: MJF Books, 1997), at 4–7.

8. "Our City Sports—Are They Ruinous?" *Daily Courier*, January 19, 1866, p. 2. ProQuest Historical Newspapers: *Louisville Courier-Journal (1851–1868)*.

9. "Match Game of Base Ball," *Daily Courier*, August 2, 1866, p. 2. ProQuest Historical Newspapers: *Louisville Courier-Journal (1851–1868)*; "Base Ball," *The Louisville Daily Journal*, August 17, 1866, p. 3. ProQuest Historical Newspapers: *The Louisville Courier-Journal (1839–1868)*; "Match Game of Base Ball at Cincinnati," *Daily Courier*, July 6, 1867, p. 1. ProQuest Historical Newspapers: *Louisville Courier-Journal (1851–1868)*; "Amateur vs Professional," *The Louisville Courier-Journal*, September 24, 1893, p. 10. ProQuest Historical Newspapers: *Louisville Courier-Journal (1869–1922)*; "Some History on Early Games," *The Louisville Courier-Journal*, November 21, 1909, p. C5. ProQuest Historical Newspapers: *Louisville Courier-Journal (1869–1922)*.

10. See: e.g., Jewell, *Baseball in Louisville*, at 9; but see Tarvin, *Seventy-Five Years*, at "The City's First Baseball Game."

11. Morris, Peter, "John Dickins," Society for American Baseball Research (sabr. org); Morris et al., *Baseball Pioneers*, at 312–313.

12. "Base Ball," *The Louisville Daily Journal*, July 18, 1866, p. 3. ProQuest Historical Newspapers: *The Louisville Courier-Journal (1839–1868)*; "Base Ball," *The Louisville Daily Journal*, July 27, 1866, p. 3. ProQuest Historical Newspapers: *The Louisville Courier-Journal (1839–1868)*.

13. "The Base Ball Match Today," *Daily Courier*, September 6, 1867, p. 2. ProQuest Historical Newspapers: *Louisville Courier-Journal (1851–1868)*.

14. Kleber, et al., *The Encyclopedia of Louisville*, "Yandell, Lunsford Pitts, Sr."

15. Johnston, William Preston, *The Life of General Albert Sidney Johnston* (New

York: D. Appleton, 1879), *republished*, (New York: Da Capo Press, 1997), "Introduction" at X.

16. *Yandell Family Papers, 1823–1887*, Filson Historical Society, Louisville, KY, Mss A Y21 43, Correspondence 1864–1867.

17. Morris, Peter, *A Game of Inches* (Chicago: Ivan R. Dee, 2006), at Sections 1.11, 1.17 and 1.33.

18. [No Title], *The Louisville Courier-Journal*, June 17, 1873, p. 2. ProQuest Historical Newspapers: *The Louisville Courier-Journal (1869–1922)*; "A Victim to Base Ball," *The Louisville Courier-Journal*, August 25, 1877, p. 1. ProQuest Historical Newspapers: *The Louisville Courier-Journal (1869–1922)*; "Death from a Base Ball," *The Louisville Courier-Journal*, April 14, 1883, p. 13. ProQuest Historical Newspapers: *The Louisville Courier-Journal (1869–1922)*.

19. Morris, et al., *Base Ball Pioneers*, at 271–273.

20. "Our National Game," *The Louisville Daily Journal*, May 15, 1868, p. 2. ProQuest Historical Newspapers: *The Louisville Courier-Journal (1839–1868)*.

21. [Display Ad], *The Louisville Daily Journal*, November 7, 1868, p. 2. ProQuest Historical Newspapers: *The Louisville Courier-Journal (1839–1868)*; Wright, *The National Association*, at 238–239.

22. "Base Ball," *The Louisville Daily Journal*, August 1, 1867, p. 2. ProQuest Historical Newspapers: *The Louisville Courier-Journal (1839–1868)*; [No Title], *The Louisville Daily Journal*, November 7, 1868, p. 2. ProQuest Historical Newspapers: *The Louisville Courier-Journal (1839–1868)*; "Base Ball," *The Louisville Daily Journal*, August 15, 1868, p. 4. ProQuest Historical Newspapers: *The Louisville Courier-Journal (1839–1868)*; "Base Ball," *Daily Courier*, August 15, 1868, p. 1. ProQuest Historical Newspapers: *The Louisville Courier-Journal (1851–1868)*; "Base Ball," *The Louisville Courier-Journal*, July 12, 1874, p. 4. ProQuest Historical Newspapers: *The Louisville Courier-Journal (1869–1922)*.

23. "Base Ball," *The Louisville Courier-Journal*, July 7, 1869, p. 7. ProQuest Historical Newspapers: *The Louisville Courier-Journal (1869–1922)*; "Base Ball," *The Louisville Courier-Journal*, July 30, 1869, p. 4. ProQuest Historical Newspapers:

The Louisville Courier-Journal (1869–1922); "The City," *The Louisville Courier-Journal*, August 2, 1869, p. 4. ProQuest Historical Newspapers: *The Louisville Courier-Journal (1869–1922)*; "Base Ball," *The Louisville Courier-Journal*, April 22, 1870, p. 4. ProQuest Historical Newspapers: *The Louisville Courier-Journal (1869–1922)*.

24. "Base Ball," *The Louisville Courier-Journal*, March 13, 1870, p. 4. ProQuest Historical Newspapers: *The Louisville Courier-Journal (1869–1922)*.

25. "The General Council," *The Louisville Courier-Journal*, January 26, 1872, p. 4. ProQuest Historical Newspapers: *The Louisville Courier-Journal (1869–1922)*; Kleber, et al., *The Encyclopedia of Louisville*, "Alfred Victor DuPont."

26. "Base Ball," *The Louisville Courier-Journal*, August 1, 1874, p. 4. ProQuest Historical Newspapers: *The Louisville Courier-Journal (1869–1922)*; Nemec, David, *The Great Encyclopedia of 19th Century Major League Baseball* (New York: Donald I. Fine Books, 1997), at 57; Morris, *A Game of Inches*, at 118.

27. "Base Ball," *Louisville Commercial*, September 9, 1871, p. 4.

28. "Base Ball," *The Louisville Courier-Journal*, July 30, 1874, p. 4. ProQuest Historical Newspapers: *The Louisville Courier-Journal (1869–1922)*; "Base Ball," *The Louisville Courier-Journal*, August 25, 1874; ProQuest Historical Newspapers: *The Louisville Courier-Journal (1869–1922)*.

29. *Haldeman Family Papers, 1843–1985*, Vol. 217, "Speeches," Filson Historical Society, Louisville, KY.

30. "Where We May Skate," *The Louisville Courier-Journal*, November 27, 1874, p. 4. ProQuest Historical Newspapers: *The Louisville Courier-Journal (1869–1922)*; [Classified Ad—No Title], *The Louisville Courier-Journal*, December 2, 1874, p. 4. ProQuest Historical Newspapers: *The Louisville Courier-Journal (1869–1922)*; [Classified Ad—No Title], *The Louisville Courier-Journal*, November 29, 1874, p. 4. ProQuest Historical Newspapers: *The Louisville Courier-Journal (1869–1922)*.

31. "Fun at the Skating Park," *The Louisville Courier-Journal*, January 7, 1875, p. 4. ProQuest Historical Newspapers: *The Louisville Courier-Journal (1869–1922)*.

32. "Amusements," *The Louisville*

Courier-Journal, January 15, 1875, p. 4. ProQuest Historical Newspapers: *The Louisville Courier-Journal (1869–1922)*.

33. "A Lively Week Ahead," *The Louisville Courier-Journal*, June 20, 1875; ProQuest Historical Newspapers: *The Louisville Courier-Journal (1869–1922)*.

34. Cook, *The Louisville Grays Scandal of 1877*, at 157; Cusick, "Gentleman of the Press," at 50–52; "Our Public Schools," *The Louisville Courier-Journal*, June 20, 1872, p. 4. ProQuest Historical Newspapers: *The Louisville Courier-Journal (1869–1922)*; "At Midnight," *The Louisville Courier-Journal*, September 17, 1899, p. 7. ProQuest Historical Newspapers: *The Louisville Courier-Journal (1869–1922)*.

35. *Haldeman Family Papers, 1843–1985*, Letter, May 31, 1874, John Haldeman to Elizabeth Haldeman; Letter, September 27, 1874, John Haldeman to Elizabeth Haldeman; and Letter, October 11, 1874, John Haldeman to Elizabeth Haldeman, Filson Historical Society, Louisville, KY, Mss A H159, Correspondence 1867, Vols 13 and 14.

36. *Haldeman Family Papers, 1843–1985*, Letter, November 8, 1874, John Haldeman to Elizabeth Haldeman, Filson Historical Society, Louisville, KY, Mss A H159, Correspondence 1867, V. 15.

37. "Base Ball," *The Louisville Courier-Journal*, July 12, 1870, p. 4. ProQuest Historical Newspapers: *The Louisville Courier-Journal (1869–1922)*; *Haldeman Family Papers, 1843–1985*, Letter, August 16, 1874, William Haldeman to Elizabeth Haldeman, Filson Historical Society, Louisville, KY, Mss A H159, Correspondence 1867, V. 13; Cusick, "Gentleman of the Press," at 120.

38. "The May Meeting," *The Louisville Courier-Journal*, April 18, 1875, p. 3. ProQuest Historical Newspapers: *The Louisville Courier-Journal (1869–1922)*; Kleber, et al., *The Encyclopedia of Louisville*, "Streets."

39. Kleber, et al., *The Encyclopedia of Louisville*, "Meriwether Lewis Clark, Jr."

40. "Our New Race Course," *The Louisville Courier-Journal*, October 28, 1874, p. 4. ProQuest Historical Newspapers: *The Louisville Courier-Journal (1869–1922)*; Kleber, et al., *The Encyclopedia of Louisville*, "Kentucky Derby."

41. "Fourth Street," *The Louisville Courier-Journal*, May 11, 1875, p. 4.

ProQuest Historical Newspapers: *The Louisville Courier-Journal (1869–1922)*.

42. Ellick, Joe, "Experiences of a Base-Ball Umpire," *Lippencotts*, Vol. 38, p. 444, 1886; "Leather Pounding," *The Louisville Courier-Journal*, April 28, 1875, p. 4. ProQuest Historical Newspapers: *The Louisville Courier-Journal (1869–1922)*.

43. "Base Ball," *The Louisville Courier-Journal*, July 4, 1875, p. 1. ProQuest Historical Newspapers: *The Louisville Courier-Journal (1869–1922)*; "The American Amusement," *The Louisville Courier-Journal*, July 22, 1875, p. 4. ProQuest Historical Newspapers: *The Louisville Courier-Journal (1869–1922)*.

44. "An Extraordinary Contest," *The Louisville Courier-Journal*, August 6, 1875, p. 4. ProQuest Historical Newspapers: *The Louisville Courier-Journal (1869–1922)*; "The Professional Club," *The Louisville Courier-Journal*, August 15, 1875, p. 4. ProQuest Historical Newspapers: *The Louisville Courier-Journal (1869–1922)*; "The Professional Nine," *The Louisville Courier-Journal*, August 31, 1875, p. 4. ProQuest Historical Newspapers: *The Louisville Courier-Journal (1869–1922)*; Letter, Charles Chase to William Hulbert, August 27, 1875, Abakanowicz Research Center, Chicago History Museum, Chicago Cubs 41D, Board of Directors, Stockholders and Other Records 1874–1876.

45. "Wholesale Liquors," *The Louisville Courier-Journal*, February 22, 1874, p. 8. ProQuest Historical Newspapers: *The Louisville Courier-Journal (1869–1922)*; "Deaths and Funerals," *The Louisville Courier-Journal*, March 28, 1920, p. 9. ProQuest Historical Newspapers: *The Louisville Courier-Journal (1869–1922)*; Caron, C.K., *Caron's Directory of the City of Louisville for 1875*, at 150.

46. Letter, William Hulbert to Charles Chase, September 2, 1875; Letter, William Hulbert to Charles Chase, August 24, 1875; and Letter, William Hulbert to Charles Chase, September 13, 1875, Abakanowicz Research Center, Chicago History Museum, Chicago Cubs Correspondence 1875–1880, Box Z

47. Macdonald, *The League That Lasted*, at 2; Allen, *The National League Story*, at 4–5.

48. Macdonald, *The League That Lasted*, at 1.

49. Allen, *The National League Story*, at 5–6; Seymour and Mills, *Baseball*, at 77–79.

50. Letter, William Hulbert to Charles Chase, October 21, 1875, and Letter, William Hulbert to Charles Chase, November 11, 1875; Letter, William Hulbert to Charles Chase, November 8, 1875; Letter, William Hulbert to Charles Fowle, December 4, 1875, Abakanowicz Research Center, Chicago History Museum, Chicago Cubs Correspondence 1875–1880, Box Z.

51. Macdonald, *The League That Lasted*, at 33; "The Professional Nine," *The Louisville Courier-Journal*, August 31, 1875, p. 4. ProQuest Historical Newspapers: *The Louisville Courier-Journal (1869–1922)*.

52. Macdonald, *The League That Lasted*, at 33; Gelzheiser, Robert P., *Labor and Capital in 19th Century Baseball* (Jefferson, NC: McFarland, 2006), at 23–24.

53. Letter, Charles Chase to William Hulbert, October 23, 1875, Abakanowicz Research Center, Chicago History Museum, Chicago Cubs 41D, Board of Directors, Stockholders and Other Records 1874–1876.

54. "What Rumor Says," *The Louisville Courier-Journal*, October 3, 1875, p. 1. ProQuest Historical Newspapers: *The Louisville Courier-Journal (1869–1922)*; Letter, William Hulbert to Charles Chase, November 16, 1875, Abakanowicz Research Center, Chicago History Museum, Chicago Cubs Correspondence 1875–1880, Box Z; "Sporting—The Professional Base Ball Association," *Chicago Tribune*, October 24, 1875, p. 12; "Base Ball Conference," *The Louisville Courier-Journal*, December 19, 1875, p. 1. ProQuest Historical Newspapers: *The Louisville Courier-Journal (1869–1922)*.

55. "Base Ball Conference," *The Louisville Courier-Journal*, December 19, 1875, p. 1. ProQuest Historical Newspapers: *The Louisville Courier-Journal (1869–1922)*; Spalding, Albert G., *Base Ball: America's National Game: 1839–1915* (San Francisco: Halo Book, 1991), at 129; Allen, *The National League Story*, at 8.

56. Morris, et al., *Base Ball Pioneers*, at 158–159; Nemec, *The Great Encyclopedia*, "The National Association Era (1871–1875," at 5–82.

57. Macdonald, *The League That Lasted*, at 16–17 and 36.

58. Letter, William Hulbert to Charles Chase, November 16, 1875, and Letter, William Hulbert to Charles Chase, November 11, 1875, Abakanowicz Research Center, Chicago History Museum, Chicago Cubs Correspondence 1875–1880, Box Z.

59. Macdonald, *The League That Lasted*, at 5; Cook, *Louisville Grays Scandal*, at 35; McCulloch, Ron, ed., *Baseball Roots* (Toronto: Warwick Publishing, 2000), at 24; Kirsch, George B., *Baseball in Blue and Gray* (Princeton, NJ: Princeton University Press, 2003), at 88; Macdonald, *The League That Lasted*, at 63.

60. Kirsch, *Baseball in Blue and Grey*, at 54–55; Seymour and Mills, *Baseball*, at 79; Macdonald, *The League That Lasted* at 45.

61. Macdonald, *The League That Lasted*, at 50–51.

62. Spalding, *Base Ball*, at 129–130; Gelzheiser, *Labor and Capital*, at 39.

63. Seymour and Mills, *Baseball*, at 80–82.

64. Sullivan, Dean A., ed., *Early Innings: A Documentary History of Baseball, 1825–1908* (Lincoln: University of Nebraska Press, 1995), at 96–99; "Base-Ball," *The New York Times*, February 7, 1876, p. 2. ProQuest Historical Newspapers: *The New York Times with Index (1857–1922)*; Macdonald, *The League That Lasted*, at 59–61; "Shut Out," *The Louisville Courier-Journal*, February 6, 1876, p. 4. ProQuest Historical Newspapers: *The Louisville Courier-Journal (1869–1922)*.

Chapter Two

1. "The Professional Club," *The Louisville Courier-Journal*, September 8, 1875, p. 4. ProQuest Historical Newspapers: *The Louisville Courier-Journal (1869–1922)*; BR Bullpen, "Jack Chapman," baseball-reference.com; Di Salvatore, Bryan, *A Clever Base-Ballist: The Life and Times of John Montgomery Ward* (Baltimore: The Johns Hopkins University Press, 1999), at 84.

2. "The Professional Club," *The Louisville Courier-Journal*, September 8, 1875, p. 4. ProQuest Historical Newspapers: *The Louisville Courier-Journal (1869–1922)*; "The Base Ball Season," *The Louisville Courier-Journal*, April 23, 1875, p. 4.

ProQuest Historical Newspapers: *The Lou-isville Courier-Journal (1869–1922)*.

3. "Preparing for Playing," *The Louis-ville Courier-Journal*, January 31, 1876, p. 4. ProQuest Historical Newspapers: *The Louisville Courier-Journal (1869–1922)*; Kleber, et al., *The Encyclopedia of Louis-ville*, "Tyler Block" at 896.

4. Letter, Charles Chase to William Hulbert, August 31, 1875, Abakanowicz Research Center, Chicago History Museum, Chicago Cubs Correspondence.

5. BR Bullpen, "Jim Devlin," baseball-reference.com; United States Census, Philadelphia, PA, 1850; Nemec, *The Great Encyclopedia*, at 47, 62 and 76; "Base Ball," *The Louisville Courier-Journal*, October 12, 1875, p. 4. ProQuest Historical Newspapers: *The Louisville Courier-Journal (1869–1922)*.

6. Faber, Charles F. "Pop Snyder," Soci-ety for American Baseball Research (sabr.org); Letter, William Hulbert to Charles Chase, October 21, 1875; Letter, Charles Chase to William Hulbert, October 23, 1875; Letter, William Hulbert to Charles Chase, October 25, 1875, Abakano-wicz Research Center, Chicago History Museum, Chicago Cubs Correspondence.

7. "The Centennial Campaign," *New York Clipper*, February 5, 1877, p. 357.

8. "The Centennial Campaign," *New York Clipper*, February 5, 1877, p. 357.

9. "Base-ball Notes," *The Louis-ville Courier-Journal*, March 12, 1876, p. 4. ProQuest Historical Newspapers: *The Louisville Courier-Journal (1869–1922)*; "Eager for the Play," *The Louisville Courier-Journal*, March 13, 1876, p. 4. Pro-Quest Historical Newspapers: *The Lou-isville Courier-Journal (1869–1922)*; Von Borries, Philip, *Louisville Diamonds: The Louisville Major-League Reader 1876–1899* (Paducah, KY: Turner Publishing Co., 1996), at 14; "Good Enough," *The Louis-ville Courier-Journal*, April 26, 1876, p. 4. ProQuest Historical Newspapers: *The Lou-isville Courier-Journal (1869–1922)*; "The New Grounds of the Louisville B.B.C.," *The Louisville Courier-Journal*, April 13, 1876, p. 4. ProQuest Historical Newspa-pers: *The Louisville Courier-Journal (1869–1922)*; "Base Ball Notes," *The Louisville Courier-Journal*, April 20, 1876, p. 4. Pro-Quest Historical Newspapers: *The Louis-ville Courier-Journal (1869–1922)*.

10. "Centennial Sport," *The Louisville Courier-Journal*, April 2, 1876, p. 2. Pro-Quest Historical Newspapers: *The Louis-ville Courier-Journal (1869–1922)*; Nemec, *The Great Encyclopedia*, at 96; "Chapman's Crew," *The Louisville Courier-Journal*, March 26, 1876, p. 4. ProQuest Historical Newspapers: *The Louisville Courier-Journal (1869–1922)*; "Good Enough," *The Lou-isville Courier-Journal*, April 26, 1876, p. 4. ProQuest Historical Newspapers: *The Louisville Courier-Journal (1869–1922)*; "Base-Ball," *Cincinnati Enquirer*, October 9, 1877, p. 2. ProQuest Historical Newspapers: *The Cincinnati Enquirer (1841–1922)*; Wat-terson, Jeremy. "Ed Somerville." Society for American Baseball Research (sabr.org).

11. "Wrath of the Winds," *The Louis-ville Courier-Journal*, April 14, 1876, p. 4. ProQuest Historical Newspapers: *The Lou-isville Courier-Journal (1869–1922)*.

12. "After the Storm," *The Louisville Courier-Journal*, April 15, 1876, p. 4. Pro-Quest Historical Newspapers: *The Louis-ville Courier-Journal (1869–1922)*.

13. "Toss Up, Captains," *The Louisville Courier-Journal*, April 23, 1876, p. 1. Pro-Quest Historical Newspapers: *The Louis-ville Courier-Journal (1869–1922)*.

14. "Louisville vs. Chicago," *The Louis-ville Courier-Journal*, April 25, 1876, p. 4. ProQuest Historical Newspapers: *The Lou-isville Courier-Journal (1869–1922)*.

15. "Diamond Dust," *The Louisville Courier-Journal*, April 16, 1876, p. 2. Pro-Quest Historical Newspapers: *The Louis-ville Courier-Journal (1869–1922)*.

16. "Amusements," *The Louisville Courier-Journal*, April 23, 1876, p. 1. Pro-Quest Historical Newspapers: *The Louis-ville Courier-Journal (1869–1922)*.

17. "Good Enough," *The Louisville Courier-Journal*, April 26, 1876, p. 4. Pro-Quest Historical Newspapers: *The Louis-ville Courier-Journal (1869–1922)*.

18. "Yesterday's Game," *Louisville Commercial*, April 30, 1876, p. 4.

19. "The Game Today," *The Louis-ville Courier-Journal*, April 27, 1876, p. 4. ProQuest Historical Newspapers: *The Louisville Courier-Journal (1869–1922)*; "Eleven Errors," *The Louisville Courier-Journal*, April 28, 1876, p. 4. Pro-Quest Historical Newspapers: *The Louis-ville Courier-Journal (1869–1922)*.

20. "Municipal Affairs," *The Louisville*

Courier-Journal, May 5, 1876, p. 4. Pro-Quest Historical Newspapers: *The Louisville Courier-Journal (1869–1922)*; "Discreditable!" *The Louisville Courier-Journal*, May 5, 1876, p. 4. ProQuest Historical Newspapers: *The Louisville Courier-Journal (1869–1922)*.

21. "Jeffersonville," *The Louisville Courier-Journal*, May 6, 1876, p. 1. ProQuest Historical Newspapers: *The Louisville Courier-Journal (1869–1922)*; "Take the People," *The Louisville Courier-Journal*, May 19, 1876, p. 4. ProQuest Historical Newspapers: *The Louisville Courier-Journal (1869–1922)*; "The Board of Aldermen," *The Louisville Courier-Journal*, May 19, 1876, p. 4. ProQuest Historical Newspapers: *The Louisville Courier-Journal (1869–1922)*; "The Base-ball Ordinance," *The Louisville Courier-Journal*, May 25, 1876, p. 4. ProQuest Historical Newspapers: *The Louisville Courier-Journal (1869–1922)*; "Municipal Crumbs," *The Louisville Courier-Journal*, May 26, 1876, p. 3. ProQuest Historical Newspapers: *The Louisville Courier-Journal (1869–1922)*.

22. "Base Ball," *The Louisville Courier-Journal*, May 30, 1876, p. 3. ProQuest Historical Newspapers: *The Louisville Courier-Journal (1869–1922)*; Macdonald, *The League That Lasted*, at 111–112; "Our Boys," *Cincinnati Enquirer*, May 31, 1876, p. 8. ProQuest Historical Newspapers: *The Cincinnati Enquirer (1841–1922)*; "The People's Interests," *The Louisville Courier-Journal*, June 2, 1876, p. 4. ProQuest Historical Newspapers: *The Louisville Courier-Journal (1869–1922)*; "The City Council," *The Louisville Courier-Journal*, July 7, 1876, p. 4. ProQuest Historical Newspapers: *The Louisville Courier-Journal (1869–1922)*; "Municipal Interests," *The Louisville Courier-Journal*, July 14, 1876, p. 4. ProQuest Historical Newspapers: *The Louisville Courier-Journal (1869–1922)*.

23. *Haldeman Family Papers, 1843–1985*, Letter, John A. Haldeman to Elizabeth Haldeman, June 6, 1876, Filson Historical Society, Louisville, KY, Mss A H159, Correspondence Vol. 25.

24. *Haldeman Family Papers, 1843–1985*, Letter, Walter N. Haldeman to John A. Haldeman, May 27, 1876, Filson Historical Society, Louisville, KY, Mss A H159, Correspondence Vol. 24.

25. "Base Ball," *The Louisville Courier-Journal*, May 31, 1876, p. 4. ProQuest Historical Newspapers: *The Louisville Courier-Journal (1869–1922)*; "Base-Ball," *New York Times*, May 31, 1876, p. 2. ProQuest Historical Newspapers: *The New York Times with Index (1857–1922)*; Macdonald, *The League That Lasted*, at 159.

26. "Base Ball," *The Louisville Courier-Journal*, July 25, 1876, p. 4. ProQuest Historical Newspapers: *The Louisville Courier-Journal (1869–1922)*; Ginsburg, Daniel, *The Fix Is In: A History of Baseball Gambling and Game Fixing Scandals* (Jefferson, NC: McFarland, 2004), at 26–27 and 30.

27. "Babblings O' Green Fields," *The Louisville Courier-Journal*, June 15, 1876, p. 4. ProQuest Historical Newspapers: *The Louisville Courier-Journal (1869–1922)*; "Big Sport To-day," *The Louisville Courier-Journal*, June 20, 1876, p. 1. ProQuest Historical Newspapers: *The Louisville Courier-Journal (1869–1922)*; "Louisville Ball Gossip," *The Louisville Courier-Journal*, July 25, 1876, p. 4. ProQuest Historical Newspapers: *The Louisville Courier-Journal (1869–1922)*; Macdonald, *The League That Lasted*, at 159.

28. "The Bechtel Expulsion," *New York Clipper*, February 24, 1877, p. 378.

29. "The League," *The Louisville Courier-Journal*, June 10, 1876, p. 4. ProQuest Historical Newspapers: *The Louisville Courier-Journal (1869–1922)*.

30. "Big Sport To-day," *The Louisville Courier-Journal*, June 20, 1876, p. 1. ProQuest Historical Newspapers: *The Louisville Courier-Journal (1869–1922)*; Macdonald, *The League That Lasted*, at 220.

31. Weatherby, Charlie. "Joe Borden." Society for American Baseball Research (sabr.org); "Notes of the Game," *The Louisville Courier-Journal*, July 24, 1887, p. 7. ProQuest Historical Newspapers: *The Louisville Courier-Journal (1869–1922)*.

32. "All Dead," *The Louisville Courier-Journal*, July 6, 1876, p. 1. ProQuest Historical Newspapers: *The Louisville Courier-Journal (1869–1922)*.

33. "General Notes," *The Louisville Courier-Journal*, July 19, 1876, p. 4. ProQuest Historical Newspapers: *The*

Louisville Courier-Journal (1869–1922); "A Panic in Chicago," *The Louisville Courier-Journal*, July 21, 1876, p. 4. ProQuest Historical Newspapers: *The Louisville Courier-Journal (1869–1922)*.

34. "Their Parting Shot," *The Louisville Courier-Journal*, July 23, 1876, p. 1. ProQuest Historical Newspapers: *The Louisville Courier-Journal (1869–1922)*.

35. "Adverse Fate," *Louisville Commercial*, August 2, 1876, p. 4.

36. "Who Says We're Pie?" *The Louisville Courier-Journal*, August 6, 1876, p. 1. ProQuest Historical Newspapers: *The Louisville Courier-Journal (1869–1922)*.

37. "Base Ball," *Louisville Commercial*, August 9, 1876, p. 4.

38. "Cheyenne," *The Louisville Courier-Journal*, August 13, 1876, p. 1. ProQuest Historical Newspapers: *The Louisville Courier-Journal (1869–1922)*; "Pistols and Rifles," *The Louisville Courier-Journal*, August 17, 1876, p. 3. ProQuest Historical Newspapers: *The Louisville Courier-Journal (1869–1922)*; Weiser-Alexander, Kathy. "Jack McCall—Cowardly Killer of Wild Bill Hickok." Legendsofamerica.

39. "Base-Ball," *The Louisville Courier-Journal*, September 5, 1876, p. 4. ProQuest Historical Newspapers: *The Louisville Courier-Journal (1869–1922)*.

40. "Holbert the Catcher," *The Louisville Courier-Journal*, June 11, 1884, p. 6. ProQuest Historical Newspapers: *The Louisville Courier-Journal (1869–1922)*; "Notes," *The Louisville Courier-Journal*, June 22, 1884, ProQuest Historical Newspapers: *The Louisville Courier-Journal (1869–1922)*.

41. "A Card from James Devlin," *The Louisville Courier-Journal*, September 20, 1876, p. 1. ProQuest Historical Newspapers: *The Louisville Courier-Journal (1869–1922)*.

42. "General Notes," *The Louisville Courier-Journal*, September 18, 1876, p. 1. ProQuest Historical Newspapers: *The Louisville Courier-Journal (1869–1922)*; "Base Ball," *The Louisville Courier-Journal*, September 24, 1876, p. 1. ProQuest Historical Newspapers: *The Louisville Courier-Journal (1869–1922)*; "A Terrible Accident," *The Louisville Courier-Journal*, September 23, 1876, p. 4. ProQuest Historical Newspapers: *The Louisville Courier-Journal (1869–1922)*; "Base Ball," *The Louisville Courier-Journal*, September 24, 1876, p. 1. ProQuest Historical Newspapers: *The Louisville Courier-Journal (1869–1922)*.

43. "Base Ball," *The Louisville Courier-Journal*, September 26, 1876, p. 1. ProQuest Historical Newspapers: *The Louisville Courier-Journal (1869–1922)*.

44. "Base Ball," *Louisville Commercial*, October 5, 1876, p. 4; "Last Man Out," *The Louisville Courier-Journal*, October 6, 1876, p. 4. ProQuest Historical Newspapers: *The Louisville Courier-Journal (1869–1922)*.

45. "Sporting," *The Louisville Courier-Journal*, September 20, 1876, p. 1. ProQuest Historical Newspapers: *The Louisville Courier-Journal (1869–1922)*; "Base Ball," *The Louisville Courier-Journal*, September 26, 1876, p. 1. ProQuest Historical Newspapers: *The Louisville Courier-Journal (1869–1922)*; "Base Ball," *The Louisville Courier-Journal*, December 14, 1876, p. 3. ProQuest Historical Newspapers: *The Louisville Courier-Journal (1869–1922)*; Nemec, *The Great Encyclopedia*, at 98.

Chapter Three

1. "Base Ball," *The Louisville Courier-Journal*, January 4, 1877, p. 4. ProQuest Historical Newspapers: *The Louisville Courier-Journal (1869–1922)*.

2. "Base-Ball Bruitings," *The Louisville Courier-Journal*, January 21, 1877, p. 4. ProQuest Historical Newspapers: *The Louisville Courier-Journal (1869–1922)*; Nemec, *The Great Encyclopedia*, at 89.

3. "Base Ball," *The Louisville Courier-Journal*, January 4, 1877, p. 4. ProQuest Historical Newspapers: *The Louisville Courier-Journal (1869–1922)*; "Devlin in the League," *New York Clipper*, January 6, 1877, p. 323; "To What Base Uses!" *The Louisville Courier-Journal*, February 18, 1877, p. 1. ProQuest Historical Newspapers: *The Louisville Courier-Journal (1869–1922)*.

4. "George Bechtel and the Louisville Club," *The Louisville Courier-Journal*, June 20, 1876, p. 1. ProQuest Historical Newspapers: *The Louisville Courier-Journal (1869–1922)*.

5. "Diamond Dust," *The Louisville*

Courier-Journal, January 17, 1877, p. 4. ProQuest Historical Newspapers: *The Louisville Courier-Journal (1869–1922)*.

6. "To What Base Uses!" *The Louisville Courier-Journal*, February 18, 1877, p. 1. ProQuest Historical Newspapers: *The Louisville Courier-Journal (1869–1922)*.

7. "Base Ball," *The Louisville Courier-Journal*, January 4, 1877, p. 4. ProQuest Historical Newspapers: *The Louisville Courier-Journal (1869–1922)*.

8. "Base Ball," *The Louisville Courier-Journal*, January 4, 1877, p. 4. ProQuest Historical Newspapers: *The Louisville Courier-Journal (1869–1922)*; "League Lingo," *The Louisville Courier-Journal*, February 11, 1877, p. 1. ProQuest Historical Newspapers: *The Louisville Courier-Journal (1869–1922)*; "Base Ball Bruitings," *The Louisville Courier-Journal*, January 21, 1877, p. 4. ProQuest Historical Newspapers: *The Louisville Courier-Journal (1869–1922)*.

9. Woodward, C. Vann, *Reunion and Reaction: The Compromise of 1877 and the End of Reconstruction*, (New York: Oxford University Press, 1966), at 110–111.

10. Cook, *The Louisville Grays Scandal*, at 86; "Base Ball," *The Louisville Courier-Journal*, January 4, 1877, p. 4. ProQuest Historical Newspapers: *The Louisville Courier-Journal (1869–1922)*.

11. "League Lingo," *The Louisville Courier-Journal*, February 11, 1877, p. 1. ProQuest Historical Newspapers: *The Louisville Courier-Journal (1869–1922)*; "Base-Ball Bruitings," *The Louisville Courier-Journal*, January 21, 1877, ProQuest Historical Newspapers: *The Louisville Courier-Journal (1869–1922)*.

12. "Around the Bases," *The Louisville Courier-Journal*, January 28, 1877, p. 1. ProQuest Historical Newspapers: *The Louisville Courier-Journal (1869–1922)*; Nemec, *The Great Encyclopedia*, at 105.

13. "League Lingo," *The Louisville Courier-Journal*, February 11, 1877, p. 1. ProQuest Historical Newspapers: *The Louisville Courier-Journal (1869–1922)*; Brunson, James E., III, *Black Baseball 1858–1900*, Vol. 1 (Jefferson, NC: McFarland, 2019), at 98.

14. "League Lingo," *The Louisville Courier-Journal*, February 11, 1877, p. 1. ProQuest Historical Newspapers: *The Louisville Courier-Journal (1869–1922)*;

"League Literature," *The Louisville Courier-Journal*, March 18, 1877, p. 2. ProQuest Historical Newspapers: *The Louisville Courier-Journal (1869–1922)*; Nemec, *The Great Encyclopedia*, at 75.

15. "Around the Bases," *The Louisville Courier-Journal*, January 28, 1877, p. 1. ProQuest Historical Newspapers: *The Louisville Courier-Journal (1869–1922)*; "The Louisville Nine," *The Louisville Courier-Journal*, February 18, 1877, p. 1. ProQuest Historical Newspapers: *The Louisville Courier-Journal (1869–1922)*; "Base-Ball," *Cincinnati Enquirer*, February 23, 1877, p. 5. ProQuest Historical Newspapers: *The Cincinnati Enquirer (1841–1922)*.

16. "League Lingo," *The Louisville Courier-Journal*, February 11, 1877, p. 1. ProQuest Historical Newspapers: *The Louisville Courier-Journal (1869–1922)*; "The Louisville Nine," *The Louisville Courier-Journal*, February 18, 1877, p. 1. ProQuest Historical Newspapers: *The Louisville Courier-Journal (1869–1922)*; "Our Nine Complete," *The Louisville Courier-Journal*, March 4, 1877, p. 1. ProQuest Historical Newspapers: *The Louisville Courier-Journal (1869–1922)*.

17. Palmer, et al., *Athletic Sports in America*, at 69; "Counting the Chicken," *The Louisville Courier-Journal*, March 11, 1877, p. 1. ProQuest Historical Newspapers: *The Louisville Courier-Journal (1869–1922)*; "Baseball," *New York Clipper*, October 13, 1877, p. 226.

18. "Diamond Dust," *The Louisville Courier-Journal*, January 17, 1877, p. 4. ProQuest Historical Newspapers: *The Louisville Courier-Journal (1869–1922)*; "League Lingo," *The Louisville Courier-Journal*, February 11, 1877, p. 1. ProQuest Historical Newspapers: *The Louisville Courier-Journal (1869–1922)*; "Louisville Nine," *The Louisville Courier-Journal*, February 18, 1877, p. 1. ProQuest Historical Newspapers: *The Louisville Courier-Journal (1869–1922)*; "Our Nine Complete," *The Louisville Courier-Journal*, March 4, 1877, ProQuest Historical Newspapers: *The Louisville Courier-Journal (1869–1922)*; "Base-Ball," *Cincinnati Enquirer*, April 15, 1877, p. 2. ProQuest Historical Newspapers: *The Cincinnati Enquirer (1841–1922)*.

19. Albertson, Matt, "George Hall,"

Society for American Baseball Research (sabr.org).

20. Ginsburg, *The Fix Is In*, at 45; Cook, *The Louisville Grays Scandal*, at 16; Nemec, *The Great Encyclopedia*, at 20, 32, 48, 59, 74 and 96.

21. Nemec, *The Great Encyclopedia*, at 91; "The Game Today—Professionals vs. Amateurs," *The Louisville Courier-Journal*, April 7, 1877, p. 4. ProQuest Historical Newspapers: *The Louisville Courier-Journal (1869–1922)*.

22. "Come, Gentle Spring," *The Louisville Courier-Journal*, February 25, 1877, p. 1. ProQuest Historical Newspapers: *The Louisville Courier-Journal (1869–1922)*.

23. "Looming Up," *The Louisville Courier-Journal*, March 25, 1877, p. 3. ProQuest Historical Newspapers: *The Louisville Courier-Journal (1869–1922)*.

24. "Base Ball," *The Louisville Courier-Journal*, May 5, 1877, p. 1. ProQuest Historical Newspapers: *The Louisville Courier-Journal (1869–1922)*; "Base-Ball," *Cincinnati Enquirer*, May 4, 1877, p. 8. ProQuest Historical Newspapers: *The Cincinnati Enquirer (1841–1922)*; "Ludlows Laid Low," *The Louisville Courier-Journal*, May 3, 1877, p. 1. ProQuest Historical Newspapers: *The Louisville Courier-Journal (1869–1922)*; Seymour and Mills, *Baseball*, at 117–118.

25. "General Notes," *The Louisville Courier-Journal*, May 13, 1877, p. 1. ProQuest Historical Newspapers: *The Louisville Courier-Journal (1869–1922)*.

26. Sullivan, Josh, "Bill Craver," Society for American Baseball Research (sabr.org).

27. Sullivan, Josh, "Bill Craver," Society for American Baseball Research (sabr.org); Nemec, *The Great Encyclopedia*, at 21; Ginsburg, *The Fix Is In*, at 44; "Base Ball," *The Louisville Courier-Journal*, August 28, 1869, p. 3. ProQuest Historical Newspapers: *The Louisville Courier-Journal (1869–1922)*.

28. "Our Nine Complete," *The Louisville Courier-Journal*, March 4, 1877, p. 1. ProQuest Historical Newspapers: *The Louisville Courier-Journal (1869–1922)*.

29. "Our Nine Complete," *The Louisville Courier-Journal*, March 4, 1877, p. 1. ProQuest Historical Newspapers: *The Louisville Courier-Journal (1869–1922)*; Nemec, *The Great Encyclopedia*, at 32 and 48.

30. "Forward March!" *The Louisville Courier-Journal*, March 11, 1877, p. 1. ProQuest Historical Newspapers: *The Louisville Courier-Journal (1869–1922)*.

31. "General Notes," *The Louisville Courier-Journal*, May 13, 1877, p. 1. ProQuest Historical Newspapers: *The Louisville Courier-Journal (1869–1922)*.

32. "In Working Harness," and "A Pleasant Evening and an Enjoyable Entertainment," *The Louisville Courier-Journal*, April 8, 1877, p. 1. ProQuest Historical Newspapers: *The Louisville Courier-Journal (1869–1922)*.

33. "A Pleasant Evening and an Enjoyable Entertainment," *The Louisville Courier-Journal*, April 8, 1877, p. 1. ProQuest Historical Newspapers: *The Louisville Courier-Journal (1869–1922)*.

34. "Base Ball," *The Louisville Courier-Journal*, May 4, 1877, p. 1. ProQuest Historical Newspapers: *The Louisville Courier-Journal (1869–1922)*; "Base Ball," *The Louisville Courier-Journal*, May 5, 1877, p. 1. ProQuest Historical Newspapers: *The Louisville Courier-Journal (1869–1922)*; "Base Ball," *The Louisville Courier-Journal*, May 6, 1877, p. 1. ProQuest Historical Newspapers: *The Louisville Courier-Journal (1869–1922)*; "Base Ball," *The Louisville Courier-Journal*, May 7, 1877, p. 1. ProQuest Historical Newspapers: *The Louisville Courier-Journal (1869–1922)*; "Base Ball," *The Louisville Courier-Journal*, May 8, 1877, p. 1. ProQuest Historical Newspapers: *The Louisville Courier-Journal (1869–1922)*.

35. "Waving the Willow," *The Louisville Courier-Journal*, May 11, 1877, p. 1. ProQuest Historical Newspapers: *The Louisville Courier-Journal (1869–1922)*.

36. "General Notes," *The Louisville Courier-Journal*, May 11, 1877, p. 1. ProQuest Historical Newspapers: *The Louisville Courier-Journal (1869–1922)*.

37. "Base Ball," *The Louisville Courier-Journal*, May 14, 1877, p. 4. ProQuest Historical Newspapers: *The Louisville Courier-Journal (1869–1922)*; "Let's Take a Walk!" *The Louisville Courier-Journal*, May 13, 1877, p. 1. ProQuest Historical Newspapers: *The Louisville Courier-Journal (1869–1922)*; "A Rattling Victory," *The Louisville Courier-Journal*, May 15, 1877, p. 1. ProQuest Historical Newspapers: *The Louisville Courier-Journal (1869–1922)*.

38. "What an Umpire Can Do," *The*

Louisville Courier-Journal, May 16, 1877, p. 1. ProQuest Historical Newspapers: *The Louisville Courier-Journal (1869–1922)*.

39. "What an Umpire Can Do," *The Louisville Courier-Journal*, May 16, 1877, p. 1. ProQuest Historical Newspapers: *The Louisville Courier-Journal (1869–1922)*; "Won by One," *The Louisville Courier-Journal*, May 17, 1877, p. 1. ProQuest Historical Newspapers: *The Louisville Courier-Journal (1869–1922)*.

40. "What an Umpire Can Do," *The Louisville Courier-Journal*, May 16, 1877, p. 1. ProQuest Historical Newspapers: *The Louisville Courier-Journal (1869–1922)*.

41. "The League Meeting at Indianapolis," *The Louisville Courier-Journal*, May 16, 1877, p. 1. ProQuest Historical Newspapers: *The Louisville Courier-Journal (1869–1922)*; "The Louisvilles Apologize," *Cincinnati Enquirer*, May 18, 1877, p. 8. ProQuest Historical Newspapers: *The Cincinnati Enquirer (1841–1922)*.

42. "At the Home Plate Again," *The Louisville Courier-Journal*, May 27, 1877, p. 1. ProQuest Historical Newspapers: *The Louisville Courier-Journal (1869–1922)*; "Base Ball," *The Louisville Courier-Journal*, May 25, 1877, p. 1. ProQuest Historical Newspapers: *The Louisville Courier-Journal (1869–1922)*; "Base Ball," *The Louisville Courier-Journal*, May 26, 1877, p. 1. ProQuest Historical Newspapers: *The Louisville Courier-Journal (1869–1922)*; "At the Home Plate Again," *The Louisville Courier-Journal*, May 27, 1877, p. 1. ProQuest Historical Newspapers: *The Louisville Courier-Journal (1869–1922)*; "Base Ball," *The Louisville Courier-Journal*, May 29, 1877, p. 1. ProQuest Historical Newspapers: *The Louisville Courier-Journal (1869–1922)*.

43. "Feeble Fielding," *The Louisville Courier-Journal*, May 30, 1877, p. 4. ProQuest Historical Newspapers: *The Louisville Courier-Journal (1869–1922)*; "Twenty-Two Base Hits," *The Louisville Courier-Journal*, May 31, 1877, p. 4. ProQuest Historical Newspapers: *The Louisville Courier-Journal (1869–1922)*.

44. "Base Ball," *The Louisville Courier-Journal*, June 16, 1877, p. 4. ProQuest Historical Newspapers: *The Louisville Courier-Journal (1869–1922)*.

45. "Base Ball," *The Louisville Courier-Journal*, June 16, 1877, p. 4.

ProQuest Historical Newspapers: *The Louisville Courier-Journal (1869–1922)*; "Base-Ball," *Cincinnati Enquirer*, June 17, 1877, p. 7. ProQuest Historical Newspapers: *The Cincinnati Enquirer (1841–1922)*; "Their Highness!" *The Louisville Courier-Journal*, June 17, 1877, p. 1. ProQuest Historical Newspapers: *The Louisville Courier-Journal (1869–1922)*; "Base Ball," *The Louisville Courier-Journal*, June 19, 1877, p. 1. ProQuest Historical Newspapers: *The Louisville Courier-Journal (1869–1922)*; "Base Ball," *The Louisville Courier-Journal*, June 20, 1877, p. 1. ProQuest Historical Newspapers: *The Louisville Courier-Journal (1869–1922)*; Cook, *Louisville Grays Scandal*, at 86 and 94.

46. Cook, *Louisville Grays Scandal*, at 94–95; Nemec, *The Great Encyclopedia*, at 99; "Base-Ball," *Cincinnati Enquirer*, June 17, 1877, p. 7. ProQuest Historical Newspapers: *The Cincinnati Enquirer (1841–1922)*.

47. "Base Ball," *The Louisville Courier-Journal*, June 21, 1877, p. 1. ProQuest Historical Newspapers: *The Louisville Courier-Journal (1869–1922)*.

48. "Base-Ball," *Cincinnati Enquirer*, June 21, 1877, p. 2. ProQuest Historical Newspapers: *The Cincinnati Enquirer (1841–1922)*.

49. "Base Ball," *The Louisville Courier-Journal*, June 23, 1877, p. 4. ProQuest Historical Newspapers: *The Louisville Courier-Journal (1869–1922)*; "Valiantly at Work," *The Louisville Courier-Journal*, June 24, 1877, p. 1. ProQuest Historical Newspapers: *The Louisville Courier-Journal (1869–1922)*; "Base-Ball," *Cincinnati Enquirer*, June 26, 1877, p. 2. ProQuest Historical Newspapers: *The Cincinnati Enquirer (1841–1922)*.

50. "Good!" *The Louisville Courier-Journal*, July 6, 1877, p. 4. ProQuest Historical Newspapers: *The Louisville Courier-Journal (1869–1922)*; Morris, *A Game of Inches*, at Sec. 9.4.2, at 432.

51. Morris, *A Game of Inches*, Sec. 6.5.1 at 341.

52. "The Same Old Story," *The Louisville Courier-Journal*, July 4, 1877, p. 2. ProQuest Historical Newspapers: *The Louisville Courier-Journal (1869–1922)*; "Base-Ball," *Cincinnati Enquirer*, July 4, 1877, p. 2. ProQuest Historical Newspapers: *The Cincinnati Enquirer (1841–1922)*.

53. "Yesterday's Game in Louisville,"

The Louisville Courier-Journal, July 5, 1877, ProQuest Historical Newspapers: *The Louisville Courier-Journal (1869–1922).*

54. "Good!" *The Louisville Courier-Journal,* July 6, 1877, p. 4. ProQuest Historical Newspapers: *The Louisville Courier-Journal (1869–1922);* "Got 'Em Again," *Cincinnati Enquirer,* July 6, 1877, p. 8. ProQuest Historical Newspapers: *The Cincinnati Enquirer (1841–1922);* "General Notes," *The Louisville Courier-Journal,* July 6, 1877, p. 4. ProQuest Historical Newspapers: *The Louisville Courier-Journal (1869–1922).*

55. "Base Ball," *Cincinnati Enquirer,* July 11, 1877, p. 7. ProQuest Historical Newspapers: *The Cincinnati Enquirer (1841–1922).*

56. "General Notes," *The Louisville Courier-Journal,* July 5, 1877, p. 4. ProQuest Historical Newspapers: *The Louisville Courier-Journal (1869–1922);* "Base Ball," *The Louisville Courier-Journal,* July 7, 1877, p. 4. ProQuest Historical Newspapers: *The Louisville Courier-Journal (1869–1922);* "General Notes," *The Louisville Courier-Journal,* July 12, 1877, p. 1. ProQuest Historical Newspapers: *The Louisville Courier-Journal (1869–1922).*

Chapter Four

1. "General Notes," *The Louisville Courier-Journal,* July 8, 1877, p. 1. ProQuest Historical Newspapers: *The Louisville Courier-Journal (1869–1922).*

2. "Base-Ball," *The Louisville Courier-Journal,* July 10, 1877, p. 4. ProQuest Historical Newspapers: *The Louisville Courier-Journal(1869–1922);* Cook, *Louisville Grays Scandal,* at 99; "General Notes," *The Louisville Courier-Journal,* July 10, 1877, p. 4. ProQuest Historical Newspapers: *The Louisville Courier-Journal (1869–1922);* "It Is All True," *The Louisville Courier-Journal,* July 12, 1877, p. 1. ProQuest Historical Newspapers: *The Louisville Courier-Journal (1869–1922);* "The Championship Record," *New York Clipper,* July 21, 1877, p. 131.

3. "General Notes," *The Louisville Courier-Journal,* July 10, 1877, p. 4. ProQuest Historical Newspapers: *The Louisville Courier-Journal (1869–1922);* "Beaten at Last," *The Louisville Courier-Journal,* July 12, 1877, p. 1. ProQuest Historical Newspapers: *The Louisville Courier-Journal (1869–1922).*

4. "We Ride the Top Wave," *The Louisville Courier-Journal,* July 13, 1877, p. 1. ProQuest Historical Newspapers: *The Louisville Courier-Journal (1869–1922).*

5. "We Ride the Top Wave," *The Louisville Courier-Journal,* July 13, 1877, p. 1. ProQuest Historical Newspapers: *The Louisville Courier-Journal (1869–1922).*

6. "We Took 'Em In," *The Louisville Courier-Journal,* April 17, 1877, p. 4. ProQuest Historical Newspapers: *The Louisville Courier-Journal (1869–1922).*

7. "A Day of Surprises," *The Louisville Courier-Journal,* July 14, 1877, p. 1. ProQuest Historical Newspapers: *The Louisville Courier-Journal (1869–1922);* "Gallant Grays," *The Louisville Courier-Journal,* July 15, 1877, p. 1. ProQuest Historical Newspapers: *The Louisville Courier-Journal (1869–1922).*

8. "As Luck Would Have It," *The Louisville Courier-Journal,* July 21, 1877, p. 4. ProQuest Historical Newspapers: *The Louisville Courier-Journal (1869–1922).*

9. "The Gray Above the Red" and "General Notes," *The Louisville Courier-Journal,* July 24, 1877, p. 4. ProQuest Historical Newspapers: *The Louisville Courier-Journal (1869–1922).*

10. "General Notes," *The Louisville Courier-Journal,* July 24, 1877, p. 4. ProQuest Historical Newspapers: *The Louisville Courier-Journal (1869–1922);* "Base Ball," *The Louisville Courier-Journal,* December 5, 1877, p. 1. ProQuest Historical Newspapers: *The Louisville Courier-Journal (1869–1922).*

11. "Base Ball," *The Louisville Courier-Journal,* July 31, 1877, p. 4. ProQuest Historical Newspapers: *The Louisville Courier-Journal (1869–1922).*

12. "Sic Semper McManus," *The Louisville Courier-Journal,* August 2, 1877, p. 4. ProQuest Historical Newspapers: *The Louisville Courier-Journal (1869–1922).*

13. "That Bribery Affair," *The Louisville Courier-Journal,* August 3, 1877, p. 1. ProQuest Historical Newspapers: *The Louisville Courier-Journal (1869–1922);* "General Notes," *The Louisville Courier-Journal,* August 10, 1877, p. 4. ProQuest Historical Newspapers: *The Louisville Courier-Journal (1869–1922).*

14. "Base Ball," *Louisville Commercial*, August 4, 1877, p. 5.

15. "Let St. Louis Investigate," *The Louisville Courier-Journal*, August 6, 1877, p. 1. ProQuest Historical Newspapers: *The Louisville Courier-Journal (1869–1922)*.

16. "The Devinney-McManus Affair," *The Louisville Courier-Journal*, August 19, 1877, p. 1. ProQuest Historical Newspapers: *The Louisville Courier-Journal (1869–1922)*.

17. "Base Ball," *The Louisville Courier-Journal*, May 30, 1876, p. 3. ProQuest Historical Newspapers: *The Louisville Courier-Journal (1869–1922)*; "Fouls and Strikes," *The Louisville Courier-Journal*, March 24, 1876, p. 4. ProQuest Historical Newspapers: *The Louisville Courier-Journal (1869–1922)*; "Base Ball," *The Louisville Courier-Journal*, May 31, 1876, p. 4. ProQuest Historical Newspapers: *The Louisville Courier-Journal (1869–1922)*. "Base Ball," *The Louisville Courier-Journal*, June 6, 1876, p. 4. ProQuest Historical Newspapers: *The Louisville Courier-Journal (1869–1922)*; "Base Ball," *The Louisville Courier-Journal*, July 25, 1876, p. 4. ProQuest Historical Newspapers: *The Louisville Courier-Journal (1869–1922)*.

18. "General Notes," *The Louisville Courier-Journal*, August 4, 1877, p. 1. ProQuest Historical Newspapers: *The Louisville Courier-Journal (1869–1922)*; "Base Ball," *The Louisville Courier-Journal*, August 5, 1877, p. 1. ProQuest Historical Newspapers: *The Louisville Courier-Journal (1869–1922)*; "General Notes," *The Louisville Courier-Journal*, August 5, 1877, p. 1. ProQuest Historical Newspapers: *The Louisville Courier-Journal (1869–1922)*.

19. "We Would Not Win Always," *The Louisville Courier-Journal*, August 7, 1877, p. 4. ProQuest Historical Newspapers: *The Louisville Courier-Journal (1869–1922)*.

20. "An Outrageous Falsehood," *The Louisville Courier-Journal*, August 10, 1877, p. 4. ProQuest Historical Newspapers: *The Louisville Courier-Journal (1869–1922)*; Cook, *The Louisville Grays Scandal*, at 104–105.

21. "Base Ball," *The Louisville Courier-Journal*, August 5, 1877, p. 1. ProQuest Historical Newspapers: *The Louisville Courier-Journal (1869–1922)*.

22. "General Notes," *The Louisville Courier-Journal*, June 12, 1877, p. 1. ProQuest Historical Newspapers: *The Louisville Courier-Journal (1869–1922)*.

23. "Sporting News," *Chicago Tribune*, June 1, 1877, p. 5; "The Field Turf," *Chicago Tribune*, June 3, 1877, p. 7.

24. "Lime Balls," *The Louisville Courier-Journal*, March 4, 1877, p. 1. ProQuest Historical Newspapers: *The Louisville Courier-Journal (1869–1922)*; "Base-Ball," *Cincinnati Enquirer*, April 18, 1877, p. 5. ProQuest Historical Newspapers: *The Cincinnati Enquirer (1841–1922)*; "Outrageous Falsehood," *The Louisville Courier-Journal*, August 10, 1877, p. 4. ProQuest Historical Newspapers: *The Louisville Courier-Journal (1869–1922)*; "Completely Squelched," *The Louisville Courier-Journal*, August 14, 1877, p. 4. ProQuest Historical Newspapers: *The Louisville Courier-Journal (1869–1922)*.

25. "We Would Not Win Always," *The Louisville Courier-Journal*, August 7, 1877, p. 4. ProQuest Historical Newspapers: *The Louisville Courier-Journal (1869–1922)*.

26. Melville, *Early Baseball*, at 91.

27. "General Notes," *The Louisville Courier-Journal*, August 8, 1877, p. 4. ProQuest Historical Newspapers: *The Louisville Courier-Journal (1869–1922)*.

28. "As a Matter of Course" and "General Notes," *The Louisville Courier-Journal*, August 9, 1877, p. 4. ProQuest Historical Newspapers: *The Louisville Courier-Journal (1869–1922)*.

29. "Onward and Upward," *The Louisville Courier-Journal*, August 14, 1877, p. 4. ProQuest Historical Newspapers: *The Louisville Courier-Journal (1869–1922)*.

30. "Gossip Over the Game," *Louisville Commercial*, August 7, 1877, p. 5.

31. "Notes, News and Miscellany," *Cincinnati Enquirer*, August 14, 1877, p. 7. ProQuest Historical Newspapers: *The Cincinnati Enquirer (1841–1922)*; "Bounce Win," *Cincinnati Enquirer*, August 14, 1877, ProQuest Historical Newspapers: *The Cincinnati Enquirer (1841–1922)*; "Onward and Upward," *The Louisville Courier-Journal*, August 14, 1877, p. 4. ProQuest Historical Newspapers: *The Louisville Courier-Journal (1869–1922)*; "Baseball," *New York Clipper*, August 11, 1877, p. 155.

32. "General Notes," *The Louisville Courier-Journal*, August 15, 1877, p. 4.

ProQuest Historical Newspapers: *The Louisville Courier-Journal (1869–1922)*.

33. "Notes, News and Miscellany," *Cincinnati Enquirer*, August 14, 1877, p. 7. ProQuest Historical Newspapers: *The Cincinnati Enquirer (1841–1922)*.

Chapter Five

1. "Base Ball," *The Louisville Courier-Journal*, August 15, 1877, p. 4. ProQuest Historical Newspapers: *The Louisville Courier-Journal (1869–1922)*; "Base Ball," *The Louisville Courier-Journal*, August 16, 1877, p. 4. ProQuest Historical Newspapers: *The Louisville Courier-Journal (1869–1922)*.

2. "Sports of the Season," *Boston Globe*, August 18, 1877, p. 5; "Accidents Will Happen," *The Louisville Courier-Journal*, August 18, 1877, p. 4. ProQuest Historical Newspapers: *The Louisville Courier-Journal (1869–1922)*; "Round the Sphere," *The Louisville Courier-Journal*, August 19, 1877, p. 1. ProQuest Historical Newspapers: *The Louisville Courier-Journal (1869–1922)*.

3. "Sports of the Season," *Boston Globe*, August 18, 1877, p. 5; Macdonald, *The League That Lasted*, at 105.

4. Nemec, *The Great Encyclopedia*, at 98.

5. Palmer, et al., *Athletic Sports in America*, at 73.

6. Palmer, et al., *Athletic Sports in America*, at 73.

7. Palmer, et al., *Athletic Sports in America*, at 73.

8. Palmer, et al., *Athletic Sports in America*, at 73; Ginsburg, *The Fix Is In*, at 46; Cook, *The Louisville Grays Scandal*, at 122.

9. Ginsburg, *The Fix Is In*, at 46; Allen, *The National League Story*, at 19; Cook, *The Louisville Grays Scandal*, at 107–108.

10. Palmer, et al., *Athletic Sport in America*, at 73.

11. Palmer, et al., *Athletic Sport in America*, at 73.

12. "Chicagoed," *Brooklyn Daily Eagle*, August 22, 1877; "What's the Matter?" *The Louisville Courier-Journal*, August 22, 1877, p. 4. ProQuest Historical Newspapers: *The Louisville Courier-Journal (1869–1922)*; "Summer Pastimes," *Boston Globe*, August 22, 1877, p. 5.

13. Palmer, et al., *Athletic Sport in America*, at 73.

14. "Fast Fading," *The Louisville Courier-Journal*, August 29, 1877, p. 4. ProQuest Historical Newspapers: *The Louisville Courier-Journal (1869–1922)*; "Base Ball," *The Louisville Courier-Journal*, September 7, 1877, p. 1. ProQuest Historical Newspapers: *The Louisville Courier-Journal (1869–1922)*; "Mitchell's Misery," *The Louisville Courier-Journal*, September 15, 1877, p. 4. ProQuest Historical Newspapers: *The Louisville Courier-Journal (1869–1922)*.

15. "Base Ball," *The Louisville Courier-Journal*, August 30, 1877, p. 4. ProQuest Historical Newspapers: *The Louisville Courier-Journal (1869–1922)*; "The National Pastime," *The Louisville Courier-Journal*, September 2, 1877, p. 1. ProQuest Historical Newspapers: *The Louisville Courier-Journal (1869–1922)*; "Base Ball," *The Louisville Courier-Journal*, September 4, 1877, p. 4. ProQuest Historical Newspapers: *The Louisville Courier-Journal (1869–1922)*; "Base Ball," *The Louisville Courier-Journal*, September 5, 1877, p. 4. ProQuest Historical Newspapers: *The Louisville Courier-Journal (1869–1922)*; "Base Ball," *The Louisville Courier-Journal*, September 7, 1877, p. 1. ProQuest Historical Newspapers: *The Louisville Courier-Journal (1869–1922)*; "Base Ball," *The Louisville Courier-Journal*, September 12, 1877, p. 4. ProQuest Historical Newspapers: *The Louisville Courier-Journal (1869–1922)*; "Base Ball," *The Louisville Courier-Journal*, September 16, 1877, p. 1. ProQuest Historical Newspapers: *The Louisville Courier-Journal (1869–1922)*; "Base Ball," *The Louisville Courier-Journal*, September 20, 1877, p. 1. ProQuest Historical Newspapers: *The Louisville Courier-Journal (1869–1922)*; "Base Ball," *The Louisville Courier-Journal*, September 26, 1877, p. 4. ProQuest Historical Newspapers: *The Louisville Courier-Journal (1869–1922)*.

16. "Base Ball," *Louisville Commercial*, August 4, 1877, p. 5; "!!!—???—!!!" *The Louisville Courier-Journal*, August 21, 1877, p. 4. ProQuest Historical Newspapers: *The Louisville Courier-Journal (1869–1922)*; "What's the Matter," *The Louisville Courier-Journal*, August 22, 1877, p. 4. ProQuest Historical Newspapers:

The Louisville Courier-Journal (1869–1922).

17. "Seven to Nothing," *Cincinnati Enquirer*, August 22, 1877, p. 2. ProQuest Historical Newspapers: *The Cincinnati Enquirer (1841–1922)*; "A Tie Game," *The Louisville Courier-Journal*, August 24, 1877, p. 4. ProQuest Historical Newspapers: *The Louisville Courier-Journal (1869–1922).*

18. "The World of Sports," *Boston Globe*, August 27, 1877, p. 2; "We May Be Happy Yet," *The Louisville Courier-Journal*, August 26, 1877, p. 2. ProQuest Historical Newspapers: *The Louisville Courier-Journal (1869–1922).*

19. "The League Championship," *New York Clipper*, September 1, 1877, p. 179.

20. "Victory Vanishes," *The Louisville Courier-Journal*, August 28, 1877, p. 1. ProQuest Historical Newspapers: *The Louisville Courier-Journal (1869–1922).*

21. "Cussed Crookedness," *The Louisville Courier-Journal*, November 3, 1877, p. 4. ProQuest Historical Newspapers: *The Louisville Courier-Journal (1869–1922)*; "The Lowells Win a Spendid Victory from the Louisvilles," *Boston Globe*, August 30, 1877, p. 4.

22. "Base Ball," *The Louisville Courier-Journal*, August 30, 1877, p. 4. ProQuest Historical Newspapers: *The Louisville Courier-Journal (1869–1922).*

23. "A Base Ball Victory," *Brooklyn Daily Eagle*, September 1, 1877, p. 2.

24. "The Boys Have Been Traveling," *The Louisville Courier-Journal*, September 1, 1877, p. 4. ProQuest Historical Newspapers: *The Louisville Courier-Journal (1869–1922).*

25. "Devlin vs Mitchell," *The Louisville Courier-Journal*, September 14, 1877, p. 4. ProQuest Historical Newspapers: *The Louisville Courier-Journal (1869–1922)*; "General Notes," *The Louisville Courier-Journal*, October 3, 1877, p. 1. ProQuest Historical Newspapers: *The Louisville Courier-Journal (1869–1922)*; Gelzheiser, *Labor and Capital*, at 36.

26. "Base Ball," "The Boys Have Been Traveling," and "General Notes," *The Louisville Courier-Journal*, September 1, 1877, p. 4. ProQuest Historical Newspapers: *The Louisville Courier-Journal (1869–1922)*; "But It Doesn't Count," *The Louisville Courier-Journal*, September 2, 1877, p. 1.

ProQuest Historical Newspapers: *The Louisville Courier-Journal (1869–1922).*

27. "Baseball," *New York Clipper*, September 15, 1877, p. 197; "Base Ball," *The Louisville Courier-Journal*, September 4, 1877, p. 4. ProQuest Historical Newspapers: *The Louisville Courier-Journal (1869–1922)*; "Cussed Crookedness," *The Louisville Courier-Journal*, November 3, 1877, p. 4. ProQuest Historical Newspapers: *The Louisville Courier-Journal (1869–1922)*; "Base Ball," *The Louisville Courier-Journal*, September 5, 1877, p. 4. ProQuest Historical Newspapers: *The Louisville Courier-Journal (1869–1922)*; "Base Ball," *The Louisville Courier-Journal*, September 6, 1877, p. 4. ProQuest Historical Newspapers: *The Louisville Courier-Journal (1869–1922)*; "Cussed Crookedness," *The Louisville Courier-Journal*, November 3, 1877, p. 4. ProQuest Historical Newspapers: *The Louisville Courier-Journal (1869–1922).*

28. "Cussed Crookedness," *The Louisville Courier-Journal*, November 3, 1877, p. 4. ProQuest Historical Newspapers: *The Louisville Courier-Journal (1869–1922).*

29. "General Notes," *The Louisville Courier-Journal*, September 4, 1877, p. 4. ProQuest Historical Newspapers: *The Louisville Courier-Journal (1869–1922)*; "General Notes," *The Louisville Courier-Journal*, September 6, 1877, p. 4. ProQuest Historical Newspapers: *The Louisville Courier-Journal (1869–1922).*

30. Palmer, et al., *Athletic Sports in America,* at 75–76.

31. Palmer, et al., *Athletic Sports in America,* at 75–76.

32. "Amateurs vs. Mutuals," *The Louisville Courier-Journal*, September 8, 1877, p. 1. ProQuest Historical Newspapers: *The Louisville Courier-Journal (1869–1922).*

33. "Weak with the Willow," *The Louisville Courier-Journal*, September 9, 1877, p. 1. ProQuest Historical Newspapers: *The Louisville Courier-Journal (1869–1922).*

34. "Professional vs. Amateurs" and "General Notes," *The Louisville Courier-Journal*, September 12, 1877, p. 4. ProQuest Historical Newspapers: *The Louisville Courier-Journal (1869–1922).*

35. "Devlin vs Mitchell," *The Louisville Courier-Journal*, September 14, 1877, p. 4. ProQuest Historical Newspapers: *The Louisville Courier-Journal (1869–1922).*

36. "Base-Ball," *Cincinnati Enquirer*, September 15, 1877, p. 2. ProQuest Historical Newspapers: *The Cincinnati Enquirer (1841–1922)*.

37. "General Notes," *The Louisville Courier-Journal*, September 15, 1877, p. 4. ProQuest Historical Newspapers: *The Louisville Courier-Journal (1869–1922)*.

38. Cook, *Louisville Grays Scandal*, at 116.

39. "Base Ball," *The Louisville Courier-Journal*, September 25, 1877, p. 4. ProQuest Historical Newspapers: *The Louisville Courier-Journal (1869–1922)*; "Cussed Crookedness," *The Louisville Courier-Journal*, November 3, 1877, p. 4. ProQuest Historical Newspapers: *The Louisville Courier-Journal (1869–1922)*; "Base Ball," *The Louisville Courier-Journal*, September 26, 1877, p. 4. ProQuest Historical Newspapers: *The Louisville Courier-Journal (1869–1922)*.

40. "Base-Ball," *Cincinnati Enquirer*, September 27, 1877, p. 2. ProQuest Historical Newspapers: *The Cincinnati Enquirer (1841–1922)*; "Monumental Muffing," *The Louisville Courier-Journal*, September 27, 1872, p. 4. ProQuest Historical Newspapers: *The Louisville Courier-Journal (1869–1922)*.

41. Cook, *The Louisville Grays Scandal* at 124 and 131.

42. Palmer, et al., *Athletic Sports in America*, at 69–70.

Chapter Six

1. "Base Ball," *The Louisville Courier-Journal*, September 16, 1877, p. 1. ProQuest Historical Newspapers: *The Louisville Courier-Journal (1869–1922)*; "General Notes," *The Louisville Courier-Journal*, September 11, 1877, p. 4. ProQuest Historical Newspapers: *The Louisville Courier-Journal (1869–1922)*; "Base-Ball," *Cincinnati Enquirer*, September 22, 1877, p. 6. ProQuest Historical Newspapers: *The Cincinnati Enquirer (1841–1922)*.

2. "The Championship," *The Louisville Courier-Journal*, September 2, 1877, p. 1. ProQuest Historical Newspapers: *The Louisville Courier-Journal (1869–1922)*; "General Notes," *The Louisville Courier-Journal*, September 12, 1877, p.

4. ProQuest Historical Newspapers: *The Louisville Courier-Journal (1869–1922)*; "Reviewing the Situation," *The Louisville Courier-Journal*, September 14, 1877, p. 4. ProQuest Historical Newspapers: *The Louisville Courier-Journal (1869–1922)*.

3. "Base Ball," *The Louisville Courier-Journal*, December 2, 1877, p. 1. ProQuest Historical Newspapers: *The Louisville Courier-Journal (1869–1922)*.

4. "Cussed Crookedness," *The Louisville Courier-Journal*, November 3, 1877, p. 4. ProQuest Historical Newspapers: *The Louisville Courier-Journal (1869–1922)*; "General Notes," *The Louisville Courier-Journal*, September 1, 1877, p. 4. ProQuest Historical Newspapers: *The Louisville Courier-Journal (1869–1922)*; "Monumental Muffing," *The Louisville Courier-Journal*, September 27, 1877, p. 4. ProQuest Historical Newspapers: *The Louisville Courier-Journal (1869–1922)*; "When We're a Mind To," *The Louisville Courier-Journal*, September 29, 1877, p. 4. ProQuest Historical Newspapers: *The Louisville Courier-Journal (1869–1922)*.

5. "The Championship" and "General Notes," *The Louisville Courier-Journal*, October 7, 1877, p. 1. ProQuest Historical Newspapers: *The Louisville Courier-Journal (1869–1922)*.

6. "Cussed Crookedness," *The Louisville Courier-Journal*, November 3, 1877, p. 4. ProQuest Historical Newspapers: *The Louisville Courier-Journal (1869–1922)*; Palmer, et al., *Athletic Sport in America*, at 74.

7. "Base Ball," *The Louisville Courier-Journal*, October 16, 1877, p. 1. ProQuest Historical Newspapers: *The Louisville Courier-Journal (1869–1922)*; "Base Ball," *The Louisville Courier-Journal*, October 17, 1877; ProQuest Historical Newspapers: *The Louisville Courier-Journal (1869–1922)*; "Vain Glory," *The Louisville Courier-Journal*, October 18, 1877, p. 1. ProQuest Historical Newspapers: *The Louisville Courier-Journal (1869–1922)*.

8. "Vain Glory," *The Louisville Courier-Journal*, October 18, 1877, p. 1. ProQuest Historical Newspapers: *The Louisville Courier-Journal (1869–1922)*.

9. "General Notes," *The Louisville Courier-Journal*, October 18, 1877, p. 1. ProQuest Historical Newspapers: *The Louisville Courier-Journal (1869–1922)*.

10. "Base Ball," *The Louisville Courier-Journal*, October 23, 1877, p. 4. ProQuest Historical Newspapers: *The Louisville Courier-Journal (1869–1922)*; "Base Ball," *The Louisville Courier-Journal*, October 24, 1877, p. 4. ProQuest Historical Newspapers: *The Louisville Courier-Journal (1869–1922)*.

11. Palmer, et al., *Athletic Sport in America*, at 74.

12. Palmer, et al., *Athletic Sport in America*, at 74.

13. "Cussed Crookedness," *The Louisville Courier-Journal*, November 3, 1877, p. 4. ProQuest Historical Newspapers: *The Louisville Courier-Journal (1869–1922)*; Palmer, et al., *Athletic Sport in America*, at 75.

14. "Cussed Crookedness," *The Louisville Courier-Journal*, November 3, 1877, p. 4. ProQuest Historical Newspapers: *The Louisville Courier-Journal (1869–1922)*.

15. "Cussed Crookedness," *The Louisville Courier-Journal*, November 3, 1877, p. 4. ProQuest Historical Newspapers: *The Louisville Courier-Journal (1869–1922)*; Palmer, et al., *Athletic Sport in America*, at 75.

16. "Cussed Crookedness," *The Louisville Courier-Journal*, November 3, 1877, p. 4. ProQuest Historical Newspapers: *The Louisville Courier-Journal (1869–1922)*.

17. "Cussed Crookedness," *The Louisville Courier-Journal*, November 3, 1877, p. 4. ProQuest Historical Newspapers: *The Louisville Courier-Journal (1869–1922)*.

18. "Cussed Crookedness," *The Louisville Courier-Journal*, November 3, 1877, p. 4. ProQuest Historical Newspapers: *The Louisville Courier-Journal (1869–1922)*.

19. "Cussed Crookedness," *The Louisville Courier-Journal*, November 3, 1877, p. 4. ProQuest Historical Newspapers: *The Louisville Courier-Journal (1869–1922)*.

20. "Cussed Crookedness," *The Louisville Courier-Journal*, November 3, 1877, p. 4. ProQuest Historical Newspapers: *The Louisville Courier-Journal (1869–1922)*.

21. "Louisville Base-Ball Club," *The Louisville Courier-Journal*, October 31, 1877, p. 4. ProQuest Historical Newspapers: *The Louisville Courier-Journal (1869–1922)*.

22. "A Louisville Scandal," *St. Louis Globe-Democrat*, October 31, 1877, p. 3.

23. "Cussed Crookedness," *The Louisville Courier-Journal*, November 3, 1877, p. 4. ProQuest Historical Newspapers: *The Louisville Courier-Journal (1869–1922)*; "Louisville," *Cincinnati Enquirer*, November 1, 1877, p. 5. ProQuest Historical Newspapers: *The Cincinnati Enquirer (1841–1922)*.

24. "Among the Sharks," *St. Louis Globe-Democrat*, November 1, 1877, p. 8.

25. "Base Ball," *The Louisville Courier-Journal*, November 4, 1877, p. 1. ProQuest Historical Newspapers: *The Louisville Courier-Journal (1869–1922)*.

26. "Base-Ball," *The Louisville Courier-Journal*, November 4, 1877, p. 1. ProQuest Historical Newspapers: *The Louisville Courier-Journal (1869–1922)*.

27. "Base-Ball," *Cincinnati Enquirer*, November 5, 1877, p 8. ProQuest Historical Newspapers: *The Cincinnati Enquirer (1841–1922)*.

28. "Base-Ball," *Cincinnati Enquirer*, November 5, 1877, p. 8. ProQuest Historical Newspapers: *The Cincinnati Enquirer (1841–1922)*.

29. "Base-Ball," *Cincinnati Enquirer*, November 13, 1877, p. 2. ProQuest Historical Newspapers: *The Cincinnati Enquirer (1841–1922)*; Cook, *The Louisville Grays Scandal*, at 161.

30. "Cussed Crookedness," *The Louisville Courier-Journal*, November 3, 1877, p. 4. ProQuest Historical Newspapers: *The Louisville Courier-Journal (1869–1922)*.

31. "Baseball," *New York Clipper*, November 10, 1877, p. 258.

32. "Cussed Crookedness," *The Louisville Courier-Journal*, November 3, 1877, p. 4. ProQuest Historical Newspapers: *The Louisville Courier-Journal (1869–1922)*.

33. "Cussed Crookedness," *The Louisville Courier-Journal*, November 3, 1877, p. 4. ProQuest Historical Newspapers: *The Louisville Courier-Journal (1869–1922)*; Palmer, et al., *Athletic Sport in America*, at 75.

34. "Base-Ball," *Cincinnati Enquirer*, November 5, 1877, p. 8. ProQuest Historical Newspapers: *The Cincinnati Enquirer (1841–1922)*; Cusick, "Gentleman of the Press," at 226.

35. "Craver Croaks," *The Louisville Courier-Journal*, November 4, 1877, p. 1. ProQuest Historical Newspapers: *The Louisville Courier-Journal (1869–1922)*.

36. "The Sporting World," *Boston Globe*, November 9, 1877, p. 1.

37. "Base Ball," *Boston Globe*, November 11, 1877, p. 8.

38. Letter, William Hulbert to Robert Ferguson, November 8, 1877, Abakanowicz Research Center, Chicago History Museum, Chicago Cubs Correspondence 1875–1880, Box Z.

39. "The League," *Cincinnati Enquirer*, December 5, 1877, p. 8. ProQuest Historical Newspapers: *The Cincinnati Enquirer (1841–1922)*; "Base Ball," *The Louisville Courier-Journal*, December 5, 1877, p. 1. ProQuest Historical Newspapers: *The Louisville Courier-Journal (1869–1922)*; "Base Ball," *The Louisville Courier-Journal*, December 6, 1877, p. 1. ProQuest Historical Newspapers: *The Louisville Courier-Journal (1869–1922)*.

40. "Base-Ball," *Cincinnati Enquirer*, November 13, 1877, p. 2. ProQuest Historical Newspapers: *The Cincinnati Enquirer (1841–1922)*.

41. Cook, *The Louisville Grays Scandal*, at 148.

42. "The Craver Case," *The New York Clipper*, December 29, 1877, p. 314.

43. Spalding, *Base Ball*, at 142.

Chapter Seven

1. "National League of Professional Clubs," *New York Clipper*, February 12, 1876, p. 2.

2. "Base-Ball," *Cincinnati Enquirer*, February 23, 1878, p. 8. ProQuest Historical Newspapers: *The Cincinnati Enquirer (1841–1922)*.

3. "No Base Ball in Louisville This Season," *The Louisville Courier-Journal*, March 8, 1878, p. 4. ProQuest Historical Newspapers: *The Louisville Courier-Journal (1869–1922)*.

4. "Base Ball," *The Louisville Courier-Journal*, April 28, 1878, p. 4. ProQuest Historical Newspapers: *The Louisville Courier-Journal (1869–1922)*.

5. "Base Ball," *The Louisville Courier-Journal*, May 1, 1878, p. 4. ProQuest Historical Newspapers: *The Louisville Courier-Journal (1869–1922)*.

6. "Base Ball," *The Louisville Courier-Journal*, May 4, 1878, p. 1. ProQuest Historical Newspapers: *The Louisville Courier-Journal (1869–1922)*.

7. "League Literature," *The Louisville Courier-Journal*, March 18, 1877, p. 2. ProQuest Historical Newspapers: *The Louisville Courier-Journal (1869–1922)*.

8. "Finley Signs Contract to Transfer Athletics to Louisville," *New York Times*, January 6, 1964; "AL Rejects A's Move, 9–1," *New York Daily News*, January 17, 1964, p. 573.

9. Macdonald, *The League That Lasted*, at 28, 56 and 212–213; Allen, *The National League Story* at 15.

10. Seymour and Mills, *Baseball*, at 106–109; "Death of W.A. Hulbert," *The Louisville Courier-Journal*, April 11, 1882, p. 2. ProQuest Historical Newspapers: *The Louisville Courier-Journal (1869–1922)*.

11. "Jack Chapman Talks of the National Game," *Brooklyn Daily Eagle*, March 26, 1905, p. 21.

12. "The City," *The Louisville Daily Journal*, July 2, 1868, p. 4. ProQuest Historical Newspapers: *The Louisville Courier-Journal (1839–1868)*; "Base Ball," *The Louisville Daily Journal*, July 3, 1868, p. 4. ProQuest Historical Newspapers: *The Louisville Courier-Journal (1839–1868)*; "Base Ball Match Yesterday," *Daily Courier*, July 3, 1868, p. 1. ProQuest Historical Newspapers: *Louisville Courier-Journal (1839–1868)*.

13. "Base Ball," *The Louisville Courier-Journal*, August 1, 1874, p. 4. ProQuest Historical Newspapers: *The Louisville Courier-Journal (1869–1922)*; "Base Ball," *The Louisville Courier-Journal*, August 2, 1874, p. 4. ProQuest Historical Newspapers: *The Louisville Courier-Journal (1869–1922)*; "Base Ball Items," *The Louisville Courier-Journal*, August 3, 1874, p. 3. ProQuest Historical Newspapers: *The Louisville Courier-Journal (1869–1922)*.

14. "River and Weather," *The Louisville Courier-Journal*, August 4, 1874, p. 3. ProQuest Historical Newspapers: *The Louisville Courier-Journal (1869–1922)*; "The River Disaster," *The Louisville Courier-Journal*, August 6, 1874, p. 1. ProQuest Historical Newspapers: *The Louisville Courier-Journal (1869–1922)*.

15. "Jack Chapman Talks of the National Game," *Brooklyn Daily Eagle*, March 26, 1905, p. 21; "Base Ball," *The Louisville Courier-Journal*, September 24, 1876, p. 1. ProQuest Historical Newspapers: *The Louisville Courier-Journal (1869–1922)*; Macdonald, *The League That Lasted*, at

197; Caron, *Directory of Louisville 1890*, at 196.

16. Dodgson, Lindsay, "Our Brains Sometimes Create 'False Memories,'—but Science Suggests We Could Be Better Off This Way," *Business Insider*, December 19, 2017, citing: Reyna, V.F. and C.J. Brainerd, "Fuzzy-Trace Theory: An Interim Synthesis," *Learning and Individual Differences* Volume 7, Issue 1 (1995): 1–75.

17. "Deaths," *The Louisville Courier-Journal*, November 29, 1882, p. 5. ProQuest Historical Newspapers: *The Louisville Courier-Journal (1869–1922)*; "The Death of Mrs. Chase," *The Louisville Courier-Journal*, November 29, 1882, p. 6. ProQuest Historical Newspapers: *The Louisville Courier-Journal (1869–1922)*.

18. "Personal," *Evansville Courier and Press*, January 17, 1885, p. 4; "Gossip on the Street," *The Louisville Courier-Journal*, May 30, 1886, p. 9. ProQuest Historical Newspapers: *The Louisville Courier-Journal (1869–1922)*.

19. "The Chapman Benefit," *The Louisville Courier-Journal*, September 2, 1892, p. 8. ProQuest Historical Newspapers: *The Louisville Courier-Journal (1869–1922)*; "Manager Chapman's Benefit," *The Louisville Courier-Journal*, September 3, 1892, p. 8. ProQuest Historical Newspapers: *The Louisville Courier-Journal (1869–1922)*; "Chapman Happy," *The Louisville Courier-Journal*, October 19, 1892, p. 5. ProQuest Historical Newspapers: *The Louisville Courier-Journal (1869–1922)*.

20. "Deaths and Funerals," *The Louisville Courier-Journal*, March 28, 1920, p. 9. ProQuest Historical Newspapers: *The Louisville Courier-Journal (1869–1922)*; "Deaths," *The Louisville Courier-Journal*, March 29, 1920, p. 9. ProQuest Historical Newspapers: *The Louisville Courier-Journal (1869–1922)*.

21. Cook, *The Louisville Grays Scandal*, at 151; "An Old Louisville League Crook," *Louisville Commercial*, September 1, 1884, p. 4; "Base-Ball Chatter," *The Louisville Courier-Journal*, November 17, 1887, p. 6. ProQuest Historical Newspapers: *The Louisville Courier-Journal (1869–1922)*; Peter Morris, "Al Nichols," https://web.archive.org/web/20070825115357/http://www.petermorrisbooks.com/al_nichols.htm.

22. "Base Ball," *The Louisville Courier-Journal*, November 4, 1877, p. 1.

ProQuest Historical Newspapers: *The Louisville Courier-Journal (1869–1922)*; Cook, *The Louisville Grays Scandal*, at 151; "Recalls an Old Base Ball Scandal," *Louisville Evening Post*, June 18, 1901, p. 8; "Recalls," *Louisville Times*, June 18, 1901, p. 10.

23. "Base-Ball," *Cincinnati Enquirer*, February 20, 1879, p. 8. ProQuest Historical Newspapers: *The Cincinnati Enquirer (1841–1922)*; "New York City," *The Louisville Courier-Journal*, December 9, 1880, p. 3. ProQuest Historical Newspapers: *The Louisville Courier-Journal (1869–1922)*; "The Boss Boom," *Cincinnati Enquirer*, December 9, 1880, p. 4. ProQuest Historical Newspapers: *The Cincinnati Enquirer (1841–1922)*.

24. Cook, *The Louisville Grays Scandal*, at 153–154.

25. "Base-Ball," *Cincinnati Enquirer*, February 6, 1879, p. 8. ProQuest Historical Newspapers: *The Cincinnati Enquirer (1841–1922)*.

26. "Base-Ball," *Cincinnati Enquirer*, November 5, 1878, p. 8. ProQuest Historical Newspapers: *The Cincinnati Enquirer (1841–1922)*; "Base-Ball," *Cincinnati Enquirer*, February 6, 1879, p. 8. ProQuest Historical Newspapers: *The Cincinnati Enquirer (1841–1922)*; *Louisville Evening Post*, March 29, 1879, p. 1.

27. "Base-Ball," *Cincinnati Enquirer*, February 19, 1879, p. 8. ProQuest Historical Newspapers: *The Cincinnati Enquirer (1841–1922)*.

28. "Base-Ball," *Cincinnati Enquirer*, February 20, 1879, p. 8. ProQuest Historical Newspapers: *The Cincinnati Enquirer (1841–1922)*.

29. "Base Ball," *Louisville Commercial*, August 15, 1880, p. 4; "Base Ball," *The Louisville Courier-Journal*, March 19, 1882, p. 10. ProQuest Historical Newspapers: *The Louisville Courier-Journal (1869–1922)*; "Ball and Bat," *The Louisville Courier-Journal*, March 20, 1883, p. 6. ProQuest Historical Newspapers: *The Louisville Courier-Journal (1869–1922)*.

30. Cook, *The Louisville Grays Scandal*, at 154.

31. Cook, *The Louisville Grays Scandal*, at 153–154.

32. Cook, *The Louisville Grays Scandal*, at 157.

33. "His Last Pitch," *Post-Gazette*, October 11, 1883, p. 2; "Diamond Dust,"

Boston Globe, October 13, 1883, p. 2; "Briefly Told," *Philadelphia Inquirer,* October 11, 1883, p. 3; "Local News," *Louisville Evening Post,* October 13, 1883, p. 1; "Death of James Devlin," *The Louisville Courier-Journal,* October 15, 1883, p. 6. ProQuest Historical Newspapers: *The Louisville Courier-Journal (1869–1922).*
34. "Baseball," *The New York Clipper,* October 27, 1883, p. 525.
35. Palmer, et al., *Athletic Sport in America,* at 75.
36. Nemec. *The Great Encyclopedia,* at 101; Gelzheiser, *Labor and Capital,* at 51; Cusick, "Gentleman of the Press," at 120.
37. Cusick, "Gentleman of the Press," at 155; "Notes of the Diamond," *Louisville Times,* April 7, 1886, p. 3; "Death of Mrs. John A. Haldeman," *The Louisville Courier-Journal,* May 26, 1885, p. 8. ProQuest Historical Newspapers: *The Louisville Courier-Journal (1869–1922);* "Little Adelaide Haldeman Dead," *The Louisville Courier-Journal,* August 8, 1885, p. 6. ProQuest Historical Newspapers: *The Louisville Courier-Journal (1869–1922);* "At Midnight," *The Louisville Courier-Journal,* September 17, 1899, p. 7. ProQuest Historical Newspapers: *The Louisville Courier-Journal (1869–1922).*
38. "At Midnight," *The Louisville Courier-Journal,* September 17, 1899, p. 7. ProQuest Historical Newspapers: *The Louisville Courier-Journal (1869–1922);* "Death of John Avery Haldeman," *The Louisville Courier-Journal,* September 19, 1899, p. 6. ProQuest Historical Newspapers: *The Louisville Courier-Journal (1869–1922);* "John A. Haldeman Is Dead," *Chicago Tribune,* September 17, 1899, p. 5; "Obituary Notes," *New York Times,* September 18, 1899, p. 7.
39. Cook, *The Louisville Grays Scandal,* at 159; *Haldeman Family Papers, 1843–1985,* Letter, 1/5/52 Walter N. Haldeman, II to Lee Allen, Filson Historical Society,

Louisville, Ky., Mss A H159, V. 109; *Haldeman Family Papers, 1843–1985,* Letter, 1/16/52 Lee Allen to Walter N. Haldeman, II, Filson Historical Society, Louisville, Ky., Mss A H159, V. 109.
40. "Gossip of the Day," *The Louisville Courier-Journal,* August 19, 1887, p. 8. ProQuest Historical Newspapers: *The Louisville Courier-Journal (1869–1922).*
41. "Gossip of the Game," *The Louisville Courier-Journal,* August 31, 1890, p. 5. ProQuest Historical Newspapers: *The Louisville Courier-Journal (1869–1922);* "Famous Baseball Case Is Recalled," *The Louisville Courier-Journal,* December 18, 1910, p. B5. ProQuest Historical Newspapers: *The Louisville Courier-Journal (1869–1922);* "Our Pioneer Sellers-Out," *The Louisville Courier-Journal,* April 17, 1938, p. 60. ProQuest Historical Newspapers: *The Louisville Courier-Journal (1923–2001);* "Ruby's Report," *The Louisville Courier-Journal,* September 6, 1951, p. 23. ProQuest Historical Newspapers: *The Louisville Courier-Journal (1923–2001);* "94 Years of Runs, Hits—and Errors," *The Louisville Courier-Journal,* April 5, 1959, *The Courier-Journal Magazine,* p. 24. ProQuest Historical Newspapers: *The Louisville Courier-Journal (1923–2001);* "A Century of Sports," *The Louisville Courier-Journal,* November 10, 1968, *The Courier-Journal Magazine,* p. 29. ProQuest Historical Newspapers: *The Louisville Courier-Journal (1923–2001);* "Those Disgraceful Grays," *The Louisville Courier-Journal,* October 9, 1977, *The Courier-Journal Magazine,* p. 21. ProQuest Historical Newspapers: *The Louisville Courier-Journal (1923–2001);* "Baseball in Louisville," *The Louisville Courier-Journal,* April 12, 2000, Opening Night at Louisville Slugger Field (Special Insert), p. 11. ProQuest Historical Newspapers: *The Louisville Courier-Journal (1923–2001).*

Bibliography

Books

Alexander, Charles C. *Our Game: An American Baseball History*. New York: Fine Communications, 1997.
Allen, Lee. *The National League Story*. New York: Hill & Wang, 1961.
Brunson, James E., III, *Black Baseball 1858–1900*. Jefferson, NC: McFarland, 2019.
Cook, William. *The Louisville Grays Scandal of 1877*. Jefferson, NC: McFarland, 2005.
Di Salvatore, Bryan. *A Clever Base-Ballist: The Life and Times of John Montgomery Ward*. Baltimore: Johns Hopkins University Press, 1999.
Gelzheiser, Robert P. *Labor and Capital in 19th Century Baseball*. Jefferson, NC: McFarland, 2006.
Ginsburg, Daniel. *The Fix Is In: A History of Baseball Gambling and Game Fixing Scandals*, Jefferson, NC: McFarland, 2004.
Goldstein, Warren. *Playing for Keeps: A History of Early Baseball*. Ithica, NY: Cornell University Press, 1989.
Jewell, Anne. *Baseball in Louisville*. Charleston, SC: Arcadia Publishing, 2006.
Johnston, William Preston. *The Life of General Albert Sidney Johnston*. New York: D. Appleton, 1879. *Republished*, New York: Da Capo Press, 1997.
Kirsch, George B. *Baseball in Blue and Gray*. Princeton, NJ: Princeton University Press, 2003.
Kleber, John E., Mary Jean Kinsman, Thomas D. Clark, Clyde F. Crews, and George H. Yater, eds. *The Encyclopedia of Louisville*. Lexington: The University Press of Kentucky, 2001.
Macdonald, Neil W. *The League That Lasted*. Jefferson, NC: McFarland, 2004.
McCulloch, Ron, ed. *Baseball Roots*. Toronto: Warwick Publishing, 2000.
Melville, Tom. *Early Baseball and the Rise of the National League*. Jefferson, NC: McFarland, 2001.
Morris, Peter. *A Game of Inches*. Chicago: Ivan R. Dee, 2010.
Morris, Peter, William J. Ryczek, Jan Finkel, Leonard Levin and Richard Malatzky eds. *Baseball Pioneers, 1850–1870: The Clubs and Players Who Spread the Sport Nationwide*. Jefferson, NC: McFarland, 2014.
Nemec, David. *The Great Encyclopedia of 19th Century Major League Baseball*. New York: Penguin Group, 1997.
Palmer, Harry Clay, J.A. Fynes, Frank Richter, W.I. Harris, *et al.*, eds. *Athletic Sports in America, England and Australia*. Philadelphia: Hubbard Bros., 1889.
Seymour, Harold, and Dorothy Seymour Mills. *Baseball—The Early Years*. New York: Oxford University Press, 1960.
Spalding, Albert G., *Base Ball: America's National Game: 1839–1915*. San Francisco: Halo Book, 1991.
Tarvin, A.H. *Seventy-Five Years on Louisville Diamonds*. Louisville, KY: Schumann Publications, 1940.

Von Borries, Philip. *Louisville Diamonds: The Louisville Major-League Reader 1876–1899.* Paducah, KY: Turner Publishing, 1996.

Wilbert, Warren N. *Opening Pitch: Professional Baseball's Inaugural Season.* Lanham, MD: Roman & Littlefield, 2007.

Woodward, C. Vann. *Reunion and Reaction: The Compromise of 1877 and the End of Reconstruction.* New York: Oxford University Press, 1966.

Wright, Marshall D. *The National Association of Base Ball Players, 1857–1870.* Jefferson, NC: McFarland, 2000.

Academic Works

Cusick, Dennis Charles. "Gentleman of the Press: The Life and Times of Walter Newman Haldeman." Master's thesis, University of Louisville, 1987.

Reyna, V.F., and C.J. Brainerd. "Fuzzy-Trace Theory: An Interim Synthesis." *Learning and Individual Differences*, Volume 7, Issue 1, 1995, pages 1–75.

Online Articles

Albertson, Matt. "George Hall." Society for American Baseball Research (sabr.org).

BR Bullpen. "Jim Devlin." Baseball-reference.com.

Dodgson, Lindsay, "Our Brains Sometimes Create 'False Memories'—But Science Suggests We Could Be Better Off This Way." *Business Insider*, December 19, 2017.

Faber, Charles F. "Pop Snyder." Society for American Baseball Research (sabr.org).

Morris, Peter. "John Dickins." Society for American Baseball Research (sabr.org).

Sullivan, Josh. "Bill Craver." Society for American Baseball Research (sabr.org).

Watterson, Jeremy. "Ed Somerville." Society for American Baseball Research (sabr.org).

Weatherby, Charlie. "Joe Borden." Society for American Baseball Research (sabr.org).

Weiser-Alexander, Kathy. "Jack McCall—Cowardly Killer of Wild Bill Hickok." Legendsofamerica.com.

Newspapers and Magazines (Including Digital Collections)

Boston Globe
Brooklyn Daily Eagle
Chicago Tribune
The Cincinnati Enquirer (ProQuest Historical Newspapers)
Daily Courier (1851–1868) (Louisville, KY)
Daily Union Press (Louisville, KY)
Lippencotts, Vol. 38, 1886, pg. 444.
Louisville Commercial
Louisville Courier-Journal (1869–1922)
The Louisville Courier-Journal (ProQuest Historical Newspapers)
Louisville Daily Journal (1839–1868)
Louisville Evening Post
New York Clipper
The New York Times
The New York Times (ProQuest Historical Newspapers)
New York Daily News
Philadelphia Inquirer
Post-Gazette (Pittsburgh, PA)
St. Louis Globe-Democrat

Reference Material

Caron's Directory of the City of Louisville (Various Years)

Index

Numbers with **bold italics** indicate pages with illustrations.